THE 50 GREATEST PLAYS
in IOWA HAWKEYES
Football History

MICHAEL MAXWELL

TRIUMPH
BOOKS

Library of Congress Cataloging-in-Publication Data

Maxwell, Michael, 1971-
  The 50 greatest plays in Iowa Hawkeyes football history / Michael Maxwell.
    p. cm.
  ISBN-13: 978-1-60078-127-8
  ISBN-10: 1-60078-127-6
  1. Iowa Hawkeyes (Football team) 2. University of Iowa—Football—History. I. Title.
  GV958.U526M39 2008
  796.332'63'09777655—dc22

2008026301

This book is available in quantity at special discounts for your group or organization. For further information, contact:

Triumph Books
542 South Dearborn Street
Suite 750
Chicago, Illinois 60605
(312) 939-3330
Fax (312) 663-3557

Printed in U.S.A.
ISBN: 978-1-60078-127-8
Design by Sue Knopf
Page production by Patricia Frey
Photos courtesy of University of Iowa—CMP Photographic Services except where otherwise indicated.

To my wife and best friend, Mary Clare, with whom my path would never have crossed were it not for The University of Iowa.

To our daughters, Rory and Cayleigh, who will have no choice but to grow up Hawkeye fans.

To dedicated sports fans everywhere who have dreamed of moonlighting as a sportswriter, but who have not been fortunate enough to have their dream come true.

Contents

FOREWORD

The University of Iowa has been a very special place for me and my family since I first arrived on campus way back in 1981. I am forever grateful to coach Hayden Fry who saw enough in me as a graduate assistant coach from the University of Pittsburgh to offer me a job as offensive-line coach. I'm not sure that there was another Division I coach in the country who would have hired me in 1981 for that position. The fact was that at that point in my career, I simply did not have the résumé suitable to the job. In reality, my wife and I had reached an agreement that I would stay two years at Pitt and not make a move until after the 1981 season. I had initially planned to just interview at Iowa, to gain the interviewing experience for when the time came to move on from Pitt. Well, I ended up being totally overwhelmed by Coach Fry, his staff, and the warmth of the great people I met at the University of Iowa. So plans changed, and we packed up and headed west to Iowa City. I knew Iowa was the place for me almost immediately as we upset a powerful Nebraska team 10–7 in my first game in 1981 (Play Number 19). It would just get better and better from there. I can't even begin to imagine what my life would be like today had Coach Fry not taken that chance on me in my younger days.

In two different stints, I have spent a total of almost 20 years here at Iowa and feel very fortunate to be a part of the football program and the university community. The rich history and tradition of the football program is something I, my staff, and my players believe is very important. So many great players and coaches have been a part of the football program over the years. I can only imagine what it would have been like to have coached the legendary Heisman Trophy winner, Nile Kinnick. He was no doubt a one-of-a-kind player, but perhaps more importantly, an incredible human being. I have no doubt that he was capable of far greater accomplishments off the field, such as some high political office, had his life not been tragically cut short while courageously serving his country with honor during World War II.

One other thing that jumps out at me about the history of the program is the strong affinity for the university that past players from all generations seem to have—no matter what decade they played—1940s, 1950s, 1960s, 1970s, 1980s, and now 1990s and 2000s. We have instituted an honorary captain's program where we invite past players back to serve as honorary captains for each home game, and I always look forward to hearing their unique perspective on their past experiences and fond memories of the university. Those players have been such a key part of so many of the plays chronicled in this book.

During my time in Iowa City, I have been fortunate enough to be part of four Big Ten Championship teams—in 1981, 1985, 2002, and 2004—and each of these teams is special for various different reasons. Numerous unforgettable plays from these special years are chronicled here. But there are plenty of others that stand out in my mind—the 1982 team got off to a very slow start, but was able to refocus and finish a strong season, winning eight of the final 10 games, including an impressive win over Tennessee in the Peach Bowl (Play Number 18); the 2001 season was also very rewarding, as we finally thought we turned a corner, capping the season with an Alamo Bowl win over Texas Tech (Play Number 9); and finally, the 2003 team may not have been as talented as the 2002 or 2004 teams, but it still managed to again reach the 10-win plateau and a Top 10 national finish, which was topped off with a memorable win over Florida in the Outback Bowl (Play Number 15).

In scanning the list of top 50 plays, I happened to find myself on the sideline as either an assistant or head coach for 28 of the 50 plays. Although I remember most of the 28 plays quite fondly, the six plays that found their way into the Top 10 were particularly memorable for me. I never get tired of reminiscing about the final play of the Capital One Bowl on New Year's Day in 2005 (Play Number 1). That play is burned into my memory bank. The play was called "All Up." It was obviously designed to gain a lot of yards on a deep pass pattern. The key to the play from my perspective was that, to a man, all 11 of our guys on the field executed their assignments almost flawlessly, including the offensive line giving Drew (Tate) enough time, the receivers running the correct routes, Drew putting the ball exactly where it needed to be, and finally Warren (Holloway) making a great grab, but still maintaining his balance as he landed. Conversely, on the other side of the ball, it only took one LSU defender missing an assignment for us to convert the big play we needed. As the clock was running out just prior to the play, our bench did not signal for a timeout until it was too late, but as fate would have it, I think not calling the timeout worked to our advantage. I'm not sure we would have executed the play if a timeout was called,

because it may have allowed LSU to better organize their defense. Of course, the other great story related to that play was one I wasn't even aware of until the next day. The game-winning play was Warren's first touchdown as a Hawkeye. He was a fifth-year senior on that team and nobody worked harder than Warren. He handled the intense spotlight and all the accolades that came his way following the game with impressive humility, class, and dignity.

Another very memorable play for me was the touchdown pass from Brad Banks to Dallas Clark on fourth-and-goal in the final minute against Purdue on homecoming in 2002 (Play Number 7). That play first and foremost was a masterful call by offensive coordinator Ken O'Keefe. The execution on the part of Dallas—hesitating just the right amount of time at the line of scrimmage before darting across the secondary—and Brad, who knew he was going to be hit as he released the ball, really made the play work. I couldn't be prouder of Dallas Clark in all he has accomplished, both here and since leaving school. He has earned everything he got—two years prior to winning the Mackey Award as the nation's best tight end that year he made the team as a walk-on third-team backup linebacker—just an incredible story of what hard work and dedication can accomplish. He is one of the most positive and energetic players I have ever been around, with a tremendous attitude that is really contagious to his teammates. I don't think it is a coincidence at all that the Indianapolis Colts have identified Clark and Bob Sanders as key players to their offensive and defensive units respectively.

The last play in the Top 10 (where I was fortunate enough to be head coach) was Nate Kaeding's clutch field goal late in the fourth quarter to beat Texas Tech in the 2001 Alamo Bowl (Play Number 9). We had been through some difficult years win-loss wise my first two seasons as head coach, and it meant an awful lot to finish that season 7–5, rather than 6–6, on the strength of that kick. Nate was a tremendous leader for our program, which tends to be somewhat unusual for a specialist.

Much like the 1984 Freedom Bowl win over Texas was the springboard to a championship year in 1985, that key bowl win gave us plenty of momentum heading into the Big Ten Championship year in 2002.

Almost equally as memorable for me were the three Top 10 plays during the 1980s when I was an assistant under Coach Fry. One play that stands out from that era is Marv Cook's game-winning catch against Ohio State in 1987 (Play Number 2). In comparison to "The Catch" in the Capital One Bowl (when the LSU defense blitzed us on the play), on that fateful play the Ohio State defense, which had been blitzing us relentlessly most of that day, for whatever reason, chose to drop into coverage instead. That allowed Chuck Hartlieb time to survey the field and to find Cook down the right side after first looking left. Ohio State was in man-to-man coverage underneath, with two safeties deep. Marv ran a great route and Chuck put the ball in a place where Marv could step back in front of the defender to make the grab and then bull his way into the end zone, just breaking the plane as he was being tackled.

While Rob Houghtlin's field goal to beat Michigan in 1985 (Play Number 3) may have been slightly more dramatic than the 2001 kick in the Alamo Bowl, given the No. 1 vs. No. 2 matchup and all the hype that goes with that, both kickers enjoyed similar careers here, fostering great reputations as clutch kickers. We all felt very comfortable when either Rob or Nate came onto the field with the game on the line. I have been a part of some tremendous environments at Kinnick Stadium over the years, but right from the moment we came out for pregame warm-ups that day against Michigan, it was as electric as I can remember the stadium ever being.

One of the best parts of the game-winning play to me was, as Coach Schembechler called timeout in a futile attempt to "ice" Rob, he sarcastically shook his hands in the direction of the Michigan bench as if to say, "Boy, now I'm really nervous." This, right before he calmly drilled probably the most memorable kick in school history.

Finally, similar to Dallas's touchdown catch in 2002 versus Purdue, Clark's bootleg run was again a tremendous call on offense by Coach Fry, but it also was executed flawlessly by our guys. Because of the great ability of Ronnie Harmon, who was certainly one of the more dynamic players in Iowa football history, the Spartans defense clearly had to honor the fake handoff. Consequently, the fake drew practically every Spartans defender to the middle of the line, giving Chuck a cake-walk into the end zone. The play was all the more satisfying because, at the same spot, on the same goal line, on another quarterback run play the year before against Michigan State, the officials ruled as short (although we all felt like we had broken the plane of the goal line on a two-point conversion that would have won the game). I still debate that call with the officials to this day. There would be no doubt about this one, as Chuck waltzed untouched into the end zone.

It has been an honor and a privilege to be associated with the great history and tradition that is Iowa football. Reliving some of the key components of that history in a book like this really does make me appreciate all the great moments we worked so hard together to build here at the University of Iowa. I look forward to the challenge of creating many new memories for the future.

—Kirk Ferentz

FOREWORD

Though it has been cultivated during my 35-year career as a play-by-play broadcaster, my passion for Hawkeye football goes back to 1958—or 50 of the 118 years Iowa has teed it up on the gridiron—when I was a youngster growing up in rural Iowa. My experiences have convinced me that there is no better place than Iowa City, and no better conference than the Big Ten, for college football.

We all have our favorite memories of Iowa football (which vary, of course, depending on your age). Tucked in those memories are many of the plays that have left an indelible impression on Iowa fans and have invoked conversations and arguments about which was the greatest ever. Now, here's a book that is as close to being a "hammer on the head" for this topic as you'll ever find. Are these 50 plays contained within the pages of this publication truly the greatest in Hawkeyes history? I think so. You and I might argue about their order of placement, but that's the fun, excitement, and joy of the read. You'll pore over the pages again and again, as I did, changing your mind, rearranging the order, calling your friends for their opinions, and—best of all—reliving the specific cadence of the calls.

There are just two of these books hitting the shelves at this time, which pay homage to schools with terrific football traditions. Iowa and Georgia caught the publisher's attention, due in large part to their passionate fan base. Congratulations Hawk fans! This book is yours. Without your loyal support, many of the great players who have worn black-and-gold since 1889 might have gone elsewhere. Who wouldn't want to play in front of sellout crowds in one of college football's greatest environments, Kinnick Stadium? It is because of your football fanaticism that Nile Kinnick, Bill Reichardt, Calvin Jones, Alex Karras, Randy Duncan, Chuck Long, Ronnie Harmon, Andre Tippett, Sedrick Shaw, Tim Dwight, Brad Banks, Dallas Clark, Bob Sanders, Robert Gallery, Drew Tate, and countless other Hawkeye greats found their way to Iowa City. They're all in this book, running, passing, blocking, and tackling their way up and down the field at Kinnick Stadium.

While it is a major challenge to chronicle the 50 greatest plays in Iowa football history, I don't think there will be much argument with the ones selected by Mike Maxwell. Some of my favorites, in no particular order:

- Bobby Jeter's 81-yard sprint to pay dirt in the Rose Bowl
- Kenny Ploen's touchdown pass to Jim Gibbons in November 1956, securing Iowa's first-ever Pasadena trip
- Chuck Long's bootleg score to beat Michigan State in a dramatic comeback

- Bruising Nick Bell's steamrolling runs that dismantled No. 3 Illinois in Champaign
- Andre Tippett almost single-handedly disrupting mighty Michigan, causing Bo Schembechler to lose more hair
- Chuck Hartlieb to Marv Cook on fourth-and-23 to pull out a rare win at Ohio State in 1987
- Rob Houghtlin kicking Iowa past Michigan on the game's final play in the infamous 1985 No. 1 versus No. 2 game
- Of course, quarterback Drew Tate to Warren Holloway, the long touchdown pass on the Capitol One Bowl's final play, allowing the Hawks to defeat defending national champion LSU

The 50 greatest plays in Iowa football history were called by some of the greatest coaching minds: Howard Jones, Dr. Eddie Anderson, Forest Evashevski, Hayden Fry, and, of course, Kirk Ferentz. This book is the complete team effort. It is a must for every Hawkeye fanatic. It is as good a resource as you'll ever need to stay in touch with the lasting memories of many Saturday afternoons in Iowa City and around the Big Ten. Enjoy!

—Gary Dolphin, radio voice of the Iowa Hawkeyes

INTRODUCTION

The University of Iowa has proudly fielded a varsity football team since 1889. Since then, the Hawkeyes have participated in more than 1,100 games, which have included more than 150,000 individual plays. During this time span, the Hawkeyes have developed as storied and rich a tradition and as loyal a following as any team in college football. From its inception into what would become the Big Ten Conference in 1900 when Iowa went undefeated in its first year, through the glory years of the early 1920s when the Hawkeyes posted back-to-back perfect seasons, to the memorable Ironmen group of 1939 led by legendary Heisman Trophy winner Nile Kinnick, to the two-time Rose Bowl Champion teams of the late 1950s, through the renaissance led by Hayden Fry in the '80s and '90s, right up to the current group led by coach Kirk Ferentz, there clearly was no shortage of great plays from which to choose.

I personally found out firsthand the special feelings between the fans and the team during my first football weekend as a graduate student at the University of Iowa in September 1994. I had come to Iowa City after living my entire life on the East Coast, where I attended a small public college in western New York State with no football team. I soon found out that I had been missing plenty all those years. I remember being out and around town that Saturday afternoon, when all the streets and stores were empty. It only took me a minute to figure out that everyone's attention was focused on the football game. To me, the season-opening game against Central Michigan seemed like a snoozer, but that didn't seem to matter to anyone else. Of course every store had the football game on over the radio. Because 1994 was a relatively down year for Iowa football (the team was just 5–5–1), it actually took me about a year to get hooked. But I had student season tickets in 1995, and have considered myself a "die hard" since then.

There is a unique bond between the Iowa Hawkeyes football team and the state of Iowa. There are no big-time professional sports in Iowa (with all due respect to the Iowa Cubs, Iowa's Arena Football League team, the Barnstormers, and the minor-league hockey franchise, The Iowa Stars, in Des Moines). This makes it unlike every other school in the Big Ten. Although there is another Division I football school in Iowa, historically the Hawkeyes have received the vast majority of attention in the state. They don't call it the "Hawkeye State" for nothing! To most people in the state, the Hawkeyes are the only game in town if you are looking for big-time football.

So then, how to select a mere 50 plays as the greatest in the history of Iowa Hawkeyes football? It took hours and hours of research—poring over historical information in books, on video, and over the Internet. Glancing at the complete list, the most common trend in each of the plays is that most of them occurred during Iowa victories. Only one play from an Iowa loss made the list; one game was also from a tie. Another important criterion was that the play needed to come from a meaningful game in a meaningful season. Therefore, the majority of the plays are from successful seasons. I hope you enjoy reading the book as much as I have enjoyed writing it.

January 2, 2003

Record Return to the National Stage

C.J. Jones's 100-yard kickoff-return touchdown gets the 2003 Orange Bowl off to a raucous start

The 2002 University of Iowa football season was as special as any in several generations. The Hawks had suffered through some difficult times in the years immediately preceding the 2002 season. The senior class during the 2002 football season had been winless in Big Ten play (0–8) during their freshman year in 1999, coach Kirk Ferentz's first season. That had turned completely around by 2002 when the Hawks posted a perfect 8–0 record in league play during the 2002 Big Ten regular season. It was Iowa's first perfect conference record since 1922.

The only blemish on an 11–1 overall record coming into the Orange Bowl was an early-season loss at home to intrastate rival Iowa State, in a game Iowa led big at the half 24–7, only to see the Cyclones come storming back in the second half for a spirited 36–31 come-from-behind victory. Iowa's sterling regular season was strong enough to earn the school's first Bowl Championship Series (BCS) bowl invitation. However, because of the BCS selection system created by the rotating National Championship game, the Orange Bowl was selected ahead of the Rose Bowl that year. The Orange Bowl selected Iowa as an at-large team before the Rose Bowl could offer Iowa a bid. Iowa was in for a January 2 date with the Pac-10 champion USC Trojans in a traditional Big Ten–Pac 10 bowl contest, but this time it was played in south Florida's Pro Player Stadium rather than at the Rose Bowl in Pasadena.

On paper, it was a dream matchup: the Heisman winner, USC quarterback Carson Palmer, versus the Heisman runner-up, Iowa

> **N**one of us had a good taste in our mouths after the game last January. It stuck with us.
>
> —COACH KIRK FERENTZ, ONE YEAR AFTER THE ORANGE BOWL LOSS TO USC

Iowa's C.J. Jones (8), with help from Jermelle Lewis (29), returns the opening kickoff past fallen USC cornerback Darrell Rideaux (22) during the FedEx Orange Bowl at Pro Player Stadium on January 2, 2003, in Miami. *Photo courtesy Getty Images*

quarterback Brad Banks. Both teams were loaded with future NFL talent, including Palmer, Troy Polamalu, Mike Williams, and Justin Fargas of Southern Cal and Bob Sanders, Dallas Clark, Robert Gallery, Eric Steinbach, Matt Roth, Sean Considine, and Nate Kaeding of Iowa. USC came into the game 10–2 and had previously beaten six top-25 teams during 2002.

The game was the only bowl game of the evening, so it had the spotlight all to itself. An estimated crowd of 45,000 Iowa supporters clad in black and gold made Pro Player Stadium more like Kinnick Stadium South.

It had been nearly 50 days since Iowa played its last game at Minnesota on November 16, but that didn't prevent the

C.J. JONES

C.J. Jones hails from Boynton Beach, Florida, just 60 miles north of Miami, which made the game-opening play all the more special because it took place in front of several local family members and friends. (Jones is also the cousin of quarterback Brad Banks.) During the 2002 season, Jones ranked 12th in the nation in kickoff return average, with 26.6 yards, and Iowa led the nation as a team in kickoff return yards, at 25.1 yards per attempt. Jones also ranked second on the 2002 team in touchdown receptions, with nine, and third on the team in receptions, with 38 for a total of 468 yards. He was named to the Honorable Mention All–Big Ten Team in 2002.

Jones's accomplishments on the football field at the University of Iowa resulted in his signing as a free agent with the Cleveland Browns in 2003, where he played through the 2004 season. He also played in NFL Europe and had preseason tryouts with the Seattle Seahawks in 2006 and New England Patriots in 2007.

Hawkeyes from getting off to a lightning-quick start. As Iowa had done most times that season, it decided to receive the opening kickoff. The kick came to Iowa's C.J. Jones at the goal line. Jones took the ball up to the wedge and cut to the left sideline. He was able to break into the clear near midfield thanks to a block by speedy running back Jermelle Lewis, who was also deep to receive the kick alongside Jones. Tim Brandt of ABC-TV quipped, "C.J. Jones, see you later," as it became clear that no Trojan would lay a hand on him. Jones scampered down the left sideline untouched for an early 7–0 lead before the first offensive snap. The 100-yard kickoff return was an Orange Bowl record, and the atmosphere in the stadium was absolutely electric. The sky was the limit for the Hawkeyes, it seemed.

Unfortunately for Iowa, the game's opening play ended up being the high point of the entire game. USC quickly moved down the field on the ensuing kickoff and capped their drive with a four-yard touchdown run by Justin Fargas. The game was tied 7–7, just over two minutes in. Iowa managed to keep the contest close in the first half, but missed opportunities and generally sloppy play proved to be their downfall. They earned two first-and-goal opportunities inside the 2-yard line in the first half, but only took away a total of three points.

A blocked 28-yard field-goal attempt by Nate Kaeding as the first half expired kept the game tied at 10–10 heading into the locker rooms, but the Hawkeyes were clearly deflated by their inability to cash in on various golden opportunities.

USC took over the ballgame in the second half, beginning with an 80-yard drive to open the third quarter. They scored on long touchdown drives of 99 yards and 85 yards on the next two possessions, which essentially sealed Iowa's fate. USC's speed and conditioning appeared to wear down Iowa, which had not played a competitive game in more than 50 days and had not competed in the heat and humidity typical of South Florida since early in the season.

The final statistics were as lopsided as the 38–17 final score. USC enjoyed a 16-minute time-of-possession advantage and outgained Iowa in total net yards, 550 to 323. Iowa was hurt by 13 penalties that lost them a total of 85 yards. However, Jones's 169 yards on kickoff returns is an Orange Bowl and an Iowa record for return yards—one of the benefits to the opponent scoring so often.

In spite of the bitter taste left by the defeat, the 2002 Iowa football team served notice that it was back and ready to perform at a high level on a national stage. The

GAME DETAILS

USC 38 • Iowa 17

Date: January 2, 2003

Location: Pro Player Stadium, Miami, Florida

Attendance: 75,971

Significance: Orange Bowl

Box Score:

Iowa	10	0	0	7	**17**
Southern California	7	3	14	14	**38**

Scoring:

IA	Jones 100-yard kickoff return (Kaeding PAT)
USC	Fargas 4-yard run (Killeen PAT)
IA	Kaeding 35-yard FG
USC	Killeen 35-yard FG
USC	Williams 18-yard pass from Palmer (Killeen PAT)
USC	Fargas 50-yard run (Killeen PAT)
USC	McCullough 5-yard run (Killeen PAT)
USC	Byrd 6-yard run (Killeen kick)
IA	Brown 18-yard pass from Banks (Kaeding PAT)

2002 season was so memorable that the opening play of the Orange Bowl made it into this book, even though it came in an Iowa loss. In fact, this is the only play from an Iowa loss in the entire book!

The 2002 campaign marked the first of three consecutive 10-or-more-win seasons for Ferentz and the Hawkeyes. Their 10–2 overall record was good enough to earn Iowa the number eight ranking in both the final Associated Press and coaches' polls.

The Hawks also learned valuable lessons from the Orange Bowl experience. The next year at the Outback Bowl in Tampa, Florida, Iowa changed its preparation schedule by coming to Florida more than a week before the game. The change in preparation strategy was later cited as one of the reasons for the completely different result in the 2004 Outback Bowl (a 37–17 drubbing of the Florida Gators—see Play Number 15 for further details).

September 9, 2006

THE GOAL-LINE STAND

Syracuse is thwarted on seven straight plays inside the
5-yard line in Iowa's overtime win

The number 49 selection in this book is so special because it was impossible to pick a single play in the final sequence of seven plays in double overtime above any other. This series of plays at the end of a grueling game represents one of the best goal-line stands not only in Iowa history, but in NCAA history as well.

The game was an early-season non-conference game against a once-proud football program from the Big East Conference that had since fallen on hard times. Syracuse had turned to new coach Greg Robinson in 2005; he replaced Paul Pasqualoni who had been at the Syracuse helm since 1991. Robinson had won two Super Bowl rings as defensive coordinator for the Denver Broncos, and it was hoped that he could return Syracuse to glory. The Orange were coming off a one-win season in 2005, with the only win coming against the lightly regarded University of Buffalo. However, perhaps awakened by the strong performance against Iowa, Syracuse would go on to collect four wins in 2006. Iowa was coming off an easy win in the season opener versus Montana the week before, but was without starting quarterback Drew Tate who

was scratched at game time with a strained abdominal muscle. Tate had started all 12 games in both 2004 and 2005, as well as the 2006 opener against Montana: 25 straight games. Senior Jason Manson got his first career start in Tate's absence.

The loss of Tate proved to be a big blow as the Iowa offense struggled to put points on the scoreboard most of the afternoon, amassing a total of just 202 yards through the air—including both of the overtimes. Iowa coughed it up on four interceptions, which kept Syracuse in the game. Despite the struggles on offense, Iowa held the lead for most of the second half. It took a 41-yard field goal by Syracuse's Patrick Shadle with six seconds remaining to force overtime, deadlocked at 10–10.

In the first extra session, Syracuse drove to the Iowa 4-yard line. The Iowa defense faced a first-and-goal, but were ready for the challenge. In what would prove to be a prelude of things to come in the second overtime, the Iowa defense stiffened at the goal line and Syracuse was forced to settle for a 19-yard field goal by Shadle, which came after Tim Lane dropped a perfectly thrown pass from Perry Patterson at the back of the

Iowa's defense, lead by Kenny Iwebema (92) and Mike Klinkenborg (40), stops Syracuse's Paul Chiara short of the end zone on fourth down in double overtime. The historic goal-line stand allowed Iowa to win 20–13 at the Carrier Dome in Syracuse, New York, on September 9, 2006. *Copyright: University of Iowa—CMP Photographic Service*

end zone on third-and-goal. On their first overtime possession, the Hawkeyes tied it on a 26-yard field goal by reliable senior kicker Kyle Schlicher.

Iowa had the ball first in the second overtime. Keyed by a pass-interference call on cornerback Tanard Jackson that moved the ball to the Syracuse 5-yard line, Iowa's Albert Young capped the overtime drive with a one-yard touchdown run. Iowa led 20–13, and now it was Syracuse's turn in the second overtime. The game was in the more-than-capable hands of the Iowa defensive unit.

Syracuse ran a total of 11 offensive plays on their second drive in overtime. However, that was only enough to gain 24 yards and get them to the 1-yard line. A pass-interference call on the sixth play of the drive against Iowa cornerback Charles Godfrey set Syracuse up first-and-goal on the Iowa 2-yard line. Iowa's defense was primed and ready to make history.

First-and-goal from the Iowa 2-yard line: Run up the middle by the fullback, gain of one yard.

Second-and-goal from the 1-yard line: Run up the middle by the fullback, loss of one yard.

Third-and-goal from the 2-yard line: Syracuse passes to the end zone, but Iowa's Marcus Paschal is called for pass interference. That gives the Orange another set of four downs from the Iowa 2.

First-and-goal from the 2-yard line: Run up the middle by the fullback, gain of one yard.

Second-and-goal from the 1-yard line: Another run up the middle by the fullback, no gain. ESPN/ABC analyst Andre Ware (a former Heisman-winning quarterback) is screaming for the quarterback sneak. Patterson, the Syracuse quarterback, is squarely built and listed at 6'4" and 242 pounds. Ware wouldn't get it.

Third-and-goal from the 1-yard line: Syracuse option run to left is kept by the quarterback, Patterson, and completely stuffed by Iowa's Mike Klinkenborg, who seemingly flies in out of nowhere to make the stop.

After having stopped Syracuse from inside the 2-yard line six straight times, Iowa now faced a Syracuse fourth-and-goal from the 1-yard line. The prior six plays would all be for naught if Syracuse scored on the seventh.

MIKE KLINKENBORG

Tragically, Mike Klinkenborg's father passed away the day after Iowa's historic goal-line stand versus Syracuse. In spite of his huge loss, Klinkenborg started the following week against intrastate rival Iowa State and recorded eight tackles, helping lead Iowa to another big win 27–17. This performance just days after the death of his father earned Klinkenborg the Walter Camp Football Foundation National Defensive Player of the Week honors. The native of Rock Rapids, Iowa, averaged 10.75 tackles per game in 2006, good for second in the Big Ten and eighth in the NCAA. Klinkenborg earned Second Team All–Big Ten Honors from the media in 2006.

Klinkenborg not only excelled on the football field, but off it as well; he earned First Team Academic All-America Honors in both 2006 and 2007. Mike was an elementary education major and as of the first semester in 2007, had earned a stellar 3.95 GPA. He is a true Hawkeyes hero both on and off the field.

Linebacker Mike Klinkenborg (40) was the heart of the defense that shut down Syracuse during Iowa's celebrated overtime goal-line stand. During his career, he earned both All–Big Ten and Academic All-American honors. *Photo courtesy AP Images*

GAME DETAILS

Iowa 20 • Syracuse 13

Date: September 9, 2006

Location: Carrier Dome, Syracuse, New York

Attendance: 37,199

You can't write a script like that.

—COACH KIRK FERENTZ, COMMENTING ON THE GAME'S FINAL SEQUENCE

Box Score:

Iowa	0	7	3	0	3	7	**20**
Syracuse	7	0	0	3	3	0	**13**

Scoring:

SYR	Smith 3-yard pass from Patterson (Shadle PAT)
IA	S. Chandler 1-yard pass from Manson (Schlicher PAT)
IA	Schlicher 24-yard FG

SYR	Shadle 41-yard FG
SYR	Shadle 19-yard FG
IA	Schlicher 26-yard FG
IA	Young 1-yard run (Schlicher PAT)

Syracuse called timeout to strategize about the fourth-down call, with the game hanging in the balance.

After all the strategizing on the sideline, the Syracuse offensive brain trust decided to go with a relatively ordinary run up the middle by the running back after a fake handoff to the wide receiver in motion; again it was stuffed by the Iowa defense well short of the goal line. Iowa had won it in double overtime, and the joyous Hawks sideline spilled onto the field to congratulate an exhausted defensive unit.

There is rarely one individual star in goal-line stand situations. In this case, most stops were made with gang tackling. Every Hawkeyes player on the field during those seven plays had a role in preventing a Syracuse touchdown that would have given Syracuse the opportunity to tie it and send it to a third overtime with an extra point. Yes, this was a team effort by the defense, especially the "big uglies" up front, so remember the names of Kenny Iwebema, Ryan Bain, Mitch King, Bryan Mattison, Edmond Miles, Mike Humpal, and Klinkenborg. Collectively, they were the stars that preserved the Iowa win and provided Hawks fans with an exhilarating goal-line stand for the ages.

We're tired but we're 2–0. Both teams played well enough to win. I never remembered a game in which we stopped a team seven times at the goal.

—FERENTZ, ON HIS DEFENSE STOPPING SU SEVEN TIMES IN A ROW

THE GOAL LINE STAND

In the second overtime session against Syracuse, the Orange needed a touchdown to match Iowa's touchdown in their frame. Given a total of seven opportunities near the goal line, it certainly looked as though the game was destined for at least a third overtime. The drama built up to a seventh play from the 2-yard line or closer. Continuing the play-calling pattern established by Syracuse during the series, the Orange attempted to run the ball up the middle on what would turn out to be the last play of the game. With quarterback Perry Patterson (10) under center, he faked a handoff to a wide receiver who was in motion from the right side, then handed off to his running back, Paul Chiara (34) who was stuffed cold yet again well short of the goal line by a whole host of Hawkeye defenders that included Kenny Iwebema (92), Mitch King (47), and Mike Klinkenborg (40), among others.

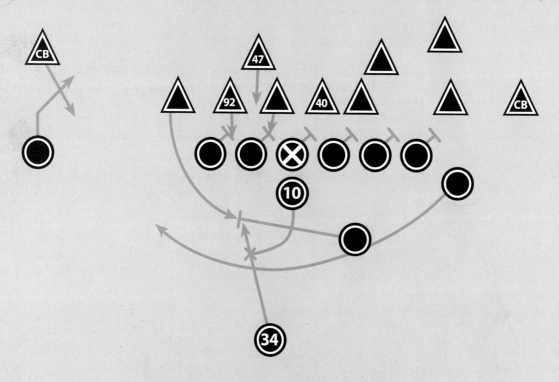

It was tough today, but we learned and we stuck together. In the overtime, we were aggressive going for the ball. Give credit to the boys up front on stopping them seven times from the 2. They must have eaten their steaks this week.

—IOWA CORNERBACK ADAM SHADA

Iowa fans congratulate defensive end Kenny Iwebema after the tenacious goal-line stand that delivered a 20–13 overtime victory over Syracuse. *Photo courtesy AP Images*

November 21, 1953

FAINTING IRISH MAKE TIME STAND STILL

"Injury" timeouts allow Notre Dame to tie Iowa, spur rulebook changes

Perhaps the most controversial game in Hawkeyes history came on the watch of coach Forest Evashevski. It was the 1953 season finale against the heavily favored Notre Dame Fighting Irish in South Bend, Indiana. It was just Evashevski's second season, and Iowa football was showing signs of coming out of a long slumber that had lasted over a decade. Iowa started the 1953 season with an even 3–3 record, but saved the best for last that year. The next two games were both decisive shutout wins for Iowa: 26–0 over Purdue and 27–0 over archrival Minnesota. That set up the game at South Bend.

Notre Dame came into the game against Iowa as an overwhelming 13-point favorite and No. 1 in the AP writers poll by the largest margin in the history of the poll. Notre Dame was coached by the legendary Frank Leahy. Leahy had coached Notre Dame for 11 seasons and had already won four national championships coming into the 1953 season. But Iowa would not be intimidated by the Notre Dame mystique.

The Hawkeyes took a 7–0 lead in the first half, led by the running of Eddie Vincent. The 7–0 lead lasted until the final seconds of the half. On the last drive of the first half, the Iowa defense stopped Notre Dame on a running play inbounds at the Iowa 13-yard line. There were only two seconds left on the clock at the conclusion of the play and Notre Dame had no timeouts. Since the clock runs following a running play that ends inbounds, the Hawks expected the clock to expire so that they would then take the 7–0 lead into the locker room at halftime. However, yards away from the play, a Notre Dame player suddenly fell injured, which stopped the clock. While the fallen player was tended to by the medical staff, Notre Dame's offense quickly moved to the line of scrimmage and was ready to run a play when the officials finally wound the clock. The extra play resulting from the apparent injury allowed Notre Dame to pass for the tying touchdown as time expired in the first half.

A defensive struggle was waged between the two teams for most of the second half.

Legendary Notre Dame coach Frank Leahy won four national championships for the Irish, but was widely criticized for instructing his players to fake injuries at the end of both halves against Iowa at Notre Dame Stadium on November 21, 1953. The ploy twice allowed Notre Dame an extra play that resulted in their only two touchdowns, which were enough to tie Iowa 14–14. *Photo courtesy of Getty Images*

Finally, late in the fourth quarter, Iowa was able to string together a long drive that culminated in a four-yard touchdown reception by Frank Gilliam. Now Iowa led 14–7 with just over two minutes remaining on the clock. However, Notre Dame was not finished. The Fighting Irish drove deep into Iowa territory in the game's waning seconds. In a scene that was eerily reminiscent of the sequence at the end of the second quarter, Notre Dame was again stopped inbounds on a pass play at the Iowa 9-yard line, again with no timeouts remaining. Again, Iowa thought that this play would end the half. But again Notre Dame turned to the same tactic. To be sure that the clock would stop, this time *two* Irish players fell to the ground with apparent injuries. With the clock stopped, the Irish were able to again set up one final play at the line of scrimmage while the Irish trainers attended to the Notre Dame players who had suddenly dropped to the ground. The players eventually walked off the field under their own power. Again, Notre Dame took advantage of an extra play to pass for a touchdown and an eventual 14–14 tie following the extra point.

Iowa's coaches, players, and fans felt strongly that the suspiciously well-timed injuries at the end of both halves had robbed them of an opportunity for an upset of historic proportions. Upon returning to Iowa City, Coach Evashevski paraphrased from a poem by legendary sportswriter Grantland Rice as follows:

"When the One Great Scorer comes to write against our name,

He won't ask whether we won or lost,

But how come we got gypped at Notre Dame."

Leahy later admitted that he had instructed his players to fake injuries at the end of both halves.

Following the game, the East Coast press made a significant issue of Notre Dame's conduct. Rice and various other national media were harshly critical of the tactics employed by Notre Dame during the game. The consensus was that Notre Dame had been able to forge the tie by cheating, period.

The controversial game did have an unintended benefit of some much-needed national exposure for the up-and-coming Iowa football program. Although

FRANK LEAHY AND FOREST EVASHEVSKI

Following the game, heaps of criticism were dumped upon Notre Dame coach Frank Leahy. But, in spite of the intense pressure stemming from the game, he did not back down. He is quoted as saying: "Feigned injuries have been a part of football since Walter Camp invented the first down more than 70 years ago. Other coaches have told their players the same thing. Just ask any coach or player you know at the college, high-school, or even the grade-school level. Yet you probably never heard about a feigned injury until our Iowa game [because] the extra seconds gained [almost always] avail a team little or nothing. It seems to me that the feigned-injury controversy was caused not by what was done, but by who did it and how

successfully." Plagued by poor health, the "Fainting Irish" game versus Iowa would turn out to be the last game Leahy would coach for Notre Dame. He missed Notre Dame's game the following week versus USC and the last game versus SMU and stepped down as head coach at Notre Dame in January 1954.

Iowa coach Forest Evashevski, on the other hand, would go on to have significant success as the head coach at Iowa. He lead Iowa to a 52–27–4 record during his coaching tenure in Iowa City, including two Rose Bowl victories following the 1956 and 1958 seasons. It should come as no surprise that plays from both these Rose Bowls are included later in the book.

GAME DETAILS

Iowa 14 • Notre Dame 14

Date: November 21, 1953

Location: Notre Dame Stadium, South Bend, Indiana

Attendance: 56,478

Box Score:

Iowa	7	0	0	7	**14**
Notre Dame	0	7	0	7	**14**

Scoring:

IA   Vincent 12-yard run (Freeman PAT)
ND   Shannon 12-yard pass from Guglielmi (Schaefer PAT)
IA   Gilliam 4-yard pass from Stearnes (Freeman PAT)
ND   Shannon 9-yard pass from Guglielmi (Schaefer PAT)

Iowa finished with a 5–3–1 record in 1953, their strong showing in the last three games was enough for a ninth-place finish in the final AP poll. It was the first time an Iowa football team had finished the season ranked since the days of Nile Kinnick and the Ironmen in 1939. Meanwhile, the tie cost Notre Dame the national title, which would have been Leahy's fifth. Notre Dame finished a distant No. 2 in the final polls.

On January 13, 1954, the NCAA rules committee released a statement outlining its position on the "serious problem" of feigned injuries. This statement from early 1954 is reflected in the rules and regulations of today. The 2006 NCAA Football Rules and Interpretations indicate on page 13 that the following is considered an "unethical practice":

"Feigning an injury for the purpose of gaining additional, undeserved time for one's team. An injured player must be given full protection under the rules, but feigning injury is dishonest, unsportsmanlike and contrary to the spirit of the rules. Such tactics cannot be tolerated among sportsmen of integrity."

October 13, 2007

PICKOFF STOPS THE BIG TEN BLEEDING

Brett Greenwood's late interception against Illinois helps Iowa snap an eight-game conference losing streak

By most accounts, the 2007 season for the Iowa Hawkeyes football program was one of disappointment and wondering what could have been. It was an up-and-down year that saw the Hawks finish with a mediocre 6–6 record in the regular season (4–4 in Big Ten play and 2–2 in nonconference games). Iowa won its first two nonconference games, then dropped four straight and followed that by winning four of five. Then, just when it appeared that things were turning the Hawks' way, a lackluster performance in a home loss to Western Michigan essentially cost Iowa a chance at a bowl game. With the six wins, the team was bowl-eligible for the seventh straight year, but the Big Ten boasted a total of 10 bowl-eligible teams. Even with Ohio State qualifying for the BCS title game against LSU, which opened up another bowl slot for the conference, there weren't enough bowl bids to go around; both Iowa and Northwestern were left bowl-eligible but deemed not "bowl-worthy."

One of the bright spots during the 2007 season came during the home game against Illinois in October. The game would come right down to the wire, with an interception by freshman safety Brett Greenwood on Illinois's final drive ultimately sealing an exciting win for Iowa.

Iowa had come into the game 0–3 in Big Ten play and had also dropped the last five league games the prior year. The eight-game losing streak in conference play was the longest since head coach Kirk Ferentz's first season at the helm in 1999. Illinois was experiencing a breakout year under third-year head coach Ron Zook and brought a perfect 3–0 league mark into Kinnick Stadium. The University of Chief Illiniwek found themselves ranked in the polls, at No. 18/19, for the first time since 2001.

At least from a scoring standpoint, the game would prove to be dominated by the defense of both teams. Although they didn't produce an abundance of points, Iowa's offense controlled most of the first half, possessing the ball 19 minutes to Illinois' 11. This was critically important, because until this game, the offense had not been able to generate many sustained drives during the

Iowa's Brett Greenwood secures an interception late in the fourth quarter against Illinois at Kinnick Stadium on October 13, 2007, sealing a Hawkeye victory. *Copyright: University of Iowa—CMP Photographic Service*

2007 campaign, which put tremendous pressure on a talented and seasoned Iowa defense. However, the only points of the half were produced on a 28-yard field goal by Iowa kicker Daniel Murray with just 26 seconds left before intermission. The kick matched a prior 46-yard field goal by Illinois's Jason Reda. The teams entered the locker rooms tied at 3–3.

The drama built in the second half. Illinois took the opening possession of the half on a 12-play, 74-yard drive that was capped by another Reda field goal, this time for 23 yards. However, Iowa was able to take some solace in limiting the Illini to a field goal, as the defense kept Illinois out of the end zone following a first-and-goal situation at the Iowa 2-yard line.

By the end of the third quarter, Iowa had grabbed a lead it would not relinquish. Iowa took over at the Illinois 46 with 4:39 to play in the quarter, and the offense—led by sophomore quarterback Jake Christensen—executed a nine-play drive that culminated in the go-ahead touchdown. Running back Albert Young carried most

of the load early in the drive, but a 20-yard touchdown pass from Christensen to Brandon Myers with six seconds left in the quarter capped the drive. Iowa now led 10–6.

Up until the final two minutes of the fourth quarter, the biggest play of the quarter had ended in a penalty on Illinois. The penalty for having an ineligible receiver downfield negated an 83-yard scoring strike from Illinois quarterback Eddie McGee to Joe Morgan. Ironically, a similar penalty that went against Iowa during the 2006 Alamo Bowl against Texas cost the Hawkeyes a touchdown, and probably the game as well—that game ended in a 26–24 loss to the Texas Longhorns. They say things have a tendency of evening out in the long run, which appeared to be true in this instance.

Iowa was clinging to the 10–6 lead when Illinois took over on a punt on their own 29-yard line with 2:28 remaining on the clock. Two big pass plays to Arrelious Benn, which were good for 28 and 24 yards, allowed the Illini to advance the ball to the Iowa 11 with just

BRETT GREENWOOD

Brett Greenwood was a redshirt freshman in 2007. The game against Illinois in October 2007 was only his second start at the college level. He would go on to start the remaining games that year for Iowa. Greenwood, a native of Bettendorf, Iowa, was a prep standout at Pleasant Valley High School where he participated in football, basketball, and track. The 6', 200-pounder was one of 29 first-year players to see football game action on either offense, defense, or special teams during Iowa's 2007 season. He is the only redshirt freshman on the team's leadership council. Greenwood joins a long list of successful walk-ons to the Hawkeyes program.

Greenwood used the game-changing play versus Illinois as the springboard to a very solid 2007 season.

In particular, Greenwood again stood out as a hitting machine during Iowa's last conference game against Minnesota, where he broke up two passes and was credited with seven tackles. Greenwood's performance in that game prompted the following quote from Iowa senior linebacker Mike Klinkenborg: "I can't say enough about our D-backs. They're tough to beat and have been all year. And in Brett's case, he's got quite a bright future. Imagine what he'll be like when he puts a little weight on."

On the year, Greenwood had two interceptions, posted 45 total tackles (25 of them solo), and broke up seven passes. Based on his performance during the 2007 season, big things are expected from Greenwood during his remaining three years of college eligibility.

GAME DETAILS

Iowa 10 • Illinois 6

Date: October 13, 2007

Location: Kinnick Stadium, Iowa City, Iowa

Attendance: 70,585

Weather: Cloudy with drizzle, 54 degrees

Box Score:

Illinois	3	0	3	0	6
Iowa	0	3	7	0	10

Scoring:

IL   Reda 46-yard FG

IA   Murray 28-yard FG

IL   Reda 23-yard FG

IA   Myers 20-yard pass from Christensen (Murray PAT)

over a minute left to play. That set the stage for redshirt freshman free safety Brett Greenwood to make one of the biggest plays of the 2007 season for the Hawkeyes. Illinois quarterback McGee thought he had spotted an open receiver, but evidently did not see Greenwood at all, because Greenwood stepped easily in front of the receiver in the end zone as the ball hit him between the numbers. He returned the ball to the 9-yard line, where Iowa was subsequently able to run out the clock and preserve a dramatic victory.

The win was Iowa's fifth straight versus Illinois and its first over a ranked opponent at home since the 2004 season finale versus Wisconsin. Although Iowa lost on the road the following week to Purdue, the Hawks appeared to build on the momentum gained by the Illinois victory as they closed the Big Ten campaign with three straight victories before falling to Western Michigan in the season finale. Illinois would recover quite nicely from the devastating loss and go on to defeat top-ranked Ohio State in Columbus in November 2007. Because eventual Big Ten champion Ohio State was able to work its way back into the BCS title game following the last several crazy weeks of the 2007 college football season, Illinois eventually earned its first trip to the Rose Bowl since the 1983 season.

Illinois was in shotgun and coach Phil Parker told Harold [Dalton] and me to basically read the quarterback. Coach told us that wherever he takes you with his eyes, just go with it. It happened so fast but actually [McGee] led me to the right place at the right time.

—IOWA'S BRETT GREENWOOD, ON THE INTERCEPTION PLAY AT THE END OF THE GAME VERSUS ILLINOIS

November 21, 1981

46 Interception Helps Hawks Smell Roses

Tracy Crocker's pick in the end zone halts a Michigan State drive and sends Iowa to its first Rose Bowl trip in 31 years

To say that Hawkeyes fans had waited a long time for this was the understatement of the century. The 1981 Iowa Hawkeyes football season was special, and the last conference game against Michigan State at home was probably the most memorable of that special season. The years preceding coach Hayden Fry's arrival in Iowa City had been as lean as any in the history of the program; Iowa had unfortunately become one of the doormats of the Big Ten. The numbers were not pretty:

- Iowa had no bowl appearances since winning the Rose Bowl following the 1958 season.
- Iowa had no winning seasons from 1962 to 1980.
- During the above time span, the program amassed an overall record of 58–133–5.
- The highest conference finish during this time was fourth in 1970 and 1980.
- Iowa went winless in Big Ten Conference play in three different seasons, and had one overall winless campaign in 1973.

- After coach Forest Evashevski's last season in 1960, the program burned through four different coaches from 1961 until Fry's arrival in 1979.

Coming into the Michigan State game, Iowa was a half game behind Michigan in the conference standings. Michigan had a date with ancient rival Ohio State to close the Big Ten season. The Ohio State–Michigan game ended before halftime of the Iowa–Michigan State game. Ohio State's Art Schlichter led Ohio State to a 14–9 upset win over Michigan, and the stage was set for Iowa's date with destiny. With its win over Michigan, Ohio State finished the conference season at 6–2; an Iowa win over Michigan State would give the Hawkeyes an identical record. In those days, the first tiebreaker that determined the Big Ten's Rose Bowl participant was length of time since the last Rose Bowl appearance. Iowa had that tiebreaker on Ohio State by a huge margin, so if Iowa could take care of business at home against the Spartans, then the Hawkeyes would be packing their bags for Pasadena.

The goal posts never had a chance...the crowd couldn't even wait until the final gun to begin a wild celebration following a 36–7 win over Michigan State that would send Hayden's Hawkeyes to their first Rose Bowl since the 1958 season. *Copyright: University of Iowa—CMP Photographic Service*

Iowa jumped out to a 16–0 lead in the first quarter. The first touchdown was cashed in following a Michigan State fumble on their first play from scrimmage. Hawkeyes running back Phil Blatcher scored on a nine-yard run to cap the Iowa scoring drive. Blatcher would go on to shoulder a large amount of heavy lifting for Iowa's offense as he gained a career-high 247 yards on the ground.

Iowa's other points of the half came on a safety following a blocked punt and another touchdown drive following the free kick. Michigan State answered with a touchdown in the last two minutes of the second quarter to make the score 16–7 at the half.

The entire Iowa team learned of the Ohio State–Michigan result during halftime, but Coach Fry did his best to focus the troops on the task at hand. However, Michigan State maintained the momentum grabbed by the late first-half touchdown drive on the first drive of the third quarter. Michigan State quarterback Bryan Clark, methodically led the Spartans to the Iowa 6-yard line. Many Hawkeyes supporters were wondering if the long hard-luck streak would continue. The next play was another pass into the end zone that was intended for Daryl Turner. However, Iowa cornerback Tracy Crocker stepped in front of the receiver, snatched the interception, and returned the ball out to the Iowa 16-yard line. The offense promptly marched down the field, putting a 26-yard Tom Nichol field goal on the board to extend Iowa's lead to 19–7.

Crocker, a senior from Cedar Rapids, atoned with his interception for some self-admitted mistakes earlier in the drive. He had been charged with a 15-yard personal foul penalty for a late hit and also felt like he had let the team down by allowing a 30-yard pass play from Clark to Otis Grant. Crocker admitted after the game that "yes, I was feeling like a goat when that interception came along."

It was Crocker's first interception of the entire year, but it couldn't have come at a more critical time for Iowa. Buoyed by the momentum gained on that play, the Hawks used a devastating rushing attack led by Batcher and backup Eddie Phillips to dominate the Spartans for the rest of the second half. As the time ticked off the clock, rambunctious celebrants from the crowd gathered in both end zones. With approximately two minutes left, a few anxious fans were able to put a serious list to the south goal post by grabbing the crossbar. As the final minute ticked away, first the south goal post, then the north fell to the ground. When the Kinnick Stadium scoreboard read 0:00, Iowa had grabbed its first Rose Bowl berth since the 1958 season.

THE START OF SOMETHING BIG

The 1981 season would prove to be the beginning of an incredible run of success for coach Hayden Fry at the University of Iowa. Fry would lead the Hawkeyes to bowl games in 13 of the next 16 seasons, including two additional Rose Bowl appearances following the 1985 and 1990 seasons. He retired after the 1998 season with an overall record at Iowa of 143–89–6.

Fry was instrumental in overcoming the perception of the Big Ten Conference as the "Big Two and Little Eight," which was based upon the dominance of Ohio State and Michigan in the 1960s and '70s. In fact, Fry used that perception as a motivational factor for his team before the Michigan State game. He was quoted after the win as saying: "I guess you can tell Mr. [Bo] Schembechler [the Michigan coach] that there was another game in the Big Ten today. I read my team what he said about it coming down to the same old story of Michigan and Ohio State being the Big Two and fighting for the Rose Bowl again."

GAME DETAILS

Iowa 36 • Michigan State 7

Date: November 21, 1981

Location: Kinnick Stadium, Iowa City, Iowa

Box Score:

Michigan St.	0	7	0	0	**7**
Iowa	16	0	20	0	**36**

Scoring:

IA   Blatcher 9-yard run (Nichol PAT)

IA   Blocked punt by Mojsiejenko out of end zone
      for safety

IA   Phillips 1-yard run (Nichol PAT)

MSU   Hodo 1-yard pass from Clark (Andersen PAT)

IA   Nichol 26-yard FG

IA   Blatcher 1-yard run (Nichol PAT)

IA   Nichol 23-yard FG

IA   Campbell 9-yard pass from Gales (Nichol PAT)

> Michigan State had been hurting us with timing patterns all along...Clark would throw when his receivers weren't even turned around because they were counting on knowing when the pass would be there...I read this one right, and the ball just came right to me. When an interception happens, the credit should go to 10 other guys, because that's the end result of good defense. We're not the type of team that big-plays an opponent to death. So we have to keep doing our jobs until we get a break.
>
> —IOWA CORNERBACK TRACY CROCKER,
> ON HIS INTERCEPTION EARLY IN THE THIRD QUARTER

RUNNING OVER A RIVAL

Tavian Banks's 82-yard touchdown run paces Iowa to a 15th consecutive victory over Iowa State

There are only two Bowl Subdivision (formerly Division 1-A) college football programs in the state of Iowa: Iowa and Iowa State. Thus, it goes without saying that the Hawkeyes game against Iowa State each year is one that both schools circle on the schedule. Since 1977, the two football programs have competed on the field for the Cy-Hawk Trophy.

Although the game with Iowa State has been an annual affair since 1977, many forget that the rivalry was dormant from 1934 to 1977. Iowa State generally pushed for the renewal of the intrastate rivalry. Iowa refused for a long time, realizing it had little to gain from the meeting. Television revenue was only a fraction of what it is now, and Iowa reasoned that it didn't need to play the little guy on the block in a stadium that was just half the capacity of Iowa's stadium.

However, in 1968, then–Iowa athletics director Forest Evashevski announced that the series would resume with two games to be played in 1977 and 1978. Evashevski reportedly realized that Iowa could not reasonably schedule other Big Eight conference rivals of Iowa State (such as Nebraska or Oklahoma) without scheduling Iowa State at least every once in a while. Four additional games were agreed to by Evashevski in 1969 to be played in 1979 through 1982. However, in May 1970, Evashevski resigned as Iowa athletics director.

Iowa was still reluctant to make the series a regular affair; the school later announced that Evashevski had acted beyond his authority in scheduling the four additional games with Iowa State and that it would only honor the first two of the scheduled meetings. The matter became a political football, and the State Board of Regents eventually sent the matter to arbitration. After hearing both sides, the arbitrator ruled that the prior commitment to play the four games needed to be honored by Iowa.

The teams have played every year on a home-and-home basis since 1981 (the first four games, from 1977 through 1980, were all played in Iowa City). Although Iowa grabbed a 12–10 victory at home on September 17, 1977, in the first meeting since 1934, Iowa State was on the upswing under coach Earle Bruce and would go on to claim

Iowa running back Tavian Banks is pursued by Iowa State defender Breon Ansley during his 82-yard touchdown run on the second play from scrimmage against the Cyclones on September 20, 1997, at Jack Trice Stadium in Ames. *Photo courtesy* The Cedar Rapids Gazette

victory in four of the next five contests. However, with the arrival of Hayden Fry in Iowa City, the fortunes of both schools in this hotly contested series were changed. Coming into the 1997 annual intrastate battle, Iowa had won 14 consecutive games against Iowa State. The streak had begun with a 51–10 whitewashing in 1983, and the most recent result prior to 1997 was a one-sided 38–13 win for Iowa.

The Iowa State game was Iowa's third nonconference game in 1997. The Hawks had destroyed their first two overmatched nonconference opponents: 66–0 versus Northern Iowa and 54–16 versus Tulsa. Coming into the game, however, Iowa's coaching staff was genuinely concerned about the matchup against the Cyclones—in particular, talented Iowa State running back Darren Davis. However, any concerns Iowa might have had evaporated quickly. Senior running back Tavian Banks rumbled 82 yards on the second play from scrimmage to break the game open very early. The touchdown run was directly up the middle, and the play was so well blocked by Iowa that the Iowa State defense practically did not even lay a hand on Banks.

After the early touchdown run from Banks, the Cyclones defense appeared to key on Banks and the Iowa rushing attack. In response, the Hawkeyes offense went to work over the air; senior quarterback Matt Sherman hooked up with fellow senior Tim Dwight for touchdown passes of 41 and 29 yards in the first half, and the rout was on. Banks would go on to score three more touchdowns on the day and totaled 127 yards rushing on 20 attempts. Dwight chipped in with eight receptions for 157 yards and three scores. Sherman finished an abbreviated day's work with 12 of 17 completions for 257 yards, with one interception and three touchdown passes, all to Dwight. As a team, Iowa ran up a total of 575 yards of total offense. The decisive win was the 15th consecutive win in the intrastate series for Fry and the Hawkeyes.

Early in the 1997 season, the Hawks looked as if they were primed for another Rose Bowl run. Iowa State coach Dan McCarney remarked after the game: "Having been with three Big Ten Conference champion teams—two with Hayden and one at Wisconsin—you stand there and don't see any weaknesses." McCarney

TAVIAN BANKS

Tavian Banks lettered at Iowa for four years: 1994, '95, '96, and '97. The first three years of Banks's Hawkeyes career overlapped with that of another standout tailback, Sedrick Shaw (mentioned in Plays 42 and 31). Various injuries, and having to play behind Shaw, slowed Banks during the early years of his career. However, he came into his own during the 1997 season. During that year, Banks set the Iowa single-season rushing record, with 1,691 yards, and the single-game rushing record, with 314 yards against

Tulsa (in the week immediately prior to the Iowa State game). For his Iowa career, Banks finished with a total of 2,977 yards rushing, which ranks him third on the all-time leading rusher list, behind Shaw and Ladell Betts.

Banks was selected in the fourth round of the 1998 NFL draft by the Jacksonville Jaguars. However, his NFL career was cut short by a devastating knee injury in 1999.

GAME DETAILS

Iowa 63 • Iowa State 20

Date: September 20, 1997

Location: Jack Trice Stadium, Ames, Iowa

Box Score:

Iowa	14	21	21	7	**63**	
Iowa St.	0	6	7	7	**20**	

Scoring:

IA Banks 82-yard run (Bromert PAT)
IA Banks 8-yard run (Bromert PAT)
IA Banks 1-yard run (Bromert PAT)
IA Dwight 41-yard pass from Sherman (Bromert PAT)
IA Dwight 29-yard pass from Sherman (Bromert PAT)
ISU Stensrud 11-yard pass from Bandhauer (PAT failed)

IA Dwight 33-yard pass from Sherman (Bromert PAT)
IA Banks 4-yard run (Bromert PAT)
ISU Stensrud 5-yard pass from Bandhauer (Kohl PAT)
IA Cooks 30-yard interception return (Bromert PAT)
ISU Watley 30-yard pass from Bandhauer (Kohl PAT)
IA Gibson 58-yard pass from Reiners (Bromert PAT)

said of the Hawks, "You see the good players they have, the experience they have, and having as good a head coach as there is in college football makes a pretty good combination."

Unfortunately, Iowa could not parlay its early-season domination in 1997 into a hugely successful conference season. While the Hawks easily won their first Big Ten game against Illinois, they dropped consecutive decisions on the road at Ohio State and Michigan. Iowa went on to lose very close games to Wisconsin and Northwestern late in the year to finish the conference season at just 4–4. The 1997 season ended with a forgettable 17–7 loss to Arizona State in the Sun Bowl in El Paso, Texas.

Personally, I'm disappointed in my yard production, but I think they were really trying to stop me. They stacked the defense to stop the run. They showed us some looks that messed us up a little, but we adjusted and made some great plays passing.

—TAVIAN BANKS, FOLLOWING THE GAME

November 22, 1986

44 MIRACLE AT THE METRODOME

Rob Houghtlin's second-chance field goal clinches a tight victory over Minnesota and a Holiday Bowl berth

The 1986 regular-season finale at the Metrodome in Minneapolis had all the makings of an Iowa classic: a rivalry game with the Floyd of Rosedale Trophy on the line, a hostile atmosphere on the road, major bowl implications, a spirited second-half comeback by the Hawks— and incredibly, two last-second field-goal attempts. The second field-goal attempt resulted in the final three points that were the ultimate difference in a 30–27 hard-fought Hawkeyes win that earned Iowa a trip to San Diego for the 1986 Holiday Bowl. The game was played in front of a Metrodome record crowd of 65,018 fans.

Coming into the game, Iowa stood at 4–3 in the Big Ten. Thus, this game was critical to the Iowa season because it would decide whether Iowa would finish with a winning conference record or just a .500 record. The Gophers came into the game sporting an overall 6–4 record, 5–2 in the Big Ten.

Iowa was facing a 17–0 deficit at halftime, and it certainly appeared as though the Gophers would win back Floyd of Rosedale and force Iowa to settle for a .500 Big Ten

record. Minnesota had capped the strong first half with a school-record 62-yard field goal by place-kicker Chip Lohmiller as the first half expired. The long field goal by Lohmiller, who would go on to star in the NFL for the Washington Redskins, fell just one yard short of the Big Ten record. Another future NFL standout, Morten Anderson of Michigan State, had set the Big Ten mark with a 63-yard field goal against Ohio State in 1981.

Iowa started the game with second-string quarterback Tom Poholsky. Poholsky got the call because senior starter Mark Vlasic had suffered a shoulder injury in the third game of the year against Texas-El Paso and had been slow to recover. The Iowa offense was able to move the ball in the first half behind Poholsky, but unfortunately was unable to produce any points. Two second-quarter drives penetrated deep into Minnesota territory, but failed to register any points. Poholsky was stripped inside the Minnesota 10-yard line to halt the first drive, and an interception in the end zone on a play from scrimmage at the Minnesota

I got lucky, didn't I? I went from goat to hero in a matter of a few minutes.

—ROB HOUGHTLIN, AFTER THE GAME

Iowa's Rob Houghtlin connects on a field goal on the last play of the game to defeat Minnesota at the Metrodome in Minneapolis, Minnesota, on November 22, 1986.

Copyright: University of Iowa—CMP Photographic Service

14 cost the Hawks their next opportunity to get on the scoreboard in the first half.

Desperately needing some type of spark to rally his troops, coach Hayden Fry turned to his senior quarterback, Vlasic, in the second half. Said Fry, "Evidently [Vlasic] just forgot about his shoulder tonight. In the pregame, [offensive coordinator] Bill Snyder noticed he was throwing better than he has since he got injured." Vlasic ended up validating Fry's move by producing 199 passing yards in the second half and leading the Hawks to a thrilling second-half come-from-behind victory.

Vlasic got the Iowa offense rolling immediately by completing his first two passes of the opening second-half drive, including a 35-yard completion to Quinn Early. The connection set up Rob Houghtlin's longest field goal of the season, a 49-yarder that came with 12:56 left in the third quarter. The Iowa defense then forced a Minnesota punt to freshman Peter Marciano. Marciano provided a huge lift by returning the punt 89 yards for a touchdown, trimming the Minnesota lead to 17–10 with 9:30 remaining in the third quarter.

Minnesota added another touchdown, but another Houghtlin field goal, this one a 38-yarder, would pull Iowa to within 24–13. The key play on the drive that set up the field goal was a pass interference call against Minnesota in the end zone on a pass from tight end Mike Flagg to Early. Flagg had taken a lateral from quarterback Vlasic.

Vlasic methodically drove Iowa downfield early in the fourth quarter for a touchdown. He completed passes of 18 yards to Jim Mauro, 15 yards to tight end Marv Cook, and 17 yards to running back Rick Bayless. The touchdown came on a short pass to Flagg in the end zone. With just over 10 minutes to play in the fourth quarter and Iowa down by five, the two-point conversion attempt failed, which kept the score at 24–19 in favor of the Gophers.

Iowa took the lead 25–24 on a one-yard touchdown plunge by Bayless with 5:27 left. The key play on the drive was a 24-yard strike from Vlasic to Flagg. After Iowa's third and final timeout to strategize, the Hawks scored on a two-point conversion on a pass from Vlasic to Kevin Harmon, which extended Iowa's first lead of the evening to 27–24.

However, Minnesota had plenty of fight left. The Gophers promptly pounded the ball on an 11-play drive that covered 39 yards to the Iowa 32-yard line where the

HAYDENISMS

Coach Hayden Fry has a wonderful sense of humor. An example of this was evident following the game when he met with the press. Just before the press conference, Fry donned a pair of overalls and a straw hat. It was intended as a jab at the Minnesota media for frequently making jokes about Iowa farmers. Iowa definitely got the last laugh in this case.

Also, owing to his west Texas routes, Fry also had an unusual way of expressing himself on occasion (at least as far as Midwesterners were concerned). He developed several catch phrases that became popular among those following the Iowa team. Included among them was "scratch where it itches," which essentially translated to "go after an opponent's weakness." An injured player was often referred to by Coach Fry as having a "hitch in his get-along" or "buggered up." In a bit of self deprecating humor, Fry would refer to himself as "an old mule with blinders on," to explain why coaching was his sole focus.

GAME DETAILS

Iowa 30 • Minnesota 27

Date: November 22, 1986

Location: HHH Metrodome, Minneapolis, Minnesota

Attendance: 65,018

Box Score:

Iowa	0	0	13	17	**30**
Minnesota	7	10	7	3	**27**

Scoring:

MN	Goetz 6-yard run (Lohmiller PAT)
MN	Thompson 8-yard run (Lohmiller PAT)
MN	Lohmiller 62-yard FG
IA	Houghtlin 49-yard FG
IA	Marciano 89-yard Punt Return (Houghtlin PAT)
MN	Foggie 23-yard run (Lohmiller PAT)
IA	Houghtlin 38-yard FG
IA	Flagg 1-yard pass from Vlasic (2-pt. conv. failed)
IA	Bayless 1-yard run (2-pt. conv.—Harmon, 2-yard pass from Vlasic)
MN	Lohmiller 49-yard FG
IA	Houghtlin 37-yard FG

drive stalled. On came the steady Lohmiller for a 49-yard field-goal attempt. Lohmiller was good and the game was tied at 27–27, with just 1:03 remaining. (Remember that there was no overtime in college football in those days.)

Another comeback would be needed if Iowa was to pull out the victory, and Vlasic was ready for the challenge. A 25-yard pass to Early got Iowa to midfield. A five-yard completion to Cook advanced Iowa to the Minnesota 45, and Cook got out of bounds to kill the clock with 23 seconds remaining. Then, an 11-yard pass from Vlasic to Mauro moved Iowa to the Minnesota 34-yard line. An incomplete pass stopped the clock with just 10 seconds remaining.

Although it was Vlasic who put Iowa in a position to win, it was Iowa's special teams that sealed the victory. Iowa trotted Houghtlin onto the field for a 51-yard field-goal attempt for the win. The kick was away and had the distance, but it sailed wide of the right upright. But, in an absolutely stunning turn of events, Minnesota had 12 men on the field, which drew a 15-yard penalty and a second opportunity for Houghtlin. The clutch junior place-kicker from Glenview, Illinois, cashed in on his second opportunity, nailing a 37-yard field goal with just one second on the clock. The classic Iowa victory was complete.

 HAWKS STEAL THE SHOW IN MADISON

Drew Tate's touchdown pass to Ryan Majerus boosts Iowa over Wisconsin in Barry Alvarez's home finale

November 12, 2005, was declared "Barry Alvarez Day" across the state by the governor of Wisconsin. On that day Alvarez, who was completing his 16th and final season as head coach, would lead his Badgers at Camp Randall Stadium for the last time against the Iowa Hawkeyes in the annual battle for the Heartland Trophy. Wisconsin came into the game at 5–2 in the Big Ten. Iowa came into the game reeling, having lost two close games in a row—to Michigan in overtime and to Northwestern in a narrow one-point defeat the week before. As a testament to the success of recent Iowa football seasons, amazingly, the two-game losing streak was Iowa's longest losing streak in four years.

Although it appeared as though a storybook ending was imminent for Alvarez and the Badgers, the Hawkeyes rained on the Wisconsin parade, pulling out a stirring comeback from a 10-point first-quarter deficit to score 20 unanswered points and win going away 20–10. The go-ahead touchdown came on a 13-yard touchdown pass from Drew Tate to seldom-used tight end Ryan Majerus in the third quarter.

Feeding off of the emotion of the crowd and the occasion, the Badgers charged to an early 10-point lead behind an offensive attack that racked up 136 yards of total offense in the first quarter. But the Badgers were forced to settle for a short field goal after marching to the Iowa 2-yard line on their third possession of the game.

This defensive stand started to turn the tide for Iowa. The stout Iowa defense would not allow another point the rest of the game.

> On one hand I have great feelings for Barry and the program up here, but the most important thing on our docket was making our team feel better....I hate to be a little selfish here, but the people I care about most are our football players.
>
> —IOWA HEAD COACH KIRK FERENTZ

Iowa tight end Ryan Majerus scores the go-ahead touchdown against Wisconsin in the third quarter at Camp Randall Stadium in Madison, Wisconsin, on November 12, 2005. Iowa came from behind for a hard-fought 20–10 road victory to spoil UW Coach Barry Alvarez's last home game. *Copyright: University of Iowa—CMP Photographic Service*

In fact, Wisconsin managed just 140 yards of offense over the final three quarters—and 68 of those yards came during the game's final drive over the last 1:21 of the game, after an Iowa victory was all but sealed.

The performance of the defense was all the more impressive considering that Wisconsin led the Big Ten in scoring coming into the game. The Badgers had scored more than 40 points per game in five of their previous 10 games. The Iowa cause was also assisted by several dropped passes by Wisconsin receivers, the most important being a dropped would-be 37-yard touchdown pass from John Stocco to Jonathan Orr in the second quarter. The driving rain in the second half almost certainly contributed to some of Wisconsin's miscues.

Iowa opened its scoring four minutes into the second quarter on a 35-yard field goal by Kyle Schlicher. It was Iowa's first penetration into Wisconsin territory in the game. That pulled Iowa to within 10–3 going into halftime.

The Hawkeyes came out firing in the second half. The first play from scrimmage was a 40-yard strike from Drew Tate to Clinton Solomon deep over the middle, perfectly placed between two Badgers defenders. The same combination hooked up for a 15-yard pass on the very next play. Then at the Wisconsin 6-yard line, Tate hit a wide-open Champ Davis for the tying touchdown with 10:11 left in the third quarter. The scoring drive covered a total of 75 yards.

With the outcome very much still in doubt and the game tied in the second half, Iowa's defense was nothing short of spectacular. The defense did not allow the Badgers into Iowa territory for five straight possessions. Wisconsin ran 24 straight plays without gaining a first down, including a string of four straight three-and-outs. Wisconsin's leading rusher, Brian Calhoun, was limited to 18 yards on 15 carries, and the entire Wisconsin team could muster only 19 yards on 31 attempts.

The Iowa offense was able to string together a seven-play drive that covered 80 yards and consumed 2:33 late in the third quarter. The drive climaxed with a 13-yard touchdown strike from Tate to tight end Ryan Majerus. Tate faked a handoff, which appeared to fool most of the Wisconsin defense, and found Majerus wide open with

RYAN MAJERUS

Ryan Majerus was a junior on Iowa's 2005 team and is a native of Oelwein, Iowa. The touchdown catch against Wisconsin was Majerus's second career touchdown and the biggest play of his Iowa career, at least on offense. His other memorable play as a Hawkeye came on special teams when he blocked a punt that led to an Iowa touchdown in the 2005 Capital One Bowl win over defending national champion Louisiana State.

Following the same unconventional path as one of Majerus's predecessors at tight end at Iowa, Dallas Clark, Majerus moved from outside linebacker to tight end after his redshirt year in 2002. He started at tight end in the first two games of the 2005 season. Majerus was named to the Academic All–Big Ten team in 2003, 2004, and 2005.

Iowa's Mike Elgin (54) congratulates Ryan Majerus (left) on his 13-yard reception that gave Iowa the lead in the third quarter against Wisconsin at Camp Randall Stadium on November 12, 2005. *Photo courtesy* The Cedar Rapids Gazette

GAME DETAILS

Iowa 20 • Wisconsin 10

Date: November 12, 2005

Location: Camp Randall Stadium, Madison, Wisconsin

Attendance: 83,184

Weather: Cloudy, rain, 62 degrees

Box Score:

Iowa	0	3	14	3	**20**
Wisconsin	10	0	0	0	**10**

Scoring:

WIS	Williams 17-yard pass from Stocco (Mehlhaff PAT)
WIS	Mehlhaff 24-yard FG
IA	Schlicher 35-yard FG
IA	Davis 6-yard pass from Tate (Schlicher PAT)
IA	Majerus 13-yard pass from Tate (Schlicher PAT)
IA	Schlicher 32-yard FG

no Badgers within five yards. Majerus turned completely around to face Tate as he caught the ball at the goal line and trotted backwards into the end zone for what would prove to be the winning points, thanks in large part to the brilliant play of the Iowa defense.

When Iowa added a 32-yard field goal by Schlicher with 9:21 remaining, all the rain-soaked Badgers supporters had left to cling to were past glories under Alvarez; there would be no joy in Madison this day. The win snapped an 11-game Wisconsin home winning streak. It was Iowa's fourth straight over the Badgers and it allowed Iowa to retain the Heartland Trophy—awarded annually to the winner of the Iowa-Wisconsin game since 2004—for the second consecutive time.

Although the Tate-to-Majerus score provided the winning points, the heroes on the Hawkeyes side were numerous. Freshman defensive lineman Mitch King and defensive end Kenny Iwebema registered two sacks apiece for a minus-17 yards combined. Tate ended the day with 21 of 34 for 224 yards, one interception, and two touchdown passes. Sophomore running back Albert Young rushed 26 times for 127 yards for the Hawkeyes. It was his sixth consecutive game of more than 100 yards rushing, and his seventh of the season.

December 29, 1996

42 Shaw Runs Over Red Raiders

A dazzling 20-yard touchdown run by Sedrick Shaw highlights a dominating Alamo Bowl victory

Iowa's opponent in the 1996 Alamo Bowl sported the best running back in the nation in Doak Walker Award winner Byron Hanspard of Texas Tech. Hanspard rushed for 2,084 yards in 1996, best in the NCAA. However, Hanspard would be held by the Iowa defense to a season-low rushing output this night at the Alamo Dome. Oh, and by the way, Iowa also brought its own pretty good running back into the game in senior Sedrick Shaw. Shaw, a native of Austin, Texas, produced more than 1,000 rushing yards in 1996, the third consecutive year he reached that plateau.

When the dust had cleared, it would be Shaw, the "forgotten man" in all the pregame publicity surrounding the Doak Walker winner from Texas Tech, who would steal the show and earn the game's offensive MVP honors. Shaw would finish with 113 yards on 20 carries, an Alamo Bowl record at the time.

Iowa came into the game with a solid 8–3 overall record, which included nonconference wins over an Arizona team that featured the famed "desert swarm" defense and intrastate rival Iowa State. Iowa's Big Ten record was 6–2, with the only league losses coming to 1996 Big Ten co-champions Northwestern and Ohio State.

Iowa was ranked No. 21 in both polls coming into the Alamo Bowl game versus Texas Tech. Texas Tech's overall record coming into the game was 7–4. It was Iowa's second Alamo Bowl appearance—they were soundly thrashed 37–3 by California

> **W**e couldn't find anything that would work against them. As a coach, the most helpless feeling is when you run the gauntlet of your offense and nothing works. We didn't have any momentum, and you can't play this game without a spark. So much of this game is momentum.
>
> —TEXAS TECH COACH SPIKE DYKES

Iowa running back Sedrick Shaw (5) led the Hawkeyes to a dominating 27–0 win over Texas Tech in the Alamo Bowl in San Antonio, Texas, on December 29, 1996. *Copyright: University of Iowa—CMP Photographic Service*

in the inaugural Alamo Bowl game in 1993, in which Iowa produced a paltry 90 yards of total offense. It was probably Iowa's worst-ever performance in a bowl game. However, this night would help take some of the sting out of that past pitiful performance and give Hawkeyes fans more pleasant memories to cherish regarding this bowl game.

The 1996 Alamo Bowl was memorable for the Iowa family for another, more somber reason. Iowa dedicated the game to linebacker Mark Mitchell and his family, following the death of his mother in a car accident south of Des Moines a few days before the game. The Mitchell family was on its way to San Antonio for the game. Many of Mitchell's teammates had spent time at the Mitchells' Iowa City home, so they took the news hard. In tribute to the Mitchell family, Iowa took the gold Tiger Hawk emblem and stripe off their helmets for the game.

"We were thinking of him," said defensive end Jared DeVries. "Our thoughts and prayers are with him and his family." The tragic news really put things into their proper perspective and made the football game seem inconsequential in the grand scheme of things, but Iowa appeared to draw energy and focus from the situation and ended up putting on perhaps their strongest performance of the entire season.

The Iowa defense set the tone for the entire game on Texas Tech's second play from scrimmage. Plez Atkins, hailing from Bartlett, Texas, intercepted a pass from Texas Tech quarterback Zebbie Lethridge and returned it eight yards to the Red Raiders' 39-yard line. Iowa took over, and the key play of the ensuing drive was a 24-yard Shaw scamper that set Iowa up first-and-goal on the Texas Tech 2-yard line. Shaw was trapped in the backfield on a draw play, but managed to elude multiple would-be tacklers in the backfield for the eventual big gain. Iowa quarterback Matt Sherman scored on a quarterback sneak two plays later. A bad snap resulted in a missed extra point, so Iowa led it 6–0 early.

The next scoring play was a brilliant second-quarter rushing touchdown by Shaw. It was one of the best runs of his stellar, record-setting Iowa career. Shaw took the handoff and spun a total of three times to dodge would-be tacklers on his way to an electrifying 20-yard jaunt to the end zone.

Shaw was so excited upon scoring that he drew a penalty for unsportsmanlike conduct for excessive celebration. Interestingly, he had been flagged for a similar foul following a long touchdown run in the Sun Bowl the previous year. Coach Hayden Fry jokingly commented after the game that Shaw's mother had run up to him during the postgame celebration and given him a big hug while telling him: "Don't say it, don't say it, you knew what he was going to do." Clearly, Shaw enjoyed every last minute of the

SEDRICK SHAW

Sedrick Shaw finished his Iowa career with 4,156 rushing yards, which is first on an impressive list of all-time Hawkeyes rushers. He rushed for more than 1,000 yards in three of his four seasons in Iowa City. He registered a career-best 1,477 yards rushing as a junior in 1995. Shaw was fortunate enough to play bowl games in his native state of Texas in both his junior and senior seasons (the 1995 Sun Bowl and the 1996 Alamo Bowl, both won by Iowa). His highest single-game rushing total was 250 yards on 42 attempts in support of a victory at Michigan State in 1995.

Shaw was a third-round draft pick of the New England Patriots in the 1997 NFL draft. In 1999 Shaw was traded to the Cleveland Browns and he ended his NFL career with the Cincinnati Bengals in 2000.

GAME DETAILS

Iowa 27 • Texas Tech 0

Date: December 29, 1996

Location: Alamo Dome, San Antonio, Texas

Attendance: 55,677

Significance: Alamo Bowl

Box Score:

Texas Tech	0	0	0	0	**0**
Iowa	6	11	0	10	**27**

Scoring:

IA	Sherman 1-yard run (Bromert rush failed)		IA	Bromert 36-yard FG
IA	Shaw 20-yard run (Knipper pass reception)		IA	Bromert 26-yard FG
			IA	Filer 14-yard run (Bromert PAT)

bowl game experience that was his last hurrah in a Hawkeyes uniform.

A two-yard pass play from Sherman to Chris Knipper on a two-point conversion made up for the missed point-after attempt and made the score 14–0, Iowa. The Hawkeyes made it 17–0 on the final play of the half when Zach Bromert hit a 36-yard field goal. The successful kick came only after he had missed a 41-yard attempt on a botched hold, but he got another chance when Texas Tech was flagged for an offside penalty. Bromert made good on this second chance from five yards closer.

The key play setting up the field goal was a 51-yard bomb from Sherman to junior wideout Tim Dwight. It was the longest pass completion in Alamo Bowl history up until that time. Dwight was another key performer on offense for the Hawks, hauling in five passes for 90 yards in the first half and finishing with six catches for 105 yards on the night. He also chipped in with his usual solid performance returning punts, totaling 23 return yards in the first half.

The Hawkeyes' dominance in all facets of the game essentially took a highly partisan and extremely disappointed Texas Tech crowd in San Antonio completely out of the game.

Iowa's defense took care of business the rest of the way. Defensive lineman Jared DeVries earned defensive MVP honors, although the entire 11-man defensive unit was worthy of the award. DeVries registered five tackles and linebacker Matt Hughes had eight, while fellow linebacker Vernon Rollins and defensive end Bill Ennis-Inge added five apiece. Hanspard had been averaging almost 200 yards rushing per game, but was held in this game to 64 yards on 18 attempts, by far a season low. Texas Tech had been averaging nearly 30 points a game, but were shut out for the first time since a 31–0 defeat at the hands of Arkansas in 1987. Texas Tech mustered just 206 yards of total offense against a stingy Iowa defense.

November 2, 1991

Air Strike in Columbus

A 61-yard touchdown pass from Matt Rodgers to Alan Cross gives Iowa only its second win in 30 years at Ohio State

Over the years, Columbus, Ohio, has been an unfriendly environment for most of Ohio State's opponents. But Iowa seems to have a particularly abysmal record at the Big Horseshoe. Since a win in 1959 in Columbus, Iowa has won only two contests at the Big Horseshoe through the 2007 season. In fact, plays from both of these wins appear in this book: one win in 1987 (Play Number 2) and this memorable win from 1991. The rare win in Columbus is special, indeed.

The Hawks were undoubtedly still stinging from a bitter defeat at the hands of the Buckeyes in Iowa City the previous year. Ohio State won that game 27–26 in stirring come-from-behind fashion after Iowa led most of the game. The winning score came on a three-yard touchdown pass with one second left in the game. Needless to say, Iowa felt like it owed Ohio State a big-time payback!

This game was also memorable for another reason completely unrelated to football—a terrible tragedy that occurred on campus the day before the game, on the afternoon of November 1, 1991. Just before

4:00 PM, Gang Lu, who had recently received his doctorate degree in physics from the University of Iowa, shot five people to death and permanently paralyzed another before killing himself. The killings plunged the campus into a state of shock, but they also drew the community together. The football game at Ohio State the next day allowed the campus community a brief diversion from the terrible events it was dealing with. In honor of the victims, Iowa stripped the gold Tiger Hawk emblem and gold stripe from their helmets for the game at Ohio State.

It was certainly a memorable win for the Hawkeyes. Coming off of a Rose Bowl appearance the prior year, Iowa was sporting a 3–1 conference record heading into the game; their only loss had been to Michigan at home in the Big Ten opener. The Hawkeyes had to overcome the loss of starting All–Big Ten quarterback Matt Rodgers to a knee injury late in the third quarter, but were able to hang on for the victory behind another stellar defensive effort.

Iowa jumped out to a 7–0 lead in the second quarter when Rodgers scored on a one-yard keeper to cap an 84-yard, 13-play

Iowa tight end Alan Cross scores on a 61-yard touchdown reception from Matt Rodgers against Ohio State at Ohio Stadium in Columbus, Ohio, on November 2, 1991. *Copyright: University of Iowa—CMP Photographic Service*

SHORT OUT PATTERN TO CROSS LEADS TO BIG PLAY

The biggest play of the game, on an emotional day for the Hawks at Ohio Stadium in 1991, came on an innocent-looking short pass play from Matt Rodgers (7) to Alan Cross (87) in the right flat. Before the snap, the play called for Danan Hughes (3), who lined up split wide right, to come in motion to the left. When Hughes went in motion, the only Ohio State cornerback on that side of the formation followed. No one remained on the left side of the Ohio State defense to cover tight end Cross. Compounding problems for the Buckeyes was the fact that the defensive call was a blitz. Once Rodgers got the ball to Cross in the flat a few yards downfield, all Cross had to do was keep from tripping over his own two feet as he scampered 61 yards down the right sideline and into the end zone. The Iowa offensive play was the perfect call for the Ohio State defensive formation and the Hawks executed the play flawlessly.

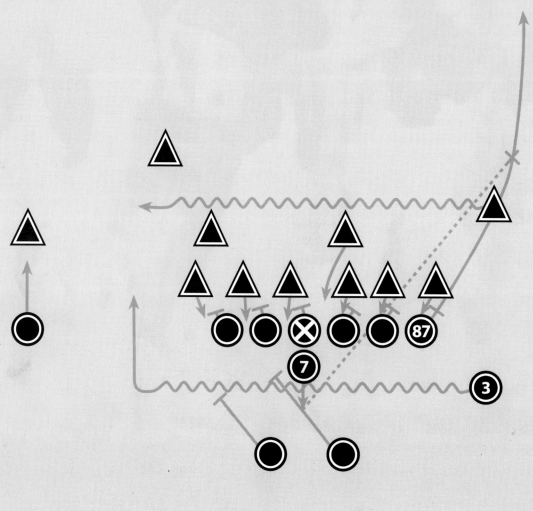

GAME DETAILS

Iowa 16 • Ohio State 9

Date: November 2, 1991

Location: Ohio Stadium, Columbus, Ohio

Attendance: 95,357

Box Score:

Iowa	0	13	3	0	**16**
Ohio St.	0	9	0	0	**9**

Scoring:

IA	Rodgers 1-yard run (Skillet PAT)
OSU	Snow 2-yard run (Williams PAT)
IA	Cross 61-yard pass from Rodgers (PAT blocked)
OSU	Simmons returns blocked PAT 85 yards for 2-pt conversion
IA	Skillet 30-yard FG

> **Y**ou're looking at the happiest man in the world right now. What a tremendous victory.
>
> —COACH HAYDEN FRY

drive. Always the innovator, coach Hayden Fry inserted two extra offensive linemen on the touchdown play, which gave Iowa a nine-man front with seven offensive linemen and two other linemen at the tight end position. Fry referred to it as the "Whale Formation," alluding to all the extra bulk up front.

Ohio State got the tying touchdown on the strength of a strong rushing attack by Carlos Snow, who carried the ball nine straight times for Ohio State, at last scoring on a two-yard touchdown run. Snow ended up accounting for all 50 yards gained on the drive, as the Buckeyes were able to have their way with the Iowa defense for one of the few times all day.

But Iowa had an answer. A spectacular answer. On a third-and-two play from their own 39-yard line, the Hawkeyes caught the Buckeyes in an all-out blitz and subsequently made them pay. Rodgers found Alan Cross all alone in the right flat for a short, soft toss, and Cross then raced 61 yards untouched down the right sideline to the end zone. That made the score 13–7, but the fireworks were not finished.

It was the Buckeyes' turn again. The point-after attempt by place-kicker Jeff Skillett was blocked by Ohio State's Greg Smith. Ohio State's Jason Simmons scooped up the bouncing ball and raced 85 yards in the opposite direction for a two-point conversion for the defense, a

> **T**here's no way you can replace those poor people who are dead, but that's why this victory has such a special meaning. The guys played their hearts out for the university family.
>
> —COACH HAYDEN FRY

new wrinkle to the rulebook adopted by the NCAA in 1990. The play ended up being a three-point swing on the scoreboard, but a huge swing in momentum. Iowa led it 13–9, rather than 14–7. Iowa took that lead into the locker room at halftime.

Both defensive units continued their strong play in the second half. Finally, late in the third quarter, Rodgers connected with Danan Hughes on a 50-yard pass play. However, Rodgers got bent awkwardly backward on a three-yard run deep in Buckeyes territory later in the drive. It was particularly unfortunate for Iowa because Rodgers was enjoying a career day, connecting on 20 of 27 pass attempts for 258 yards and one touchdown pass. Rodgers was later diagnosed with a sprained knee and was expected to be sidelined for a few weeks with the injury.

Ironically, Iowa's backup quarterback that day was Jim Hartlieb. Jim was the younger brother of Chuck Hartlieb, who had lofted the unforgettable pass to Marv Cook in the last minute of the game to stun the Buckeyes in this same stadium four years earlier (Play Number 2). Jim said after the game that he was thinking about Chuck and that dramatic 1987 game during the pregame warm-ups. Although Iowa wasn't able to score the touchdown on the drive, Skillett connected on a 30-yard field goal to make it a 16–9 Hawkeyes advantage.

Hartlieb's capable job of running time off the clock—and the more-than-capable Iowa defensive unit—took care of the rest. In particular, Iowa's Leroy Smith essentially took over the game. The senior from Sicklerville, New Jersey, set a school record with five quarterback sacks of Ohio State quarterback Kent Graham. He also recorded 14 tackles to lead the team.

Ohio State's last gasp came on a 50-yard pass into the end zone from Graham to Joey Galloway with 90 seconds remaining in the game, but Iowa's Gary Clark managed to bat the ball harmlessly away to preserve the Iowa win. In the end, many of the game statistics decisively favored Iowa, which outgained Ohio State 443–221 and enjoyed a 12-minute advantage in time of possession.

When the game was finally over, Iowa players joyously celebrated the victory in the northeast corner of the stadium with a group of loyal fans who had followed them to Columbus. Some of the players jumped into the stands and traded hugs. As the postgame celebration continued, they enjoyed a Hayden Fry original—the hokey-pokey dance—in the locker room.

MATT RODGERS

Senior quarterback Matt Rodgers saw significant action during his sophomore, junior, and senior seasons. As he surely can attest, playing quarterback for Iowa comes with a good-size helping of pressure. He struggled during his sophomore season when he made his fair share of mistakes as he learned the ropes, and the team finished 5–6 with no bowl appearance in 1989. But he stuck with it, put the experience gained during his tough sophomore year to good use, and rebounded nicely the following year. In 1990, he led Iowa to an 8–4 record, a Big Ten championship, and a Rose Bowl berth. Following the Ohio State game in 1991, Rodgers missed the next two games against Indiana and Northwestern. However, he would return in glorious fashion to lead Iowa to a season-ending victory over Minnesota to reclaim the Floyd of Rosedale Trophy. In that game, Rodgers tossed three perfectly thrown touchdown passes in snowy conditions. The 1991 Hawkeyes finished the regular season with a 10–1 record and would go on to tie Brigham Young University in the 1991 Holiday Bowl. Although Iowa led early, BYU rallied behind Heisman Trophy winner Ty Detmer to forge the tie.

Senior quarterback Matt Rodgers (shown looking for an open receiver during the 1991 Rose Bowl) led Iowa to the November 1991 win over Ohio State, but he paid a price: A sprained knee suffered in the OSU contest kept him out of the next two games. *Photo courtesy Getty Images*

December 30, 1987

WRIGHT MAKES HIS POINT

Anthony Wright's interception-return touchdown secures Iowa's second consecutive one-point Holiday Bowl victory

Following the completion of a 9–3 regular season and a second-place finish in the Big Ten, Iowa accepted a bid to the Holiday Bowl in 1987—its second straight appearance in the Holiday Bowl. Just like the previous year in 1986, the Hawkeyes' Holiday Bowl opponent was the champion of the Western Athletic Conference, which turned out to be the Wyoming Cowboys that year.

Iowa came into the game red-hot, having won five consecutive games, primarily with a high-powered offense—it averaged 36 points per game over the final five games of the regular season. However, during the Holiday Bowl, the special teams and defense certainly stood up to be counted, leading the team to a narrow victory. Three blocked kicks and an interception returned for a touchdown by Anthony Wright were instrumental in the narrow 20–19 win over Wyoming.

The exciting finish closely followed the script set during prior games in the bowl's 10-year history. Four of the previous games had been decided by a single point. The 1987 one-point Iowa win made three straight one-point games. Nine of the first 10 Holiday Bowl games were decided by a touchdown or less.

A fast start by Wyoming put Iowa in an early hole. Wyoming took the opening kickoff and quickly drove 43 yards. The two key plays were 19-yard and 24-yard pass plays from quarterback Craig Burnett (the game's offensive MVP) to Scott Joseph and James Loving. However, the drive stalled at the Iowa 26 and Wyoming was forced to settle for a 43-yard field goal from place-kicker Greg Worker.

Wyoming's next score was set up by its defense. A sack deep in its own territory and a poor punt gave the Cowboys the ball at the Iowa 44. Wyoming grabbed a 6–0 lead on a 38-yard field goal following two more passes from Burnett.

It got even worse for Iowa on Wyoming's next possession. The Cowboys engineered a 63-yard, eight-play drive again dominated by the passing attack of Burnett. Fifty-eight of the 63 yards were gained through the air. (Burnett would end up with 51 pass attempts, completing 28 for 332 yards. The

Iowa's Anthony Wright (10) celebrates in the end zone following a 33-yard interception return for a touchdown during the Hawks' win over Wyoming in the Holiday Bowl in San Diego on December 30, 1987. *Copyright: University of Iowa— CMP Photographic Service*

51 attempts broke the Holiday Bowl record previously held by Jim McMahon.)

Iowa was outgained 144–28 and could muster just one first down in the game's first 15 minutes. The Wyoming two-point conversion following the touchdown failed, but nevertheless, it didn't look good for the Hawkeyes as the first quarter ended, with Wyoming enjoying a 12–0 advantage.

Iowa finally got on the scoreboard when Merton Hanks, a sophomore from Dallas, blocked a Tom Kilpatrick punt attempt in the second quarter. Safety Jay Hess was able to coral the ball at the Wyoming 10 and run it in for the touchdown. Rob Houghtlin's point-after attempt made it 12–7, Wyoming.

However, any momentum gained by the big special teams play quickly dissipated as Wyoming answered swiftly and efficiently

on the ensuing drive, again led by the passing of Burnett. A three-yard touchdown run by Gerald Abraham put Wyoming in front 19–7.

A late second-quarter drive by the Hawkeyes set up a Houghtlin 30-yard field-goal attempt that was no good. The 13-play drive was the Hawks' only sustained offensive drive of the half. Wyoming led at halftime 19–7.

The Iowa defense was able to find an answer to the Cowboys' high-powered passing attack in the second half, shutting out the Cowboys the rest of the way. The Wyoming defense matched Iowa's in the third quarter, so the game entered the fourth quarter with Iowa still down 19–7.

The Iowa offense effectively moved the ball between the 20s, but couldn't push the ball over the goal line. The biggest weapons were the tight-end duo of Marv Cook and Mike Flagg, who caught a total of nine passes. Kevin Harmon was within inches of the goal line on a sweep, but he fumbled the ball out of the end zone, turning the ball over to the Cowboys. Early in the fourth quarter, Iowa was denied on a fourth-and-two play from the Cowboys' 5-yard line as Wyoming's Reggie Berry tipped a pass away from Cook. At that point, it certainly didn't look as if it would be the Hawkeyes' night.

But then, Iowa finally figured out the Wright stuff. Cornerback Wright picked off one of the few mistakes Wyoming quarterback Burnett had made all night. Burnett badly overthrew his intended target and sent the ball sailing right into the arms of Wright, who made the catch and scampered 33 yards through the stunned Wyoming offense for a huge Iowa touchdown. It was Wright's first interception of the season and the biggest play in Iowa's season up to that point. The big play pulled Iowa to within five points at 19–14.

With all the momentum, when Iowa got the ball back after stopping Wyoming again, the offense was finally able to string together a quality drive that covered 10 plays and 86 yards. The key play was a 48-yard pass from quarterback Chuck Hartlieb to a diving Travis Watkins at the Wyoming 20-yard line. The bomb set up a one-yard touchdown plunge by fullback David Hudson. With 7:33 remaining in the game, Iowa had grabbed its first lead 20–19.

However, Wyoming still had life and was perfectly comfortable facing this tough situation. The Cowboys had won four games in the final two minutes during the regular year. Burnett had the Iowa defense on its heels and marched Wyoming to the Iowa 35-yard line before the Iowa defense stiffened and forced three consecutive incompletions.

Wyoming was forced to attempt a desperation 52-yard field goal by Worker. It would be the longest of his career, if good. However, it never got near the goal posts; Hanks rushed in from the left to deflect the ball, and it landed harmlessly at the Iowa 20-yard line. Hanks's heroics saved the day for the Hawks, earning a second straight heart-stopping victory in the Holiday Bowl.

HAYDEN FRY ACCEPTS A CHALLENGE

Prior to the arrival of coach Hayden Fry in Iowa City in December 1978, Iowa had been to two postseason bowl games in the 20th century (two Rose Bowls following the 1956 and 1958 seasons). The Hawks and their fans had endured 17 consecutive nonwinning seasons when Hayden showed up on campus. Nevertheless, Coach Fry saw something in the Iowa program. He found the lack of recent success for the program difficult to comprehend. Iowa had strong financial support, played in a state with no major professional team, and got widespread coverage from the news media. Moreover, in spite of the heavy doses of losing, the films on the 1978 season suggested that the home games were still well attended. It seemed that the fans showed great enthusiasm, even for just a first down. Fry wondered what the reaction would be like when Iowa scored touchdowns! Fry thought he could make a winner out of Iowa and willingly took on the challenge. He ended up being right. The 1987 Holiday Bowl marked the seventh consecutive bowl game in the 1980s. The streak would be extended to eight with a visit to the Peach Bowl in 1988. In all, Iowa earned spots in 14 bowl games during Fry's 20-year tenure, a truly remarkable turnaround forged by one of the great coaches in college football history. Mostly on the strength of his great success at Iowa, Fry was inducted into the College Football Hall of Fame in 2004.

GAME DETAILS

Iowa 20 • Wyoming 19

Date: December 30, 1987

Location: Jack Murphy Stadium, San Diego, California

Attendance: 61,892

Weather: Clear, 50s

Significance: Holiday Bowl

Box Score:

Iowa	0	7	0	13	**20**
Wyoming	12	7	0	0	**19**

Scoring:

W	Worker 43-yard FG
W	Worker 38-yard FG
W	Loving 15-yard pass from Burnett (pass failed)
IA	Hess 10-yard blocked punt return (Houghtlin PAT)
W	Abraham 3-yard run (Worker kick)
IA	Wright 33-yard interception return (Houghtlin PAT)
IA	Hudson 1-yard run (pass failed)

> **I** thought the ball was right on line. I thought it would hit [the receiver] right on the head, but it just sailed.
>
> —WYOMING QUARTERBACK CRAIG BURNETT, ON WRIGHT'S INTERCEPTION

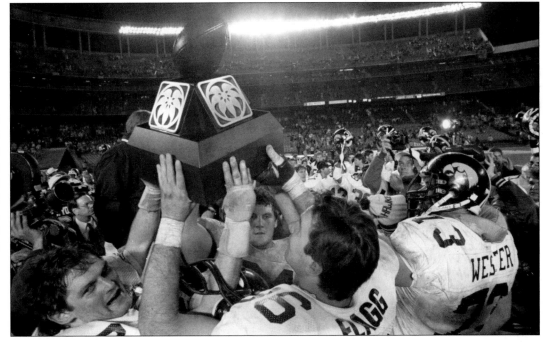

Happy Hawkeyes hold aloft the Holiday Bowl Trophy following a tight 20–19 win over Wyoming in December 1987.
Photo courtesy The Cedar Rapids Gazette

October 17, 1925

39 HAWKS LASSO THE GALLOPING GHOST

"Cowboy" Kutsch provides all the points as Iowa upsets Illinois and Red Grange

As of 1925, the Roaring Twenties were shaping up to be the best period of sustained success in the relatively short history of Iowa football. Coach Howard Jones had led the Hawkeyes to back-to-back perfect Big Ten championship seasons in 1921 and 1922—and two mythical national championships. From late in the 1920 season until the early part of the 1923 season, Iowa reeled off a 20-game winning streak, a truly amazing accomplishment so early in the history of Big Ten football.

During the run, Iowa halted Notre Dame's own 20-game winning streak in 1921 (Play Number 8). The team produced winning records in 1923 and 1924. After the 1923 season, coach Howard Jones, a Yale man from the East Coast, moved on to become the head man at the University of Southern California, where he built USC into a perennial power during the late 1920s and '30s. Five of Jones's USC teams were victorious in the Rose Bowl.

New Iowa coach Burt Ingwersen (who had played at Illinois and later served as

an assistant coach under head coach Bob Zuppke) took over the Iowa program in 1924 and led the team to a very respectable 6–1–1 record. Iowa's only loss that season came at the hands of Illinois, who was led in those days by the legendary Red Grange, the Galloping Ghost. The Hawkeyes were soundly thrashed by the Fighting Illini 36–0 in Champaign in 1924.

Based on the previous year's whipping, Coach Ingwersen likely did not have much trouble motivating his troops against Illinois during the 1925 season. As it turned out, Iowa really needed just one player—Nick "Cowboy" Kutsch accounted for all 12 of Iowa's points that day, and they were good enough to defeat Illinois 12–10.

The Illinois game in 1925 just happened to fall on Iowa's homecoming weekend. It was played at old Iowa Field, which served as Iowa's home field prior to the construction of Iowa Stadium (later renamed Kinnick Stadium), which opened for business during the 1929 season. The old stadium was located along the east bank of the Iowa

Iowa's all-everything back Nick "Cowboy" Kutsch scores Iowa's only touchdown of the game in a 12–10 victory over Illinois at Iowa Field on October 17, 1925. *Copyright: University of Iowa—CMP Photographic Service*

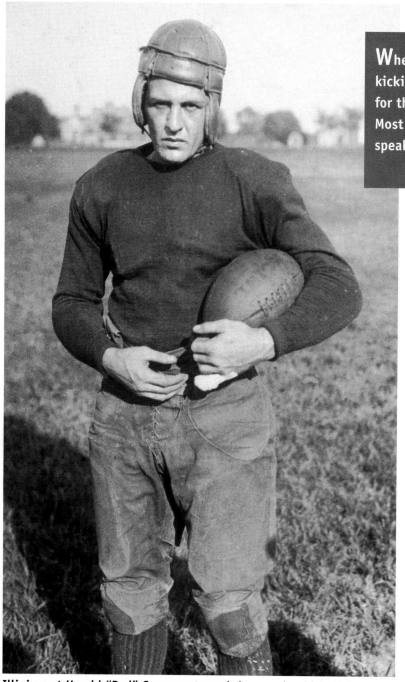

Illini great Harold "Red" Grange returned the opening kickoff for a touchdown to start the 1925 game against Iowa, but the Hawkeyes kept "The Galloping Ghost" out of the end zone after that to secure the upset victory. *Photo courtesy Getty Images*

River, just west of the present university library.

A record crowd of nearly 28,000 was on hand to witness the battle. Before the game, the Iowa team received a telegram from Ledrue Galloway, a tackle on the 1924 team. The telegram read: "There will be twelve men on the field to beat Illinois...I am with you." Galloway was laid up sick—and in reality, dying from tuberculosis. Nevertheless, the pregame message likely provided another intangible edge to Iowa as it took the field against its bitter rival one state to the east.

Grange certainly lived up to the large reputation that preceded him. As many were still settling into their seats in the bleachers along the river, Grange returned the opening kickoff 89 yards for an Illinois touchdown. After a successful point-after attempt, Illinois led the game 7–0 just seconds into the contest.

However, on this day, Iowa got all the points it needed to defeat the Illini from halfback Kutsch. Kutsch would drop-kick two field goals later in the game.

GAME DETAILS

Iowa 12 • Illinois 10

Date: October 17, 1925

Location: Iowa Field, Iowa City, Iowa

Attendance: 27,712

Box Score:

Illinois	7	0	0	3	**10**
Iowa	0	3	3	6	**12**

Scoring:

IL	Grange 89-yard kickoff return (Britton PAT good)
IA	Kutsch 25-yard FG
IA	Kutsch 25-yard FG
IL	Britton 31-yard FG
IL	Kutsch 2-yard run (PAT failed)

However, Illinois still led 10–6 late in the game when Kutsch scored the go-ahead touchdown on a two-yard plunge with less than two minutes to play, sealing an Iowa upset. The winning touchdown was set up by a 25-yard scamper from Kutsch.

The touchdown set off a wild celebration at Iowa Field. In the final statistics, the Ghost outrushed the Cowboy 172–122, but Kutsch threw for 44 yards to Grange's 16 as both players completed seven passes from their halfback position.

COWBOY KUTSCH

Nick "Cowboy" Kutsch was born in Dubuque, Iowa, in 1904, but he and his family moved to Sioux City where he eventually took a job at the local stockyards. It was there that he picked up his nickname by roping cows in the stockyard. He also developed a heroic reputation in Sioux City as a lifeguard; he was credited with saving 35 swimmers one summer. The nickname suited him well later in his football career at Iowa because he was known to ride his opponents on many exciting runs.

During his time in Iowa City, Kutsch was known primarily for his toughness. In early November of his senior season in 1926, the *Iowa City Press-Citizen* wrote: "Oh, he's pretty tough all right. He's not afraid of man or devil. That baby juke likes to fight. You can't handle him too rough to suit him on the football field. But when the game's over and he has donned his street clothes, he's a different fellow. Instead of Nick the fighter, Nick is the most bashful guy you ever saw. This hero stuff that is being slipped him rolls right off."

December 26, 1984

FLYING TO FREEDOM ON LONG'S ARM

Iowa routs Texas thanks to Chuck Long's 33-yard touchdown pass and a 31-point third-quarter outburst

Iowa finished the 1984 regular season with a record of 7–4–1 overall (5–3–1 in the Big Ten, which was good for a fourth-place tie in the final standings). The 1984 team started and ended the season slowly, but managed to put together five straight wins in the middle of the year. These wins accounted for all their Big Ten victories that year.

Unfortunately, back-to-back conference losses to open and conclude the Big Ten season plagued the 1984 Hawks and kept them out of a much more attractive bowl game. In those days of fewer bowl games, the Hawks were very much on the bowl bubble. However, their regular-season showing was enough to garner a bid to the inaugural Freedom Bowl in Anaheim, California.

The opponent that night was the University of Texas Longhorns. The Horns certainly had a proud football tradition. In fact, for several weeks in 1984, Texas held the number-one ranking in the national polls. Texas was still in the running for the Southwest Conference championship

and a Cotton Bowl bid late in the season, but back-to-back conference losses—similar to Iowa's—concluded the season in disappointing fashion and relegated Texas to a date in the Freedom Bowl with Iowa.

It would be a memorable rainy night in Southern California for Iowa and a nightmare to forget for Texas. Behind a superhuman performance by Iowa quarterback Chuck Long, the Hawks battered the Longhorns 55–17. Long set multiple school records in the process. The dominating performance by Iowa ended up being the worst loss suffered by the Texas Longhorns in 80 years—since 1904, when the University of Chicago (a Big Ten team at the time) handed Texas a 68–0 defeat.

The game was actually very competitive in the first half. Iowa led by just 24–17 at halftime. Amazingly, Long also started slowly on a rainy night. He missed his first three pass attempts, but didn't take long to catch fire from there. Iowa's first score was set up by a Mike Stoops interception on Texas's sixth play from scrimmage. He stepped in front of receiver Rob Moerschell

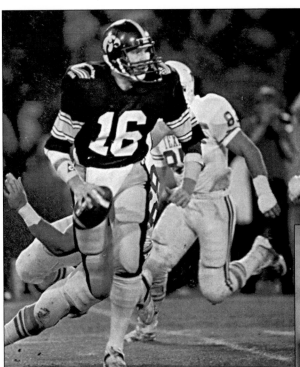

Iowa quarterback Chuck Long looks for a receiver as he rolls out during the first half of the Freedom Bowl against the Texas Longhorns on December 26, 1984, at Anaheim (California) Stadium. A dominant performance from Long and the Iowa passing attack buried the Longhorns 55–17. *Photo courtesy AP Images*

Bill Happel caught one of Chuck Long's six touchdown passes in the 1984 Freedom Bowl win over Texas. *Copyright: University of Iowa—CMP Photographic Service*

and picked off Todd Dodge's pass, returning the ball 18 yards deep into Texas territory.

On the third play of the ensuing drive, Long got Iowa on the board with the first of his eventual six touchdown passes, a six-yard strike to a wide-open Jonathan Hayes. Iowa's next possession led to another touchdown. This time, it was an 11-yard touchdown pass from Long to freshman Mike Flagg. A 41-yard pass play from Long to Flagg on third-and-three was the key play setting up the touchdown.

Texas made things interesting with a strong second quarter. The Horns got on the scoreboard following an 80-yard touchdown drive that comprised 12 plays. The scoring play came on a Dodge touchdown pass to Bill Boy Bryant. The successful point-after attempt made it 14–7, Iowa, with 13:35 to play in the first half.

CHUCK LONG

Chuck Long was just a junior in 1984, and many thought that the dominating Freedom Bowl win against Texas would be his last game in an Iowa uniform; he really didn't have much left to prove at the college level.

Two months passed before Long announced his decision in February 1985. Fortunately for the Hawkeyes, Long decided to return for his senior season. He provided the following rationale for his decision: "It boiled down to three reasons. I wanted to continue my education. Second, I wanted to be with a team that could be one of the most exciting in Iowa history. Most important, though, I'd like to have another chance to go to the Rose Bowl."

Long used his historic performance in the 1984 Freedom Bowl as the springboard for another stellar campaign in 1985. He would lead Iowa to a number one national ranking for several weeks, a Big Ten title, and a Rose Bowl appearance.

The appearance in the bowl game was the fifth of his career; he is the only NCAA player to appear in five different bowl games. He got into the game for just a few plays during the 1982 Rose Bowl, but that didn't count against his eligibility because they were his only plays of the season. Long still had four years of eligibility remaining, and he led Iowa to a bowl game in each of those memorable seasons.

But the Horns couldn't keep the momentum and Iowa's offense continued to shine. Iowa subsequently drove 77 yards in 10 plays for another touchdown. The drive was capped by a one-yard touchdown run by Fred Bush—the first touchdown of his career—with 10:14 left in the half.

However, Texas again had an answer; the Horns pounded out another 80-yard drive for a touchdown, eventually making it a seven-point 21–14 game. The touchdown came in dramatic fashion on a fourth-and-goal play from the 1-yard line. During the next drive, Iowa's first miscue of the evening was a fumbled snap at their own 27-yard line. It was recovered by Texas, who turned the lost fumble into three points, making it a 21–17 game with just over two minutes to play in the half.

The 46-yard field goal came after a roughing penalty on a 51-yard attempt that was no good. However, Iowa got the last laugh in the first half, running the two-minute drill, which ended with a 27-yard Tom Nichol field goal on the last play of the half—making it 24–17 Iowa, going into the locker rooms.

Although it seemed unlikely based on all the scoring in the first half, Texas had scored its final points of the evening by halftime. Iowa, however, was just getting warmed up. The Hawkeyes came out in the third quarter and quickly took a stranglehold on the game. Iowa took the opening kickoff 70 yards on five plays, capping the drive with a 35-yard field goal by Nichol. On Texas's second play on the ensuing drive, Iowa linebacker Larry Station stripped the ball from Jerome Johnson. Iowa recovered at the Texas 33.

Iowa would cash in immediately on the turnover. On Iowa's first play on the ensuing drive, Long heaved a beautiful 33-yard touchdown pass to Bill Happel. The Cedar Rapids junior broke free of Texas defender Tony Griffin at the line of scrimmage and raced down the sideline, hauling in Long's pass in the end zone. That key play signaled the beginning of the end for Texas, for whom the game would deteriorate quickly.

Iowa used the Long-to-Happel touchdown strike as the springboard to a devastating offensive outburst in the third quarter. An amazing three more touchdown passes were still to come from Long:

GAME DETAILS

Iowa 55 • Texas 17

Date: December 26, 1984

Location: Anaheim Stadium, Anaheim, California

Attendance: 24,093

Weather: Rain, 55 degrees

Significance: Freedom Bowl

Box Score:

Texas	0	17	0	0	**17**	
Iowa	14	10	31	0	**55**	

Scoring:

IA	Hayes 6-yard pass from Long (Nichol PAT)
IA	Flagg 11-yard pass from Long (Nichol PAT)
TX	Bryant 11-yard pass from Dodge (Ward PAT)
IA	Bush 1-yard run (Nichol PAT)
TX	Harris 1-yard pass from Dodge (Ward PAT)
TX	Ward 46-yard FG
IA	Nichol 27-yard FG
IA	Nichol 35-yard FG
IA	Happel 33-yard pass from Long (Nichol PAT)
IA	Smith 49-yard pass from Long (Nichol PAT)
IA	Helverson 4-yard pass from Long (Nichol PAT)
IA	Hayes 15-yard pass from Long (Nichol PAT)

- A 49-yard scoring strike to Robert Smith that capped a five-play, 94-yard drive
- A four-yard connection for a touchdown to Scott Helverson that concluded a four-play, 53-yard drive
- A 15-yard touchdown pass to Jonathan Hayes with 2:19 remaining in the third quarter, which capped a 65-yard drive and concluded the scoring

When the dust cleared, Iowa had put up an offensive showcase of historic proportions. The Iowa offense lit up the scoreboard for 31 points in the third quarter, grabbing a 55–17 advantage and blowing the game wide open in the process. The final offensive statistics were as lopsided as the final score:

- Iowa outgained Texas in total yards 560–300
- Iowa had 28 first downs to the Longhorns' 15
- Long finished the game with 29 completions for 39 attempts, 461 yards, six touchdowns, and no interceptions. The 29 completions, 461 yards, and six touchdowns were all school records. The six touchdown passes also tied the Big Ten mark set by Dave Wilson of Illinois in 1980.

The historic victory was most satisfying for a certain Texas native and Iowa head coach. Fry indicated after the game that "this is definitely the biggest win of my career. Being from Texas, you don't get the chance to beat the U of T very often. I have never had a victory more meaningful to me."

October 16, 2004

37

PICKOFF PUNCTUATES BUCKEYES BLOWOUT

Marcus Paschal's end-zone interception highlights Iowa's largest-ever victory over Ohio State

Even a casual Iowa football fan will likely be able to tell you that the program has historically struggled against Ohio State and Michigan. The numbers do not lie. Iowa's historic record against Ohio State is 14–44–3, and against Michigan it's 10–40–4. Of course, Iowa is not alone in struggling against these perennial Big Ten powers—and in fact has a much better record against these teams than some of its Big Ten rivals.

The reasons behind the struggle could be another book in and of themselves. It just boils down to being able to draw from a much deeper talent pool in more populated areas of the country. Iowa is the least populous Big Ten state. Teams like Iowa are able to draw quality talent to field a strong first team, but if injuries knock out a starting player for any period of time, the Michigans and Ohio States of the world have plenty of talent waiting in the wings to fill the position, while teams like Iowa may have difficulty.

Given the limited success Iowa has had against these two teams, a recurring theme in this book is seemingly ordinary plays that end up extraordinary because they happen to come in a win against one of the big two. This is already the second time Ohio State has appeared in the book, and it will appear again two more times. There are five plays from games against Michigan yet to come.

The 2004 season produced Iowa's second Big Ten championship in three seasons under coach Kirk Ferentz. However, the 2004 team did something even the 2002 team—which went undefeated in Big Ten play—could not do: it beat Ohio State. (The Hawkeyes and the Buckeyes did not play in 2002.)

Iowa sophomore quarterback Drew Tate was the clear offensive star for Iowa on this day. He passed for three touchdowns and ran for another in leading Iowa to the historic win. But the key play in the game was an interception by Marcus Paschal—in the end zone with 2:33 to play in the second

Iowa's Clinton Solomon (88) catches a touchdown pass in front of Ohio State's E.J. Underwood during the second half of Iowa's win against Ohio State at Kinnick Stadium in October 2004. *Photo courtesy AP Images*

quarter—that kept Ohio State off the scoreboard, with no momentum going into halftime. The interception halted a 13-play, 68-yard drive by the Buckeyes that had lasted six minutes and 22 seconds. Paschal leaped in the air to grab the ball at its highest point in front of the Ohio State receiver in the back right corner of the end zone; he managed to stay inbounds as he came down for a touchback.

Although the final score didn't suggest a close game, at the time of the interception an Ohio State touchdown would have pulled the Buckeyes to within 10–7—and perhaps more importantly, Ohio State would have had the momentum going into the second half. But, although so many prior Buckeyes teams had found a way to get it done against Iowa, it wasn't meant to be this day for Ohio State.

Iowa struck first in the contest with 3:14 to play in the first quarter. Tate led a 10-play drive that marched the ball 61 yards. The drive ended with an 11-yard touchdown connection from Tate to junior wide receiver Clinton Solomon. Kyle Schlicher extended the lead to 10–0 on a 45-yard field goal with 12:50 left in the second quarter. It was Schlicher's career best. Thanks to Paschal's interception, that would be all the scoring in the half.

Iowa got off to a fast start early in the second half. Ohio State had the ball to begin the half, but on the second play from scrimmage at their own 28-yard line, Iowa defensive lineman Derreck Robinson forced a fumble from Ohio State quarterback Justin Zwick. The ball was recovered by linebacker George Lewis, and Iowa was in business at the Ohio State 30.

Iowa capitalized on the fumble by converting a touchdown on a five-play drive. Tate capped the drive with an eight-yard touchdown pass to Scott Chandler. Chandler caught the ball on the run in the right flat

MARCUS PASCHAL

Marcus Paschal was a sophomore from Largo, Florida, on the 2004 team. Like many Iowa recruits, it wouldn't be a stretch to say that he wasn't exactly a much sought after blue-chip recruit coming out of high school. He was "discovered" by secondary coach Phil Parker during a recruiting trip to Florida in 2001. Coach Parker didn't even visit the area specifically to see Paschal. He was visiting another recruit from a nearby school but was referred to Paschal's high school coach by another coach. Paschal was an option quarterback in high school who rushed for nearly 1,000 yards and passed for more than 1,700 yards during his senior season. He didn't even play defense until his senior year, but also excelled on that side of the ball, making 61 tackles and hauling in eight interceptions.

Although his parents preferred that he be a big fish in a small pond and attend either Hofstra or Troy State, he ended up choosing Iowa. Paschal worked extremely hard in the weight room, bulking up to 196 pounds, compared to a paltry 165 pounds during his recruiting visit to Iowa City (when he was significantly weakened by the flu). He started 10 games at strong safety and two at free safety during the 2004 season. Paschal went on to start most of the games during his junior and senior seasons. He earned Honorable Mention All–Big Ten recognition by the coaches in 2005 and Second Team All–Big Ten recognition by the coaches in 2006.

GAME DETAILS

Iowa 33 • Ohio State 7

Date: October 16, 2004

Location: Kinnick Stadium, Iowa City, Iowa

Attendance: 70,397

Weather: Cloudy, 45 degrees

> We've been playing pretty well on defense. The defensive team has aspirations to be considered a top team. I think today we started to prove that.
>
> —IOWA COACH KIRK FERENTZ

Box Score:

Ohio St.	0	0	0	7	**7**	
Iowa	7	3	14	9	**33**	

Scoring:

IA Solomon 11-yard pass from Tate (Schlicher PAT)

IA Schlicher 45-yard FG

IA S. Chandler 8-yard pass from Tate (Schlicher PAT)

IA Solomon 36-yard pass from Tate (Schlicher PAT)

IA Tate 1-yard run (Schlicher PAT blocked)

IA Schlicher 41-yard FG

OSU Nichol 23-yard pass from Smith (Nugent PAT)

on the 7-yard line. He was able to keep his momentum going forward and dive to the front right end-zone pylon for the score, extending Iowa's lead to 17–0.

Back-to-back touchdown drives late in the third quarter staked Iowa to a 30–0 lead with 14:53 left in the fourth quarter. Iowa stayed with the pattern that had been successful earlier in the game—the vast majority of the yards came through the air. The scoring plays were a beautiful 36-yard touchdown pass down the middle from Tate to Solomon and a one-yard run by Tate. Schlicher added another field goal, this time from 41 yards out, for the final Iowa points.

There were stars aplenty on the defensive side of the ball as well. The defensive unit as a whole posted eight tackles for a loss, a season high. Linebacker Abdul Hodge registered a game-high 12 tackles (nine of them

solo). Defensive end Matt Roth chipped in with five tackles (three solo) and two quarterback sacks.

Ohio State's lone score came late in the game against the second- and third-team defense, after Iowa had pulled most of its starters. The starting defense yielded just 105 total yards to Ohio State. With the starting defense in the game, Iowa enjoyed a 24–8 advantage in first downs.

Iowa's first two Big Ten wins in 2004—over Ohio State and the previous week against Michigan State—came primarily as a result of a potent passing attack, combined with solid if not spectacular defense. Against Ohio State, Iowa amassed a total of 331 net yards passing to 117 net yards rushing (24 by Tate).

The Iowa offense was more or less forced to rely on the pass as the primary weapon because it had lost four running backs to injury. Jermelle Lewis started the season as the number one back, but he went down for the year with a serious knee injury. Both of Lewis's replacements, Albert Young and Marcus Schnoor, suffered the same fate. The fourth-stringer, Marques Simmons, was also out of action indefinitely with a sprained ankle. That left Iowa with two running backs standing: walk-on Sam Brownlee and true freshman Damien Sims. Although the historical pattern for Iowa (and for most other teams) has been that rushing is the key to victory, the 2004 Hawkeyes defied conventional logic, at least during the early part of the Big Ten season.

The 2004 season was a special one, and the Ohio State win was a signature win during that year. It extended Iowa's home-field winning streak to 16, which was a Kinnick Stadium record. And although it wasn't as flashy as a few of the scoring plays against Ohio State, Paschal's interception was critically important to the Hawkeyes' big win over a team against which it had experienced limited success.

Iowa quarterback Drew Tate (5) runs from Ohio State defenders Mike Kudla (57) and Donte Whitner (9) during the second half of Iowa's convincing 33–7 victory over Ohio State at Kinnick Stadium on October 16, 2004. *Photo courtesy AP Images*

You have to take advantage of every chance. We missed one right at the end of the first half and then turned it over again almost right away in the second half.

—OHIO STATE COACH JIM TRESSEL, ON THE KEYS TO THE GAME

36

FORCED FUMBLE SPURS ROSE BOWL RUN

Fred Harris's ferocious hit gives Iowa the ball, a win over Purdue, and momentum for its first trip to Pasadena

Coming into the 1956 season, most so-called experts picked Iowa to finish near the bottom of the Big Ten… again. It seemed like a safe bet at the time, given that Iowa had finished the conference season with a winning record just once since 1939—the year of the Ironmen, led by Nile Kinnick. (Iowa posted a 4–3 conference mark in 1954.)

However, a new offensive system was implemented by coach Forest Evashevski during the spring practice in 1956. It was known as the wing-T offense and it would prove to be highly effective during Evashevski's coaching tenure at Iowa. The wing-T offense is best characterized by frequent ball fakes and numerous bootlegs.

The new offense appeared to pay off for Iowa immediately. Iowa routed Indiana in the first game of the 1956 season 27–0. The first two drives of the season went 82 and 69 yards for touchdowns. The new wing-T offense produced a total of 242 rushing yards against the Hoosiers.

Iowa went on to win the next three games to come into the match against

Purdue at Ross-Ade Stadium with a perfect record, the only unbeaten, untied team in the Big Ten. However, Purdue was led by the talented All–Big Ten and future Super Bowl–winning quarterback Len Dawson, and it boasted a great offense of its own.

Both offenses would assert themselves early. Iowa scored on a 14-yard touchdown pass from quarterback Kenny Ploen to split end Jim Gibbons. The extra point following the touchdown made it 7–0, Iowa.

Dawson would hold forth on the next Purdue drive. The senior quarterback from Alliance, Ohio, tossed three perfect passes of 17, 20, and six yards to set up the tying touchdown. Purdue fullback Mel Dillard was credited with the touchdown on a six-yard run.

Iowa kept the touchdown volleys going by scoring on a six-yard run by Billy Happel early in the second quarter. However, Dawson again provided an answer to the second Iowa touchdown—and this time he used both his arm and his legs to lead the Boilers into the end zone. Dawson scampered for seven and 24 yards to help set Purdue up at the Iowa

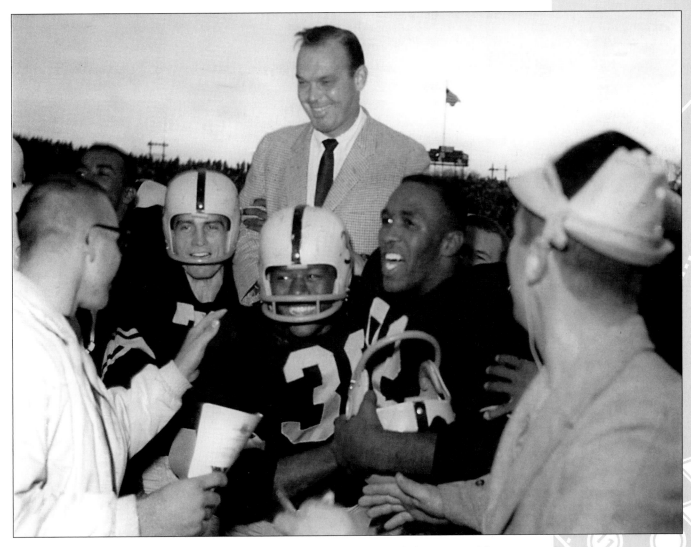

Coach Forest Evashevski, shown celebrating with his jubilant players, led Iowa to a Big Ten title in 1956. The conference championship also delivered the school's first Rose Bowl berth. *Copyright: University of Iowa—CMP Photographic Service*

18-yard line. From there, he dropped back to pass and fired a strike to Tim Fletcher, who caught the pass on the 10-yard line and ran it the rest of the way for an 18-yard score. Following another successful extra point, the game was again tied at 14.

Following Purdue's second touchdown, Iowa again was able to march down the

field on the Purdue defense. This time, the drive was capped by a 30-yard rushing touchdown by Happel. Iowa held a 21–14 lead at halftime.

In a radical departure from the first half, the defensive units stiffened and both teams were held scoreless in the third quarter. However, Purdue's offense was more effective, invading Iowa territory three times in the second half, but without coming away with a score. Finally, midway through the fourth quarter, Dawson was able to engineer a 10-play drive that covered 71 yards. The scoring play was a 20-yard touchdown pass to split end Lamar Lundy, who stood 6'6" and happened to also be the center on the Boilermakers' basketball team. Lundy hauled the ball in at the 10 and navigated through two Iowa defenders to the end zone.

The touchdown brought Purdue to within one point of Iowa at 21–20. However, the "automatic" point-after attempt would prove to be not so automatic this time: Dawson hooked the ball just left of the left upright. As is often the case when a point-after attempt is missed, it would come back to haunt the Boilermakers by making the difference in the contest. Amazingly, Dawson had also missed an extra point in the game against Iowa the prior year—which again cost Purdue the game, as the contest finished in a 20–20 tie.

As the game clock wound down, it would be Iowa fullback Fred Harris who assured an Iowa victory. Harris delivered with two clutch plays in the game's last three minutes. With Iowa still clinging to the 21–20 lead, the Purdue defense forced an Iowa punt with just three minutes remaining in the fourth quarter. It just so happened that Harris also handled the punting duties. Under extreme pressure with the game hanging in the balance, Harris boomed an almost perfect punt, which ultimately rolled out of bounds at the Purdue 4-yard line.

In spite of the terrible field position, Purdue was driving when Harris made the decisive play that would end the Boilermakers' hopes this day. His ferocious tackle was able to separate Purdue halfback Erich Barnes from the ball. The fumble was recovered by Iowa's Frank Bloomquist with just 1:13 remaining in the game. Iowa was subsequently able to run out the clock and maintain their perfect record on the season.

Although Purdue outgained Iowa in total yards, 405 to 349, it was Iowa's multiheaded running attack

COACH FOREST EVASHEVSKI

Iowa head coach Forest Evashevski was certainly one of the most successful coaches in school history. He was hired in January 1952, choosing the Iowa job over another offer from Indiana because he felt it would be easier to attain statewide support in Iowa than in Indiana. Also instrumental in Evashevski's decision to accept the Iowa job was Fritz Crisler, the athletic director and long-time head coach at Michigan, who recommended that Evashevski accept the Iowa offer. Crisler called Evashevski "the greatest quarterback I ever had." The Wolverines won 20 of 24 games during Evashevski's three years as the quarterback.

The partnership of Evashevski and the University of Iowa proved to be a long and fruitful one. Evashevski is the only coach to lead Iowa to a Rose Bowl victory—and he did it twice—in 1957 and 1959. While still in his early 40s, he decided to give up his position as head football coach to become Iowa's athletic director. Although he had wanted to serve as both Iowa's coach and athletic director, the university's Board in Control of Athletics wouldn't allow it. He had to choose one job or the other. One can only imagine the success that would have resulted had Evashevski been allowed to stay on as both coach and AD. When he stepped down as coach, he really was in his prime and had made a habit of dominating the Big Ten—he sported a Big Ten record of 22–7–1 over his last four years of coaching. Evashevski served as Iowa's athletic director until 1970.

GAME DETAILS

Iowa 21 • Purdue 20

Date: October 27, 1956

Location: Ross-Ade Stadium, Lafayette, Indiana

Attendance: 41,415

Box Score:

Iowa	7	14	0	0	**21**
Purdue	7	7	0	6	**20**

Scoring:

IA	Gibbons 14-yard pass from Ploen (PAT)		P	Fletcher 18-yard pass from Dawson (PAT)
P	Dillard 6-yard run (PAT)		IA	Happel 30-yard run (PAT)
IA	Happel 6-yard run (PAT)		P	Lundy 20-yard pass from Dawson

(a staple of the wing-T offense) that proved too much for the Boilers to overcome. In the end, Iowa had two individual backs with more than 90 yards rushing each: Happel had 99 yards rushing on 12 attempts and Don Dobrino added 94 on 15 carries. Mike Hagler also contributed 45 rushing yards on 11 carries.

Once again, the new wing-T offense installed at the beginning of the season was paying big dividends for Iowa. The players appeared to be gaining more confidence—and the rewards would keep getting greater—as the 1956 football season progressed. Although Iowa lost a closely contested game the following week at home to Michigan by a score of 17–14, the Hawks would run the table the rest of the way to finish the regular season with an 8–1 mark, good enough for an outright Big Ten Championship and their first-ever Rose Bowl berth.

The week prior to that 1956 contest [against Purdue], Evy held secret sessions at Iowa. He was an advisor with the Wilson Sporting Goods Company and had his name on a football...Everybody else in the Big Ten used the Spalding J5B, but when we went to Iowa we had to use the Wilson ball. When they came to Purdue to play, we figured they'd have to use the Spalding J5B, giving us the advantage. But Evy was crafty...He brought his own Wilson ball with him so when they got possession of the ball they'd exchange it for one of their own. Our coaches were infuriated!

—PURDUE QUARTERBACK LEN DAWSON

November 3, 1990

BELL RINGS IN CHAMPAIGN

Nick Bell's 44-yard gallop on Iowa's first play sets the tone as Hawks spoil homecoming for No. 5 Illini

The 1990 Iowa Hawkeyes football team was coming off a rather disappointing 1989 campaign that saw the Hawks post a 5–6 record, their first losing season since going 4–7 in Hayden Fry's second year in 1980. However, the Hawks would get off to a very fast start in 1990. Back-to-back non-conference blowout wins against Cincinnati and Iowa State at home were followed by a 48–21 loss to the mighty Miami Hurricanes in the Orange Bowl. The Hawks entered Big Ten play at 2–1. Iowa then swept to victories in each of its first four Big Ten games, whipping Wisconsin and Northwestern at home and narrowly winning road tests at Michigan State and Michigan. It was the first time in Iowa football history that the team had won at East Lansing and Ann Arbor in the same year.

However, the next game was at fifth-ranked Illinois, who also came into the game undefeated in the Big Ten at 4–0. Iowa entered the game at Champaign with a No. 13 national ranking and was not intimidated by the big homecoming crowd that witnessed the game at Memorial Stadium. The partisan crowd of almost 73,000 would be taken out of the game almost immediately.

Illinois took possession following the opening kickoff, but promptly coughed up a fumble on their second play of the game. The fumble was recovered by Iowa linebacker John Derby. On Iowa's first play from scrimmage, senior running back Nick Bell broke into the Illinois secondary for a 44-yard gain. The touchdown-saving tackle came from future NFL star (with the Buffalo Bills) Henry Jones, who forced Bell out of bounds at the Illini 17-yard line. However, that just delayed the inevitable, as Iowa scored three plays later on a five-yard touchdown pass from quarterback Matt Rodgers to Mike Saunders.

Iowa's second possession would result in their second touchdown. This one came on one of Fry's favorite exotic plays: the halfback-option pass. The pitch, on third-and-goal, went to Tony Stewart on the right side, who lofted a perfect pass to Danan Hughes in the back right corner of the end zone, just over the Illini defender. It would go down as a three-yard touchdown pass.

I wonder if anyone has seen anybody like Nick Bell at the college level. I thought I knew everything about Nick Bell, until the first half. He was incredible.

—IOWA COACH HAYDEN FRY

I've never seen Nick run as hard as he ran today. He's probably the best back in the nation. Once he's in the secondary, there's no way you're going to knock him down.

—IOWA QUARTERBACK MATT RODGERS

Iowa running back Nick Bell powered Iowa to a dominating 54–28 win over Illinois at Memorial Stadium in Champaign, Illinois, on November 3, 1990. *Copyright: University of Iowa—CMP Photographic Service*

Iowa's third possession produced a third touchdown. The scoring play came on a 26-yard touchdown run by Bell.

The first quarter ended with the Hawks dominating Illinois 21–0 in every facet of the game, but the most impressive performance came from Bell, who had rushed for 130 yards in the first quarter alone. He wouldn't be slowed down early in the second quarter, either. The 6'2", 255-pound punishing back added another touchdown run on Iowa's fourth possession, bowling over two Illini near the goal line and spinning into the end zone to make it 28–0, Iowa.

Illinois finally got on the board on a 20-yard touchdown pass from quarterback Jason Verduzco to Shawn Wax. However, Illinois could not capitalize on any momentum gained from the scoring play. On Iowa's fifth possession, the Illini appeared to win at least a moral victory by holding Iowa to a field-goal attempt. But it was just a few days past Halloween and Fry had another trick up his sleeve, one that would prove to be no treat for Illinois.

The ball holder, backup quarterback Jim Hartlieb, quickly spun away and spotted Matt Whitaker open in the end zone. Hartlieb lofted a 14-yard touchdown pass, increasing the Iowa lead to 35–7. That play capped an amazing offensive display by Iowa that saw the Hawks light up the Memorial Stadium scoreboard for a perfect five touchdowns in five possessions.

Everything was clicking on high cylinders for Iowa, and what made the feat all the more amazing was the caliber of the defense Iowa faced that day. Entering the game, the Illinois defense was ranked third in the nation; it had allowed just one touchdown in the previous three games combined and had allowed just two touchdown passes during the entire seven-game season. Iowa tore those numbers and the Illinois defense to shreds—and needed less than a half to do it.

Iowa took a 35–14 lead into halftime. Realizing that the powerful Illinois team still had the means to mount a comeback, Iowa kept the pressure on in the third quarter. Rodgers found Hughes with a perfect 17-yard touchdown strike and Jeff Skillett added a 29-yard field goal in the third quarter to make the score 44–14, which gave the large homecoming crowd little hope for a historic Illini comeback and little reason to stick around.

NICK BELL

The 1990 season proved to be a magical one for Nick Bell. He was voted the Big Ten's most valuable offensive player for the 1990 season. He also won the Silver Football, awarded by the *Chicago Tribune* to the Big Ten's MVP. He was voted First Team All-Conference by the coaches, Second Team by the media, and First Team All-American by *Football News*. He was one of eight finalists for the Doak Walker Award, given to college football's best running back.

Bell finished the 1990 season with 1,009 rushing yards on 166 carries (an average of 6.1 yards per carry) and 12 touchdowns. He also caught 21 passes for 308 yards and two additional scores despite splitting time during the season with Tony Stewart, who also figured prominently in the big win at Illinois.

Following his strong senior year in 1990, Bell was drafted in the second round of the NFL draft by the Los Angeles Raiders. Bell played three seasons with the Raiders before retiring from the NFL after the 1993 season.

GAME DETAILS

Iowa 54 • Illinois 28

Date: November 3, 1990

Location: Memorial Stadium, Champaign, Illinois

Attendance: 72,714

Box Score:

Iowa	21	14	9	10	**54**
Illinois	0	14	0	14	**28**

Scoring:

IA Saunders 5-yard pass from Rodgers (Skillett PAT)

IA Hughes 3-yard pass from Stewart (Skillett PAT)

IA Bell 26-yard run (Skillett PAT)

IA Bell 1-yard run (Skillett PAT)

IL Wax 20-yard pass from Verduzco (Higgins PAT)

IA Whitaker 14-yard pass from Hartlieb off fake FG (Skillett PAT)

IL Lester 2-yard pass from Verduzco (Higgins PAT)

IA Hughes 17-yard pass from Rodgers (Skillett PAT failed)

IA Skillett 29-yard FG

IL Wax 9-yard pass from Verduzco (Higgins PAT)

IA Rodgers 1-yard run (Skillett PAT)

IL Wax 5-yard pass from Verduzco (Higgins PAT)

IA Skillett 22-yard FG

When all the dust finally settled, the Iowa players and coaches were celebrating a 54–28 victory with some 5,000 or so Iowa backers in the southwest corner of the stadium. The final numbers certainly were sparkling for Iowa and ugly for Illinois. Iowa produced a total of 335 yards rushing (202 through the air), 24 first downs, a 13½–minute advantage in time of possession, and no turnovers. The 54 points were the most ever allowed by a John Mackovic team at Illinois and the most points Iowa had scored in Champaign since putting up 58 way back in 1899.

Iowa had set themselves up for a very special season following the win at Illinois in 1990. The season would produce Iowa's third Rose Bowl appearance under Fry,

but it was bittersweet because Iowa could not finish the regular season strongly. The week after the big win at Illinois, Iowa dropped a heartbreaker at home to Ohio State on a short touchdown pass on the game's final play, and went on to lose the season finale at Minnesota.

But the 6–2 conference record was good enough for a share of the Big Ten title with three other teams that had identical 6–2 records: Illinois, Michigan, and Michigan State. It was the first and only time that four teams finished tied for the Big Ten lead. However, because Iowa had beaten each of these teams head to head (and all three on the road), Iowa won the tiebreaker and would head west to Pasadena for the holidays.

TOUCHDOWN CAPS UPSETTING DEBUT

Mark Fetter finds the end zone and gives coach Bob Commings a win over nationally ranked UCLA in his first home game

As is the case with most college football programs, the Iowa program has had plenty of ups and downs in its 118-year history. And there is no denying that the period from the mid-1960s to the early 1980s was a horrifically bad period for Iowa football. However, one of the few bright spots in an otherwise dark era occurred during head coach Bob Commings's first year at the helm in 1974, in his first game at recently renamed Kinnick Stadium against the nationally ranked UCLA Bruins. A monumental upset win over UCLA was clinched as a long 14-play drive in the fourth quarter culminated in a four-yard touchdown run by Mark Fetter.

UCLA entered the contest in 1974 ranked number 12 in the nation. The program was a well-established national powerhouse under the guidance of head coach Dick Vermeil. On the field, UCLA was led by quarterback John Sciarra. Sciarra came into the game with the reputation as a one-man gang. He had personally rolled up 390 total yards against a very good Tennessee team.

The Iowa program, on the other hand, was essentially in shambles, engulfed in the longest losing streak in school history—a 12-game skid. The streak encompassed all 11 games of the 1973 season (under previous coach Frank Lauterbur) and Commings's first game in 1974, a loss at Michigan the week before the UCLA game.

The oddsmakers made UCLA a 24-point favorite on the road, and the early stages of the first quarter generally played out as expected. Iowa kick returner Earl Douthitt, who incidentally led the nation in kickoff returns the previous year, bobbled the opening kickoff from UCLA at the goal line and managed only a four-yard return. It didn't get much better on the Hawkeyes' first three plays from scrimmage, either. The three plays went for minus-1, minus-2, and no gain.

Iowa was able to garner a small moral victory, though, when the UCLA drive that began at the Iowa 34-yard line following the Iowa punt bogged down at the Iowa 4-yard line, forcing a field-goal attempt by UCLA. Brett White booted it through from 21

Iowa's Mark Fetter caps a 14-play drive with a 4-yard touchdown run with under two minutes to play, sealing Iowa's 21–10 victory over UCLA at Kinnick Stadium on September 21, 1974.
Copyright: University of Iowa—CMP Photographic Service

yards out to give UCLA the early lead 3–0. The large opening-day crowd certainly had seen this show before!

In spite of the shaky start, Iowa was able to dominate the second quarter. Iowa quarterback Rob Fick led the Hawks to the first touchdown of the game, which came on a brilliant 38-yard pass play to Dave Jackson. Both players were seniors who entered the program in 1970, which was former coach Ray Nagel's last season. But, neither player had enjoyed much success in the program. Fick saw little playing time under Lauterbur, and Jackson was actually kicked off the team as a sophomore, but managed to claw his way back into the team's good graces and earn some playing time the last two seasons.

Iowa's second touchdown was set up by a UCLA turnover. Following Iowa's first touchdown, UCLA coughed it up on a fumble and Iowa recovered at the UCLA 30-yard line. It would take Iowa just a single play to capitalize on the UCLA miscue: a well-executed 30-yard screen pass from Fick to running back Fetter, against a UCLA defense that appeared to be looking for some other call following the turnover. The teams went to the half with the score Iowa 14 and UCLA 3.

The drama would continue to build through a scoreless third quarter. UCLA's offense was able to string together back-to-back drives deep into Iowa territory. The first drive was halted on a fumble by Sciarra at the Iowa 6-yard line. But UCLA would not be denied on their next drive. The next time they had the ball, they again drove deep into Iowa territory, this time pushing the ball over the goal line for a touchdown on the opening play of the fourth quarter to pull to within 14–10. However, behind a boisterous crowd that finally saw a close game worth hanging around for into the fourth quarter, the Iowa defense forced punts on UCLA's next two possessions.

Following the second UCLA punt of the fourth quarter, Iowa maintained a 14–10 advantage. With the Iowa offense taking over at its own 10-yard line, at last the hometown crowd would be rewarded for all their loyal support over some very, very lean years. On this day, with the outcome of this game against the overwhelming favorite still very much in doubt, the Iowa offensive unit as a whole stood up and snatched a game that was there for the taking.

Iowa ground out a game-clinching drive that would cover 90 yards, require 14 plays to execute, and take six minutes off the game clock. All Sciarra and the high-powered UCLA offense could do was watch helplessly from their vantage point on the visitors' sideline. Each and every one of the 14 plays was a running play. The run blocking was so solid during the drive that Fick never once even faked a pass. They lined up and

BOB COMMINGS

Bob Commings played guard at Iowa in the mid-1950s under one of the great coaches in Iowa history, Forest Evashevski. He was honored as team MVP during his senior year, 1957, during which he was instrumental in leading Iowa to a 7–1–1 record. Commings was named head football coach at Iowa on December 15, 1973, replacing Frank Lauterbur. The 1973 football season saw the Hawks go winless (0–11) for the first time since 1889, when Iowa lost the only game played that year. Commings was hired as head coach following five years as coach at Massillion (Ohio) High School, where he compiled a 44–5–1 record. Commings actively campaigned for the job and at his introductory news conference, told reporters, "If they had told me I had to pick corn in the off-season to get the job, I'd have done it." Unfortunately, Commings could not parlay the big upset win over UCLA in his first game as coach into sustained success. He would see a few more key victories during his five-year tenure in Iowa City, but the losses far outnumbered the wins and the Commings era ended after the 1978 season, when Iowa turned to Hayden Fry. Commings's career record at Iowa was 18–37.

Game Details

Iowa 21 • UCLA 10

Date: September 21, 1974

Location: Kinnick Stadium, Iowa City, Iowa

Attendance: 47,500

Box Score:

UCLA	3	0	0	7	**10**
Iowa	0	14	0	7	**21**

Scoring:

UCLA White 21-yard FG

IA   Jackson 38-yard pass from Fick (Quartaro PAT)

IA   Fetter 30-yard pass from Fick (Quartaro PAT)

UCLA Sciarra 1-yard run (White PAT)

IA   Fetter 4-yard run (Quartaro PAT)

rammed it right down the throats of the UCLA defense in an incredible display of old-time football that would certainly have made both legendary Big Ten coaches Woody Hayes and Bo Schembechler jealous.

The last play of the drive was perhaps its best. Fetter bounced off the left tackle, but was hit at the line of scrimmage and appeared to be stopped cold. However, with a great second effort, Fetter was able to stay on his feet and spin away from the defense, shed another tackler, and find the end zone on a four-yard run with just 1:38 to play.

Immediately after the touchdown, Fetter tossed the ball high into the air, overwhelmed by the moment.

Who could blame him, given the struggles of the Iowa program over so many of the previous years? The officials flagged him for a 15-yard penalty on the ensuing kickoff, but it was of little consequence; the Iowa team could not blow this lead.

When Iowa's monumental 21–10 upset win was complete, the overjoyed Iowa fans swarmed the Astroturf field and managed to tear down the huge iron goal post in the north end zone of Kinnick Stadium. The long drought was over and Hawks fans could celebrate, at least for a day.

You have a chance to show people all over America what desire and determination can prove...It may be that you are the chosen children.

—IOWA COACH BOB COMMINGS,

ADDRESSING HIS TEAM BEFORE HIS FIRST HOME GAME AS IOWA COACH AGAINST UCLA

October 22, 1960

FUMBLE RUMBLE KEEPS IOWA NUMBER ONE

Lineman Dayton Perry's 84-yard fumble-return touchdown helps lead top-ranked Iowa to victory over Purdue

The 1960 season ended up being Forest Evashevski's last as head coach at Iowa. Following another strong season that saw Iowa grab the No. 1 ranking in both wire service polls for three weeks and post an 8–1 record, Evy moved on to become Iowa's athletics director. At the time, he appeared to be at the height of his coaching career. Over the last five years under his leadership, Iowa had essentially dominated the Big Ten.

Evashevski was only in his early 40s when he made the move to athletics director. The Iowa Board of Athletics was leery about having an ambitious man such as Evy be both the head football coach and the athletics director, and would not allow Evy to hold both posts. He had indicated in the past that he did not want to grow old coaching, and therefore decided that the athletics director position would be best for him.

Coming into the homecoming game at Iowa Stadium with Purdue, Iowa sported a perfect 4–0 record, which included big wins over Northwestern and Michigan State

and a close win the week before against Wisconsin.

The rivalry with Purdue in the years leading up to the 1960 game was intense. The last three contests with Purdue had each been decided by a touchdown or less, and this one would also follow that pattern. This game featured one of the most exciting plays of the entire 1960 season, one that would provide Iowa with loads of momentum heading into halftime and end up being the decisive score.

Iowa got off to a shaky start. A Larry Ferguson fumble on Iowa's 43-yard line gave Purdue a golden opportunity in the opening stages of the first quarter. Ferguson attempted to atone for the fumble by dropping the Purdue running back for a five-yard loss on the next play, and Purdue was eventually forced to punt. Purdue was able to advance as far as the Iowa 26 in the game's first 20 minutes, but was unable to put any points on the board.

Iowa's first touchdown was the first of quarterback Wilburn Hollis's two rushing touchdowns on the day. Various

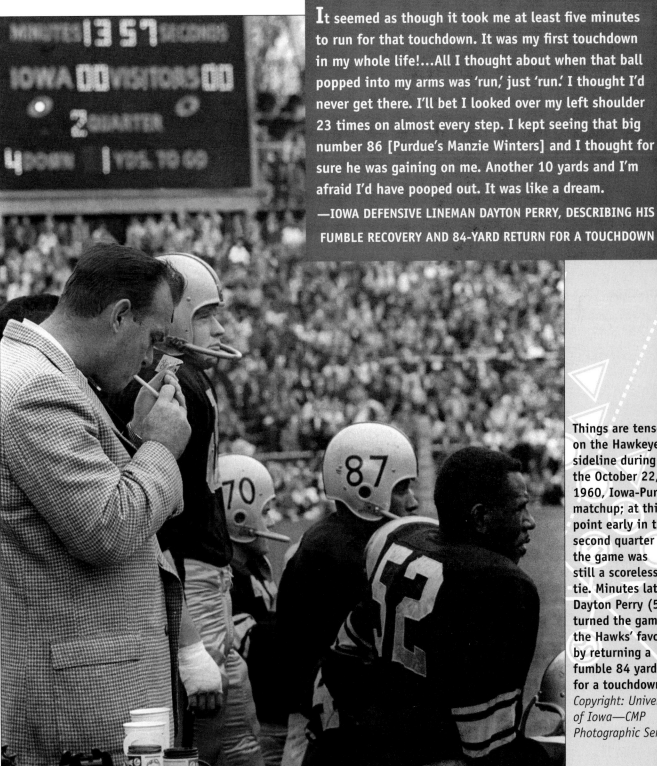

It seemed as though it took me at least five minutes to run for that touchdown. It was my first touchdown in my whole life!...All I thought about when that ball popped into my arms was 'run,' just 'run.' I thought I'd never get there. I'll bet I looked over my left shoulder 23 times on almost every step. I kept seeing that big number 86 [Purdue's Manzie Winters] and I thought for sure he was gaining on me. Another 10 yards and I'm afraid I'd have pooped out. It was like a dream.

—IOWA DEFENSIVE LINEMAN DAYTON PERRY, DESCRIBING HIS FUMBLE RECOVERY AND 84-YARD RETURN FOR A TOUCHDOWN

Things are tense on the Hawkeyes' sideline during the October 22, 1960, Iowa-Purdue matchup; at this point early in the second quarter the game was still a scoreless tie. Minutes later, Dayton Perry (52) turned the game in the Hawks' favor by returning a fumble 84 yards for a touchdown. *Copyright: University of Iowa—CMP Photographic Service*

penalties, interceptions, and poor execution hampered the Hawkeyes offense for most of the first half and prevented them from building on the 7–0 lead.

Then, late in the second quarter, Purdue managed to advance the ball down to the Iowa 16-yard line and had a first-and-10 situation, setting up the game's biggest play. Purdue quarterback Bernie Allen dropped back to pass, saw nothing downfield, and started to run, but then had a notion to pass again before he got too far. As he raised his arm to pass, Iowa end Felton Rodgers and tackle Al Hinton came together at the quarterback, and the impact caused the ball to squirt up in the air. It came down into the waiting arms of Iowa sophomore Dayton Perry, who had no Purdue player near him. The 6'1", 215-pound lineman was then able to lumber 84 yards the other way. Touchdown Iowa. It was the type of play most defensive linemen dream about, but very few ever get to experience. The score came with just 50 seconds remaining in the first half; it gave Iowa a 14–0 halftime lead after a Tom Moore extra point.

With all the momentum, the Hawks came out in the second half smoking. Iowa forged ahead 21–0

in the third quarter when Hollis scored on a six-yard touchdown run, which featured a major stiff-arm on a Purdue defender on his way to the end zone.

It seemed like the game was in hand with less than 24 minutes to play and Purdue facing a 21-point deficit. But Iowa had given up a big lead the previous week against Wisconsin, so there was still a palpable uneasiness in the crowd. The fears would prove to be well-founded, as Purdue mounted a furious rally for the rest of the game.

The next series was the beginning of the Purdue assault. Similar to Iowa's big fumble return for a touchdown, Lady Luck would play a prominent role in Purdue's first touchdown. Quarterback Allen tossed a pass from Iowa's 16-yard line that was deflected by Purdue end John Elwell. However, the ball managed to carom directly into the arms of Purdue's Jimmy Tiller in the end zone for Purdue's first points of the afternoon; now the score was 21–7.

Purdue's second touchdown came from a 92-yard, 16-play drive. The touchdown was set up by a pass-interference call on Iowa's Bernie Wyatt, on a

THE RIVALRY WITH PURDUE

Iowa's rivalry with Purdue dates back to 1910. Overall, Purdue leads the series with 45 wins, compared to 32 for Iowa; there have been three ties. The series was almost even until the 1960s and 1970s when the fortunes of the Iowa program plummeted while Purdue teams shined. In fact, this 21–14 win over Purdue during the 1960 season would be the last time the Hawkeyes would taste the sweet pleasure of a victory over the Boilermakers until Hayden Fry's 1981 Rose Bowl team finally was able to break through with a big 33–7 victory over the Boilers.

During the span from 1961 to 1980, Purdue won an astonishing 20 straight games against Iowa, many by large margins. But Fry's Hawkeyes started to turn the tide back in Iowa's favor, reeling off a string of nine consecutive victories from 1983 to 1991. The rivalry was nearly even during most of the 1990s and into the early 2000s. However, Kirk Ferentz's Hawks have put four of the last six contests against the Boilermakers into the win column, including a memorable win on Homecoming by the 2002 team (Play Number 7).

GAME DETAILS

Iowa 21 • Purdue 14

Date: October 22, 1960

Location: Iowa Stadium, Iowa City, Iowa

Attendance: 59,200

Box Score:

Purdue	0	0	7	7	**14**
Iowa	0	14	7	0	**21**

Scoring:

IA   Hollis 1-yard run (Moore PAT)

IA   Perry 84-yard fumble recovery (Moore PAT)

IA   Hollis 6-yard run (Moore PAT)

PUR   Tiller 16-yard pass from Allen (Allen PAT)

PUR   Allen 1-yard run (Allen PAT)

pass intended for Purdue's Dave Miller, setting the Boilermakers up at the Iowa 1-yard line. Allen scored on the next play, a quarterback sneak, and also converted the point-after attempt to make it 21–14, Iowa. Now there was serious concern on the part of the faithful Iowa homecoming crowd.

With the game on the line, Iowa managed to string together a solid drive on the ensuing possession. The Hawks advanced to the Purdue 26; the key play was a risky double-handoff reverse by Sammie Harris that would ultimately be good for 29 yards, with Iowa facing a key third-and-14. With the line of scrimmage at the Purdue 26, quarterback Hollis rolled out on the pass-run option and sighted split end Bill Perkins, seemingly all alone at the goal line. Hollis attempted to hit Perkins, but Purdue's Tiller leaped high in the air to grab the

interception on the 3-yard line; he returned the ball back to the Purdue 22.

Purdue would have one last shot to tie or win the ball game. Allen subsequently called seven straight pass plays as the Boilermakers desperately attempted to move the ball downfield. However, the clock was the ally of the Hawkeyes, and it ran out on Purdue when the Boilers had gotten to the Iowa 42-yard line.

Although they gave it their best shot, that long fumble return in the first half proved to be just too much for Purdue to overcome. That play would surely last a long time in the memories of Hawks fans everywhere. The gutsy win allowed Iowa to maintain their No. 1 national ranking in both major polls, the first time in school history any team had reached this lofty status.

November 13, 2004

FIVE TIMES THREE EQUALS VICTORY

Kyle Schlicher's fifth field goal allows Iowa to defeat Minnesota and keep its title hopes alive

Ever since the days of Hayden Fry, it seems like the Hawkeyes have always been able to rely upon a solid corps of place-kickers and punters on special teams. It has always been a point of emphasis because both Fry and Kirk Ferentz realize that special-teams plays can often make the difference in the game. Note that Play Number 32, by place-kicker Kyle Schlicher, is already the third special-teams play to appear on this list.

There is no question that without the spectacular play of sophomore place-kicker Kyle Schlicher during this key late-season game at rival Minnesota in 2004, Iowa would not have won the game that kept alive their hopes of a second Big Ten title in three years under Ferentz. On this day in Minneapolis, Schlicher's five…count 'em…five field goals provided more than half of Iowa's 29 points. And the difference in the game would end up being a thrilling fourth-quarter 49-yard field goal by Schlicher. But the outcome was not decided until a Minnesota missed a field-goal attempt with just 28 seconds remaining in the fourth quarter.

Iowa came into the annual battle for Floyd of Rosedale in 2004 with a 5–1 Big Ten mark and aspirations for another Big Ten crown. To keep those hopes alive, it needed a win at 3–4 Minnesota. Although the game may not have been pretty from a statistical standpoint, the 2004 team was never about statistics. Wins were much more important than statistics.

However, one key statistic the Hawks did dominate was the turnover category. Iowa forced a total of four Minnesota turnovers while not giving it up to Minnesota once.

Even with the 4–0 advantage in turnovers, Minnesota gave the Hawks all it could handle behind a two-headed monster of a running attack in running backs Marion Barber III and Laurence Maroney. These two future starting running backs in the NFL did end up with the pretty statistics: Barber had 167 yards rushing on 29 attempts, for an average of 5.8 yards per carry, and Maroney posted 156 yards on 19 carries, for a stunning average of 8.2 yards per attempt, and added three rushing touchdowns. Iowa's run defense was ranked number four in the

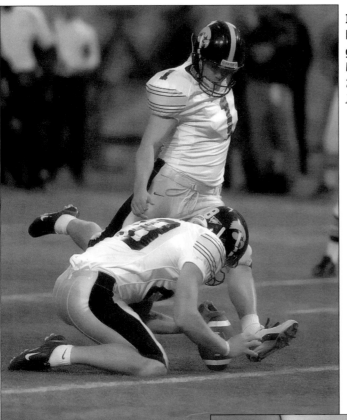

Iowa place-kicker Kyle Schlicher hits the game-winning field goal against Minnesota at the Metrodome on November 13, 2004. *Copyright: University of Iowa—CMP Photographic Service*

You grow with each field goal, or anytime you're on the field with a kickoff, an extra point, or a field goal. But I think being comfortable with every situation is a must. I don't think of this as my first season—I've had two seasons already. To everybody else it's my freshman year, but to me in my head, it's not...I've had my time to prepare and now it's my time to shine.

—KYLE SCHLICHER, AFTER THE GAME

Iowa players George Lewis (50), George Eshareturi (72), and Charles Godfrey, right, hoist the Floyd of Rosedale Trophy as the Hawkeyes retain the prize after defeating Minnesota 29–27 in Minneapolis on November 13, 2004. *Photo courtesy AP Images*

country coming in, allowing a stingy 68 yards per game, but behind Barber and Maroney, the Iowa defense was gashed for 337 yards on the ground.

It was a turnover on Minnesota's first series that got the Hawks off to a fast start. Senior safety Sean Considine intercepted a pass from Minnesota's Bryan Cupito that put Iowa in business at the Minnesota 44-yard line, less than three minutes into the game. The turnover was converted into the game's first three points on a 36-yard field goal by Schlicher.

After Minnesota answered with its own field goal to tie it, Iowa put together a seven-play, 76-yard drive capped by a 41-yard touchdown pass from quarterback Drew Tate to wide receiver Clinton Solomon. Schlicher added two more short field goals in the second quarter—the second coming off another interception by Chad Greenway, giving Iowa possession at the Minnesota 34-yard line. The two field goals made it 16–3, Iowa.

However, Minnesota would answer quickly and in spectacular fashion. Maroney took a handoff on the second play of the ensuing drive for a 79-yard touchdown run, keeping Minnesota within one score at 16–10.

The seesaw game continued as Iowa marched 83 yards on eight plays on the following possession. The drive was capped by a long 60-yard touchdown pass from Tate to James Townsend, extending Iowa's lead to 23–10, which would be the halftime score.

Minnesota added another field goal of their own and another Maroney rushing touchdown in the third quarter, to pull to within 23–20. But late in the third quarter Schlicher converted his fourth field goal of the day, increasing the lead to 26–20.

A Maroney fumble early in the fourth quarter was recovered by Iowa linebacker Abdul Hodge at the Iowa 49. Iowa would subsequently drive 31 yards on 10 plays to the Minnesota 18-yard line, but Tate was sacked on the next play on third down for a 14-yard loss, which would make the field-goal attempt much more difficult. However, Schlicher was up to the task *again*, as he calmly split the uprights for the fifth time on the day, this one a 49-yard attempt that would give Iowa the winning points, making it 29–20.

On the ensuing possession, Minnesota scored again on another Maroney rushing touchdown at the end of a long drive, this touchdown on a five-yard run. But Maroney's third one came with just 4:40 left on the fourth-quarter clock. Minnesota then forced an Iowa three-and-out and took over following an Iowa punt on the Gophers' 46-yard line, with just 2:50 left in the

KYLE SCHLICHER

Kyle Schlicher was a sophomore on the 2004 team. He certainly had big shoes to fill—he replaced All-Everything place-kicker Nate Kaeding, who had moved on to the NFL's San Diego Chargers. Schlicher appeared to gain confidence as his first season progressed, and the Minnesota game was the culmination of all the hard work prior to and during his first season as Iowa's first-team kicker. He handled all field-goal and point-after attempts and all kickoff duties in all 12 games in 2004. He was recognized as an Honorable Mention All–Big Ten selection in 2004.

Schlicher would go on to star on two more Iowa teams in 2005 and 2006 and was an All–Big Ten selection in those years as well. His 260 points during his Iowa career ranks fourth on the all-time scoring list behind fellow place-kickers Kaeding, Rob Houghtlin, and Tom Nichol.

GAME DETAILS

Iowa 29 • Minnesota 27

Date: November 13, 2004

Location: HHH Metrodome, Minneapolis, Minnesota

Attendance: 64,719

Box Score:

Iowa	10	13	3	3	**29**
Minnesota	3	7	10	7	**27**

Scoring:

IA	Schlicher 36-yard FG
MN	Lloyd 25-yard FG
IA	Solomon 41-yard pass from Tate (Schlicher PAT)
IA	Schlicher 22-yard FG
IA	Schlicher 20-yard FG
MN	Maroney 79-yard run (Lloyd PAT)
IA	Townsend 60-yard pass from Tate (Schlicher PAT)
MN	Lloyd 20-yard FG
MN	Maroney 37-yard run (Lloyd PAT)
IA	Schlicher 38-yard FG
IA	Schlicher 49-yard FG
MN	Maroney 5-yard run (Lloyd PAT)

fourth quarter. Minnesota trailed just 29–27 and needed only a field goal for the win.

A 10-yard rush by Barber on the first play of the drive advanced the ball into Iowa territory and put Iowa on its heels. Two additional runs gained another first down to the Iowa 33. However, that would end up being the Gophers' last first down. On second-and-eight, Greenway was able to drop Barber behind the line of scrimmage for a four-yard loss, setting up a third-and-12.

The defense came up with another big play on third down, holding Barber to just a one-yard gain and setting up a dramatic, potentially game-winning 51-yard field-goal attempt by Minnesota's Rhys Lloyd. Thanks largely to a heavy rush by Greenway, the field-goal attempt sailed well wide left, preserving the Iowa win.

Schlicher's five field goals and 17 kicking points were both Iowa school records. Schlicher's predecessor,

Nate Kaeding, had converted four field goals in a game on four different occasions. A Big Ten kicker had made five field goals in a game just 17 times in the history of the conference. Schlicher converted 21 of 26 field goals and 29 of 32 extra points on the year—for a team-high 92 points—in 2004.

From a team standpoint, the win put Iowa in position to earn at least a share of another Big Ten title. It would need a win at home against Wisconsin in the season finale the following week, coupled with a Michigan loss at rival Ohio State.

The stars ended up being aligned for Iowa that year; the Hawks took care of business in a decisive 30–7 win over Wisconsin (see Play Number 20 for more details) and Ohio State knocked off Michigan, giving Iowa a share of the 2004 Big Ten title. Iowa finished in a tie with Michigan, with a 7–1 conference mark.

December 29, 1995

31 SHAW BASKS IN THE SUN

Sedrick Shaw's 58-yard touchdown scamper catapults Iowa to an easy bowl victory over Washington

The 1995 edition of the Hawkeyes was about as streaky a team as you could find anywhere in the country. As had been the pattern in recent years, Iowa dominated various lesser nonconference foes to open the season. In 1995, Northern Iowa, Iowa State, and New Mexico State were thrown to the wolves early. In dominating these three opponents, Iowa won by an average score of 40–14.

The momentum gained in the weaker, nonconference portion of the schedule carried over into Iowa's first two Big Ten contests against Michigan State and Indiana. The Hawks came into the third Big Ten game against Penn State with a perfect 5–0 overall mark.

However, the Penn State game would be the beginning of a nasty four-game losing streak in the middle of the conference season. Going into Madison to play the Wisconsin Badgers in mid-November, the team was burdened by the four-game losing streak and faced intense media pressure and plenty of negative energy. Coach Hayden Fry tried to take as much of the pressure off his players as possible—by scorching the media and some "fair-weather" fans

of the program—during his weekly press conference the week of the game.

As often was the case during Fry's tenure, the team responded to Fry's psychological ploys. In a gutsy win that would be dedicated to their beloved coach who had taken so much heat during the losing streak, Iowa stormed into Madison and left with a season-changing 33–20 victory over the Badgers. It improved Coach Fry's record as head coach against Wisconsin to a sparkling 14–0–1. It is safe to say that Hayden had the Badgers' number.

Building on the momentum gained in Madison the week before, the Hawkeyes closed the regular season on Thanksgiving weekend with a dominating 45–3 win at Kinnick Stadium against traditional rival Minnesota, keeping the Floyd of Rosedale Trophy in Iowa City for another year.

Iowa finished the regular season with a 7–4 record, but the team was an attractive pick for the Sun Bowl in El Paso, Texas, for several reasons: Iowa has always traveled well to postseason bowl destinations (especially warm-weather ones!); they had finished the season very strong; and Fry was from west Texas and was presumably still a good draw.

Iowa ended up finishing sixth in the Big Ten with a 4–4 Big Ten record and was matched with the Washington Huskies who were co-champions of the Pac-10. The Huskies were coming into the game with an overall record of 7–3–1 (6–1–1 in conference) and a No. 20 national ranking. Fry had never beaten a Pac-10 team in a bowl game; he was 0–4, which included two losses to Washington in the Rose Bowl in 1982 and 1991.

Iowa was instilled as a five-point underdog, and Fry would use this to his advantage. Longtime Iowa sports information director George Wine believes that no game in the Fry era was a better fit for Fry's coaching methods than the 1995 Sun Bowl. "We're only a five-point underdog?" Fry asked. "Lawdy, lawdy, 20 to 25 points seems more like it to me!" A pregame survey of 16 reporters covering the game for various news media found that just two of 16 picked Iowa to win. These numbers certainly played a prominent role in Fry's pregame speech to his team.

Whatever Fry said to his team before the game, it clearly inspired the Hawkeyes; Iowa jumped all over a mistake-prone Washington team from the opening moments. Washington held Iowa to a punt on the first possession of the game, but fumbled the punt to turn it back over to Iowa.

The Iowa offense quickly took advantage of the Washington mistake. Sedrick Shaw, one of 17 Texans on the Iowa roster, put Iowa up 7–0 on a 58-yard touchdown run off right tackle that came just one minute and 52 seconds into the game. Iowa would never look back.

Iowa coach Hayden Fry rides on top of the shoulders of his players following the Hawkeyes' 38–18 victory over Washington in the 1995 Sun Bowl. *Photo courtesy AP Images*

On Washington's first play from scrimmage, they again turned it over on a fumble. Iowa cashed that in on a 49-yard field goal by Brion Hurley to make it 10–0.

As a result of Washington's early miscues, the Huskies had only run one offensive play in the game's first eight minutes, and it got worse from that point for the hopeless Huskies. A high snap in punt formation deep in their own territory resulted in a safety, making it 12–0. Iowa would add three more field goals to make it 21–0 at the half. Iowa's deadly combination of place-kickers,

Sedrick Shaw's Scintillating Sun Bowl Scamper

Heavily favored Washington knew they had their hands full early in the 1995 Sun Bowl. Iowa was able to immediately capitalize on a muffed punt by the Huskies following the game's first possession by Iowa. On the first play on the ensuing series, quarterback Matt Sherman (12) handed the ball to running back Sedrick Shaw (5), who was deep in the backfield in the I formation. Shaw darted through a hole in the middle of the line forged by the blocking of center Casey Wiegmann and guard Matt Purdy. Once into the Washington secondary, Shaw found daylight because both cornerbacks were in man-to-man coverage on the outside, shadowing receivers who were running deep sideline patterns. Once he broke the tackle of the last safety near midfield, Shaw split both cornerbacks on his way to a 58-yard touchdown run—his longest of the 1995 season. It put the Huskies on their heels in the game and they never recovered as the underdog Hawks would go on to dominate Washington the rest of the way.

Hurley and Zach Bromert, broke school and bowl records by going five for five on field goals.

Iowa didn't let up in the second half. Hurley nailed another field goal—this one from 50 yards out. Then Tavian Banks got into the act with a 74-yard jaunt, the longest of his career, which set up fullback Mike Burger for an eight-yard touchdown run that put Iowa in the lead 31–6 midway through the third quarter. Burger added a second touchdown run in the fourth quarter, which closed out the Iowa scoring.

Shaw won the game MVP award for posting 135 rush yards on 21 carries and the early touchdown. Banks, who missed the first half of the season with a broken wrist, contributed mightily with 122 yards rushing on 13 attempts.

The win against a ranked team broke an 11-game streak of losses to ranked teams. The postseason victory was Iowa's first since a dramatic 20–19 win over Wyoming in the 1987 Holiday Bowl. (The team had been 0–3–1 in bowl games since that Wyoming game, including a demoralizing 37–3 drubbing at the hands of California in the 1993 Alamo Bowl in San Antonio, the last time Iowa went bowling in Texas.)

It took a while, but at last the Hawkeyes were able to take a fond memory away from a bowl game in Fry's home state. But it was Shaw who set the tone early, with this long touchdown run before the game was even two minutes old.

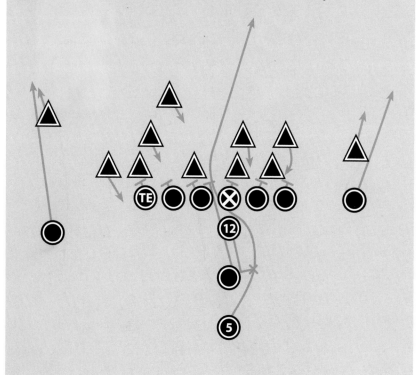

GAME DETAILS

Iowa 38 • Washington 18

Date: December 29, 1995

Location: Sun Bowl, El Paso, Texas

Attendance: 49,116

Significance: Sun Bowl

Box Score:

Iowa	10	11	10	7	**38**
Washington	0	0	6	12	**18**

Scoring:

IA	Shaw 58-yard run (Bromert PAT)
IA	Hurley 49-yard FG
IA	Safety, punt snap out of end zone
IA	Bromert 33-yard FG
IA	Bromert 34-yard FG
IA	Hurley 47-yard FG
IA	Hurley 50-yard FG
WAS	Pathon 30-yard pass from Fortney (pass failed)
IA	Burger 8-yard run (Bromert PAT)
IA	Burger 1-yard run (Bromert PAT)
WAS	Coleman 10-yard pass from Huard (pass failed)
WAS	Conwell 20-yard pass from Huard (run failed)

ONE-TWO PUNCH

Sedrick Shaw's 135 rushing yards in the 1995 Sun Bowl gave the junior running back 1,477 yards on the year, which was a single-season school record. But that record would only stand for two years. It would be broken in 1997 by Shaw's backfield teammate in the Sun Bowl, Tavian Banks, who accumulated 1,691 yards on the ground during his senior season in 1997.

However, Shaw is currently number one on the all-time Iowa career rushing list, with 4,156 career rushing yards, and Banks is number three, with 2,977 yards. Having both of them at the disposal of Iowa offensive coordinator Don Patterson during the 1995 season proved to be a very potent weapon, one that was unmatched at any time in Iowa history. Shaw's long first-quarter run in the 1995 Sun Bowl certainly set an early tone and allowed Iowa to cruise to a surprisingly easy victory over the heavily favored Washington team.

October 28, 1939

HEISMAN HAWK SOARS PAST BADGERS

Nile Kinnick's touchdown pass—and other highlights—gives Iowa its first victory over Wisconsin in six years

There is no question that Nile Kinnick is the most famous Hawkeye player ever to take to the gridiron. Fans are reminded of that during each and every home game at the stadium at Melrose Avenue and Hawkins Drive that now bears his name. Kinnick makes his first of three appearance in the top 50 plays here at Number 30.

All legends must begin with some memorable performance. Although Kinnick posted nothing less than spectacular numbers in all facets of the game during the 1939 season, the Wisconsin game in late October was special. Following that game, which saw Kinnick lead the Hawkeyes back from a second half-deficit, Iowa coach Dr. Eddie Anderson first used the term "Ironmen" with the press to describe Kinnick and his teammates, who had played the entire 60 minutes of the football game. The intriguing "Ironmen" expression drew instant national headlines, and the 1939 Iowa team was well on its way to attaining the legendary status it enjoys today.

The momentum that was initiated with this win at Wisconsin would build the

following week in a win at Purdue, followed by back-to-back wins at home against Notre Dame and Minnesota to close out the season. Kinnick would ride this momentum all the way to the most prestigious trophy in sports—the Heisman Trophy.

The team was coming off a decisive loss at Michigan the week before, which had dropped Iowa's record to 2–1. Because of a 1–6–1 season the prior year, not much was expected of the 1939 team. But despite the loss to Michigan, the good start to the season put them in position to contend for the Big Ten title, because the Big Ten race was wide open that year.

In this game, Wisconsin drew first blood with a first-quarter touchdown and a successful point-after attempt to lead it 7–0. The Badgers took another brief lead in the third quarter with another touchdown and a failed conversion. But in between those Wisconsin scores, it was pretty much all Kinnick.

You name it and Kinnick did it in this game. He almost single-handedly beat a gritty Badgers team. Among his exploits on the day:

Halfback Nile Kinnick's third of three touchdown passes was the difference in a 19–13 win over Wisconsin at Camp Randall Stadium on October 28, 1939. *Copyright: University of Iowa—CMP Photographic Service*

- Kinnick intercepted a pass to halt a Wisconsin threat.
- He set up an Iowa touchdown with a long kick return.
- He connected on a 60-yard punt to ease pressure on the defense during a furious comeback attempt by the Badgers in the fourth quarter.
- He threw three touchdown passes (to Bill Green, Al Couppee, and Dick Evans).

Iowa completed seven of 14 passes, and Kinnick threw every Iowa one. He faced a heavy pass rush from the Wisconsin defense all day because the Badgers knew Iowa's running game was weak. Kinnick rushed 11 times for a measly 12 yards. Murphy gained 20 yards on four attempts, and Green added 47 yards on five carries.

The game-winning drive in the fourth quarter was set up on an interception of a Billie Schmitz pass by

NILE KINNICK: THE FOOTBALL PLAYER

The numbers associated with Nile Kinnick's performance during the 1939 football season at Iowa are beyond compare, especially relative to statistics posted in this modern era of specialization. Today, many teams' offensive strategies rely heavily on a "third down" running back or a run-oriented quarterback in running situations. Defensive coordinators can substitute that big run stopper on running downs or the "nickel" or "dime" packages in obvious passing situations on defense.

In stark contrast to today's game—in which most players participate only on offense, defense, or special teams—Kinnick was on the field for literally every play during the Wisconsin game and also the two previous games against Indiana and Michigan. He also played all 60 minutes the following week at Purdue in a 4–0 Iowa triumph. The win at Purdue set up the classic matchup at home against Notre Dame (Play Number 4).

Kinnick either scored or passed for all but 23 of the points scored by the team during the 1939 season. He was second in the nation with eight interceptions and led the country with 377 kickoff return yards. He would go on to lead Iowa to an overall 6–1–1 record in 1939. He was on every All-American List and won nearly every award possible: the Heisman Trophy, the Maxwell Award, and the Walter Camp Trophy. As another sign of his national recognition and star power, he was named the Associated Press Male Athlete of the Year, over larger-than-life professional sports figures of the day including the Yankees' Joe DiMaggio and boxer Joe Louis.

Kinnick won the Heisman Trophy on the eve of the country's entrance into World War II. The acceptance speech he gave at the Downtown Athletic Club in New York is universally recognized as one of the most eloquent and moving addresses ever given by a Heisman Trophy winner. Kinnick's speech exuded wisdom beyond his years. He demonstrated humility, a sincere appreciation for his coaches and teammates, and gratitude toward those who had voted for him for the award. But what made the speech memorable was his keen, comprehensive understanding of the complicated world he lived in. Perhaps the most famous portion of the speech was his closing remarks:

"I thank God I was warring on the gridirons of the Midwest and not on the battlefields of Europe. [interrupted by lengthy applause] I can speak confidently and positively that the football players of this country would much more, much rather struggle and fight to win the Heisman award, than the Croix de Guerre."

Calling him "Nile Kinnick the football player" only begins to describe his many interests and achievements. Kinnick's equally impressive off-the-field achievements are described in Play Numbers 17 and 4.

GAME DETAILS

Iowa 19 • Wisconsin 13

Date: October 28, 1939

Location: Camp Randall Stadium, Madison, Wisconsin

Box Score:

Iowa	0	6	6	7	**19**
Wisconsin	7	0	6	0	**13**

Scoring:

WI	Gage 14-yard pass from Gradising (Gage PAT)
IA	Couppee 19-yard pass from Kinnick (PAT failed)
WI	Lorenz 4-yard pass from Schmitz (PAT failed)
IA	Evans 39-yard pass from Kinnick (PAT failed)
IA	Green 24-yard pass from Kinnick (PAT Kinnick)

Iowa's Floyd Dean. Iowa took over on their own 48-yard line. The ensuing drive saw Kinnick connect on two key passes to set up the touchdown play. The first was to Erwin Prasse for a first down at the Wisconsin 40, and the second was to Couppee for another first down at the 29-yard line. Kinnick then found Bill Green open over the middle right in front of the goal post for the go-ahead score. Kinnick converted his first drop-kick point-after conversion in three attempts, giving Iowa a 19–13 lead in the fourth quarter.

Later in the fourth quarter, following a 60-yard punt by Kinnick, Wisconsin took over in their own territory trailing by a score of 19–13 with approximately five minutes left in the game. They promptly converted a big play down the field; Cone somehow found Gile among three Iowa defenders for a 41-yard pass play that pushed Wisconsin to a first-and-goal at the Iowa 9-yard line late in the fourth quarter.

But this Iowa team had come too far to let it slip away. Three straight Badgers pass attempts followed, and each was batted away by the inspired Iowa defense. Wisconsin then brought in Gradisink, one of the most talented players on the team. He dropped back to pass on fourth down, attempting a game-winning pass that was batted away by Iowa's Bruno Andruska; the Wisconsin threat was averted.

It was Wisconsin's last gasp of the day. Iowa was able to efficiently run out the clock from there, driving the ball to the Wisconsin 20-yard line as the final gun sounded.

October 14, 1922

EAST VS. WEST, BROTHER VS. BROTHER

Leland Parkin's touchdown run provides the game's only points in the battle of the coaching Jones brothers

The 1922 game against Yale was played so long ago that at the time, Iowa was considered the "West," at least in college football geography. Yale was a perennial power in the late 19th and early 20th centuries, and this was the first time it had been defeated by a "Western" team in New Haven. To add additional intrigue to the matchup, it was only the second time in history that two brothers had met as head coaches of opposing teams. Iowa was led by head coach Howard Jones and Yale by Tad Jones. Ironically, the first matchup had also been between the Jones brothers, in 1909 when Howard's Yale squad, which was unbeaten and unscored upon in 10 games that season, beat Tad's Syracuse team by a score of 15–0.

The 1922 Iowa team was coming off a perfect 7–0 season in 1921, but it had lost several key contributors: All-American halfback Aubrey Devine, lineman Fred "Duke" Slater, and Lester Belding. In the week prior to the road trip east to Connecticut, Iowa thrashed Knox College 61–0, in the opening game of the 1922 season.

The elder Jones would again get the better of the family quarrel this day inside the Yale Bowl. The winning margin was only 6–0, but the game actually was not as close as the final score might indicate. The Yale team looked slow and feeble against their bigger, faster, stronger foes from Iowa. The game was a grudge-match test of stamina; Iowa played only 12 men the entire game, while 14 men saw action for Yale.

The key performer on the Iowa side was quarterback Leland Parkin, who scored the game's only touchdown. Parkin took the place of the great triple-threat halfback Devine, who had skillfully led the Hawkeyes backfield the prior year.

The Elis likely first realized that they were in for a real battle late in the first quarter when Iowa launched the only scoring drive of the game. Iowa received a Yale punt at midfield, but a Yale penalty set Iowa up in Yale territory at the 45 to start the scoring drive. With Parkin at the controls, Iowa methodically drove toward the Yale goal line, using the run as the primary attack.

A huge crowd gathered at the train station to welcome back the Iowa team following its victory over eastern power Yale in 1922. *Copyright: University of Iowa—CMP Photographic Service*

Parkin was the primary ball carrier, but big fullback Gordon Locke also played a prominent role.

Parkin's rushing was able to advance the team as far as the Yale 3-yard line, but the Hawkeyes were offside on the next play, which moved them back to the 8-yard line. The net result of the next three plays was a one-yard loss, which meant that Iowa faced a fourth-and-goal at the Yale 9-yard line.

Parkin took the snap from center, quickly moved to his right, and spotted an opening directly ahead. He made a quick dash toward the goal line for the hole, eluding a Yale would-be tackler. Parkin then cut sideways, but knocked himself off-balance in the process. Trying to keep his balance, he fell forward toward the goal line, but landed a foot short. In an indication of how good the Iowa blocking scheme was, he momentarily lay untouched on the ground. He was then able to crawl over the goal line just before the nearest Yale defender futilely dove on him after the touchdown was secure. The point-after attempt was no good, but Iowa had all the points they needed with Parkin's magical run.

Yale managed to step up its game a notch in the second half, but could not cash in on two opportunities to draw even—one in the third quarter and the other in the fourth. In the first opportunity, Yale blocked an Iowa punt on the Hawkeyes' 30-yard line and took over on the 43-yard line. They were subsequently able to drive as far as the Iowa 20-yard line, and the hometown crowd thought they would finally see the true Yale team show up. However, it wasn't meant to be; the drive was halted on a bad exchange from the

COACH HOWARD JONES

Iowa coach Howard Jones led the Hawkeyes to a second straight perfect 7–0 season in 1922. In all, Jones racked up 20 consecutive wins from 1920 to 1923. The brilliant winning streak came to an end when Iowa met a sophomore phenom by the name of Red Grange who led Illinois to a 9–6 victory in Iowa City in October 1923.

The 1923 season was Jones's last as head coach at Iowa. He moved on to Duke University for one year before landing at the University of Southern California. He led the Men of Troy to five Rose Bowls during the 1930s. Sadly, Jones died of a heart attack at age 55 in 1941. Close associates were convinced that his obsession with football may have played a role in his untimely passing.

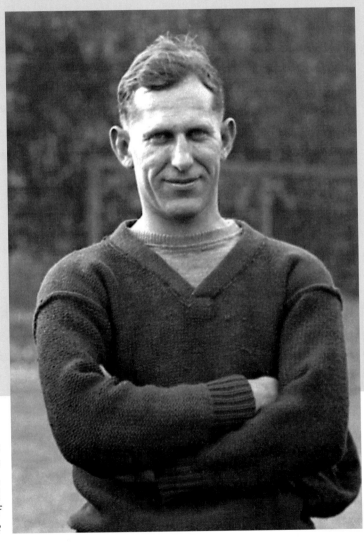

Iowa coach Howard Jones led the Hawks to a 6–0 victory over Yale at the Yale Bowl in New Haven, Connecticut, on October 14, 1922. That Yale team happened to be coached by his brother, Tad. *Copyright: University of Iowa—CMP Photographic Service*

GAME DETAILS

Iowa 6 • Yale 0

Date: October 14, 1922

Location: Yale Bowl, New Haven, Connecticut

Attendance: 35,000 (est.)

Box Score:

Iowa	0	6	0	0	**6**
Yale	0	0	0	0	**0**

Scoring:

IA   Parkin 9-yard run (PAT failed)

center that lost six yards. Yale later missed a drop-kick from the 30-yard line.

The game's outcome was in doubt until the waning minutes of the fourth quarter. Yale's final push began with a drive from their own 30-yard line. The Elis managed to string together four straight first downs to move the ball to the Iowa 17-yard line. However, the Iowa defense would not allow the team to lose this day. A failed pass attempt eventually ended Yale's last hope with less than a minute remaining on the game clock.

When word of the Iowa victory came over the wire to Iowa City, thousands of residents and students danced in the streets. As darkness fell, bonfires burned brightly and thousands of rockets and Roman candles lit up the Iowa City skies. The celebratory crowd was estimated at 7,000 and was led by the university band, which had not accompanied the team to Connecticut. The yelling, cheering multitude was reminiscent of New Year's Eve celebrations at Broadway and 42nd Streets in New York City. A large crowd of fans also gathered at the train station to greet the team upon their return home.

One of the features of the season which has provoked probably more discussion than almost any other, is that of the use of the 'huddle system' in giving signals. Those Easterners who saw Iowa defeat Yale... were first given an illustration of this system, which is becoming quite popular in the Middle West.

—WALTER CAMP, COMMENTING ON ONE OF THE INNOVATIONS IOWA EMPLOYED IN THE GAME

October 4, 2003

28 CHANDLER'S HOMECOMING HEROICS

A fourth-quarter touchdown pass caps a comeback win over Michigan in front of the Iowa City faithful

During the 2002 season, the Iowa team and coach Kirk Ferentz burst back onto the national scene and became a force to be reckoned with in the Big Ten. Play Number 50, which opened the book, was from the Orange Bowl game following the 2002 season, and several plays from the 2002 regular season are yet to come in the countdown. But just one dominant season doesn't make a team a perennial power. Thus, the 2003 season was important because it could demonstrate whether Iowa under Coach Ferentz would be just a flash in the pan or a sustained perennial power.

The 2002 team lost several star leaders to graduation or the NFL draft, including quarterback Brad Banks, tight end Dallas Clark, and a good portion of a dominant offensive line, including senior center Bruce Nelson and senior guard Eric Steinbach. But the Hawks started the 2003 regular season right where they left off in the 2002 regular season: they won each of the four nonconference games that opened the year, which included the first win against Iowa State since 1997. However, Iowa had lost

the Big Ten opener at Michigan State, which gave their Big Ten home opener against Michigan added significance.

The Wolverines jumped quickly on the Hawkeyes; with just over four minutes remaining in the first quarter they led 14–0 after a five-yard touchdown run by Chris Perry and a 14-yard touchdown pass from John Navarre to Braylon Edwards.

Iowa was finally able to put together a drive on its fourth possession. Big gains were made on the drive using the fake handoff play to Fred Russell, including a 23-yard pass play from senior quarterback Nathan Chandler to tight end Erik Jensen. Then Chandler was just able to dive into the end zone near the right pylon on a six-yard run to get Iowa on the board and in the game. It was 14–7 after the conversion by Nate Kaeding. The touchdown was followed by three straight field goals, two by Michigan and one by Iowa.

The high-powered Michigan offense was still able to effectively move the ball against a strong Iowa defense. Michigan went up 10 points on a 47-yard field goal by Garrett

Iowa's Ramon Ochoa hauls in a 31-yard touchdown pass from Nathan Chandler, keying Iowa's victory over Michigan at Kinnick Stadium on October 4, 2003. *Copyright: University of Iowa— CMP Photographic Service*

Rivas on their next possession, but that was matched by the first of three Nate Kaeding field goals on the day, a 34-yarder. Michigan again answered with a 26-yard field goal by Rivas to increase the lead to 20–10.

Michigan was able to maintain the 10-point lead for most of the second quarter as the Iowa offense struggled to put together a sustained drive. However, Iowa's special teams, which were stellar all day, provided a special lift on Michigan's punt with approximately two minutes to play in the half. When it appeared that Michigan would take at least a two-score lead into halftime, Iowa's Ramon Ochoa returned a Michigan punt 38 yards to the Michigan 18-yard line.

A personal foul by Michigan moved the ball to the 9-yard line, and Iowa took just 19 seconds of game clock to punch the ball into the end zone. The touchdown came on a six-yard pass from Chandler to Calvin Davis. Iowa now trailed the Wolverines by just three points, taking all the momentum into halftime.

The teams traded punts early in the third quarter; neither offense could sustain a drive. Michigan began their third drive of the half after a punt by Iowa at their own 35-yard line midway through the third quarter. Navarre's second pass on the drive was intercepted by Antwan Allen and returned 24 yards to the Michigan 28-yard line. Russell's strong running advanced the ball as far as the 1-yard line, but Michigan's defense would not give up the touchdown, and Iowa settled for a 25-yard Kaeding field goal to tie the game at 20–20.

Michigan went three-and-out on their next possession and came out on fourth down in punt formation. Following the long punt return at the end of the second quarter, Michigan coach Lloyd Carr changed his punt strategy. Hoping to strengthen kick coverage and keep the ball out of the hands of the dangerous Ochoa, he replaced punter Adam Finley with freshman Rivas and had Rivas roll right with the ball upon receiving the snap before kicking it diagonally downfield.

The new strategy was successful on Michigan's first two punts of the second half, as both were downed with no return. But the Iowa special-teams unit finally figured out the gimmick strategy on Michigan's third punt attempt of the half and got to Rivas for the block. Rivas covered the blocked punt at the Michigan 14-yard line, and Iowa was poised to take the lead for the first time all day. But once again, the Michigan defense was up to the challenge, forcing another Kaeding field-goal attempt. It was good from 32 yards, and Iowa had its first lead 23–20.

In a repeat of the first several possessions of the third quarter, the teams traded punts early in the fourth quarter. Iowa began its second possession of the quarter with 9:39 to play, still clinging to the three-point lead. Behind a sharp passing attack led by Chandler, Iowa moved downfield. Two critical third-down pass completions to Jensen put Iowa in position at the Michigan 31-yard line.

Ramon Ochoa

Senior Ramon Ochoa, hailing from Maywood, California, was a key offensive and special-teams contributor to Iowa's 10–3 record in 2003, which included a decisive win against Florida in the 2004 Outback Bowl on New Year's Day. On the year, Ochoa scored touchdowns by rushing, pass reception, and punt return, notching a total of eight touchdowns. He led the team in receiving, punt returns, and kickoff returns his senior season. Ochoa's 40 punt returns and 495 punt-return yards are both Iowa single-season records.

Ochoa was named Iowa's special teams co-player of the year in 2003 and also won the Next Man In award on offense in 2003. The Next Man In concept has been one of the cornerstones of coach Kirk Ferentz's philosophy during Iowa's rise to national prominence. It is intended to mean that the team works with the players available on any given day. If someone goes down and is unable to perform, the next man in is expected to step in for the starter and not miss a beat.

GAME DETAILS

Iowa 30 • Michigan 27

Date: October 4, 2003

Location: Kinnick Stadium, Iowa City, Iowa

Attendance: 70,397

Weather: Partly cloudy, 70 degrees

Box Score:

Michigan	14	6	0	7	**27**
Iowa	7	10	6	7	**30**

Scoring:

MI	Perry 5-yard run (Rivas PAT)
MI	Edwards 14-yard pass from Navarre (Rivas PAT)
IA	N. Chandler 6-yard run (Kaeding PAT)
MI	Rivas 47-yard FG
IA	Kaeding 34-yard FG
MI	Rivas 26-yard FG
IA	Davis 6-yard pass from N. Chandler (Kaeding PAT)
IA	Kaeding 25-yard FG
IA	Kaeding 32-yard FG
IA	Ochoa 31-yard pass from N. Chandler (Kaeding PAT)
MI	Edwards 41-yard pass from Navarre (Rivas PAT)

For dramatic effect, Iowa then called timeout. The Iowa offensive brain trust conferred with Chandler on the sideline and came up with a play that eventually sealed the game. On a play action fake to Russell, Chandler tossed a perfect pass just over two Michigan defenders to the front right corner of the end zone, where Ochoa made the touchdown catch. The officials conferred to be sure Ochoa had possession of the ball before falling out of bounds. It was ruled he had possession, and Iowa had grabbed a 10-point lead with just 5:16 to play in the fourth quarter.

But this time, Michigan had an answer. Navarre drove the Wolverines 86 yards for a touchdown in just one minute and 30 seconds, with the touchdown coming on a 41-yard pass to Braylon Edwards. The restlessness in the homecoming crowd grew as Michigan held the Hawks to a three-and-out on the next possession. Iowa was forced to punt the ball back to Michigan.

David Bradley, who performed well all day, boomed a clutch 52-yard punt, and Michigan took over at their own 27-yard line with 2:44 left. Michigan quickly crossed midfield but found themselves facing a fourth-and-12 at the Iowa 49. The Iowa victory was secure following an incomplete pass intended for Jason Avant.

The big win over Michigan marked only the second time in school history that Iowa had defeated Michigan twice in a row; the 2003 game followed a 34–9 victory at Michigan Stadium in 2002. (Iowa also defeated Michigan in back-to-back years was 1984 and 1985.)

November 4, 2000

STEALING A WIN IN HAPPY VALLEY

Ryan Hansen's interception in double overtime ends a Penn State thriller and turns the tide for the Hawks

Penn State's Beaver Stadium has been a house of horrors for many an opponent over the years. Yet for some reason, Iowa has had numerous big wins at Happy Valley over the years. Prior to a 27–7 loss in 2007, Iowa had won six of its last seven games at Beaver Stadium—a run that dated back to 1976, before Penn State even entered the Big Ten conference.

Iowa's final record in the 2000 season was just 3–9 overall, 3–5 in the Big Ten conference. Glancing at the top 50 top plays, one will notice there aren't too many plays from this type of year that made their way into the book. So, what makes this play in this game so special? It is widely believed to be the single turning point of the Kirk Ferentz era: the point at which the Hawkeyes started heading in the right direction under Ferentz's leadership.

The numbers would seem to back up this theory. The 2000 season was just Ferentz's second at the helm, and the Penn State game was his 21st game as head coach. In Ferentz's first 20 games, Iowa had posted

a dismal record of 2–18. But Iowa would close the 2000 season by winning two of its final three games, including this memorable win at Penn State. And from this game until the end of the 2005 season, Iowa's record under Ferentz was a stellar 47–18.

As has been a staple of Ferentz-coached teams, Iowa started quickly. Junior quarterback Kyle McCann led the team 80 yards in six plays for the game's first touchdown, on a six-yard pass to Kahlil Hill. McCann skillfully avoided a heated Penn State rush and rolled to his right to make the connection with Hill. McCann's running ability was an important part of Iowa's offensive success and something the Penn State defense hadn't seen before.

McCann would turn in a career day, connecting on 25 of 37 passes for 232 yards, one interception, and one touchdown. He also rushed 16 times for another 78 yards. And in what would prove to be a prelude to many nice things to come, this game was also the first real impact game for the freshman place-kicker from Coralville, Nate

Iowa's Ryan Hansen (14) secures the interception in the second overtime that seals Iowa's win against Penn State on November 4, 2000, at Beaver Stadium in University Park, Pennsylvania.
Photo courtesy The Cedar Rapids Gazette

Kaeding. Kaeding built Iowa's lead to 13–0 on 48-yard and 49-yard field goals, both of which were career bests. The 49-yarder in particular had plenty of distance and would have been good from 60 yards out.

Iowa would hold onto the 13–0 lead late into the second quarter. But just before halftime, Penn State drove the ball 55 yards in nine plays to set up a 42-yard field goal by Ryan Primanti, making it 13–3 in favor of Iowa heading into halftime. Penn State built on the momentum from the late first-half score and came out more determined in the second half. Another Primanti field goal in the third quarter pulled the Nittany Lions to within a touchdown and an extra point.

Then, early in the fourth quarter, Penn State took advantage of one of the rare mistakes by McCann on the day; the Lions' Justin Kurpeikis leaped to intercept a McCann pass and returned the ball to Iowa's 38-yard line. Penn State quarterback Rashard Casey then promptly led Penn State on a six-play touchdown drive. The two-yard touchdown catch by John Gilmore knotted the game at 13–13.

Both teams exchanged field goals later in the fourth quarter, which made the score 16–16. Penn State had one last chance to win the game in regulation when two long runs by Casey and Eric McCoo moved the ball to the Iowa 39-yard line with four seconds left. But a 56-yard field goal as time expired fell just a few yards short, sending the game into overtime. It would be the first-ever overtime game for each school.

RYAN HANSEN

Ryan Hansen's clutch interception was the third of the year for the senior cornerback, who led the team in that category in 2000. The Penn State game came during the week that Hansen was featured in a *People Magazine* photo spread as its sexiest American athlete. In addition to his football skills and good looks, Hansen also apparently studied hard while at Iowa; he received three straight All–Big Ten Academic awards in 1998, 1999, and 2000.

The win sealed by Hansen's interception was also special to coach Kirk Ferentz, who is a native of Pittsburgh. Ferentz would go on to have plenty of success during the coming years in his home state against coaching legend Joe Paterno, posting big road wins in 2002 and 2004, for a total of three straight at Beaver Stadium.

Ryan Hansen celebrates his game-winning interception following the second overtime session against Penn State.
Copyright: University of Iowa—CMP Photographic Service

I was just looking to go in and make the tackle. I thought I was going to have a chance to make the play, but before I knew it, the ball got away from the receiver and bounced right back to me. I caught it and fell on it...I really didn't know if the game was over or what. I just tried to hold on to it. All I remember hearing is Matt Stockdale yelling, 'The game's over. We won.' This feels great. It's one I'll remember for a long, long time.

—IOWA CORNERBACK RYAN HANSEN

GAME DETAILS

Iowa 26 • Penn State 23

Date: November 4, 2000

Location: Beaver Stadium, University Park, Pennsylvania

Attendance: 95,437

Box Score:

Iowa	7	6	0	3	7	3	**26**
Penn St.	0	3	3	10	7	0	**23**

Scoring:

IA	Hill 6-yard pass from McCann (Kaeding PAT)
IA	Kaeding 48-yard FG
IA	Kaeding 49-yard FG
PSU	Primanti 42-yard FG
PSU	Primanti 32-yard FG
PSU	Gilmore 2-yard pass from Casey (Primanti PAT)
IA	Kaeding 46-yard FG
PSU	Primanti 28-yard FG
PSU	Casey 6-yard run (Primanti PAT)
IA	Betts 11-yard run (Kaeding PAT)
IA	Kaeding 26-yard FG

Iowa won the overtime toss and decided to play defense first, so they would know what would be needed to win or tie the game after Penn State's possession. Penn State registered a touchdown on a six-yard run by Casey, and Iowa then matched Penn State with an 11-yard rushing touchdown by Ladell Betts.

Iowa had the ball first in the second overtime. Kaeding connected on a 26-yard field goal, his fourth of the day, to put Iowa in front 26–23. The game was now in the hands of the Iowa defense, and it wouldn't take long for Iowa to seal the deal.

On Penn State's first play, Casey dropped back to pass and spotted tight end Tony Stewart open downfield. The pass from Casey was a good one; it hit Stewart square in the chest, but he couldn't hold on. The ball caromed to Iowa cornerback Ryan Hansen, who secured the ball at the 14-yard line—and with it, the first overtime win in school history.

Hansen was buried in a mass of happy Hawkeyes on the field, and the wild celebration continued into Iowa's locker room, where the first hokey-pokey dance of the Ferentz era commenced after the Iowa seniors were presented with the game ball. The hokey-pokey dance was a postgame ritual started by coach Hayden Fry following big wins.

The win was huge on so many levels. It was Iowa's first road victory in more than two years (the previous win had come at Illinois in September 1998). Iowa would close the 2000 season with a win at home against Northwestern and a close loss at Minnesota in the season finale. However, history would show that this game and this play were the point in which Iowa got things going in the right direction under Ferentz. This game was the springboard to six consecutive bowl appearances for the Hawkeyes, beginning with the 2001 season and ending with the 2006 season.

November 19, 1994

FRESHMEN FOOL THE GOPHERS

Tim Dwight's nine-yard touchdown pass to Matt Sherman helps the Hawkeyes keep Floyd of Rosedale

Similar to Play Number 27, Play Number 26 is from a season that wasn't exactly one of Iowa's best. The Hawks finished the 1994 campaign with a mediocre 5–5–1 record. But this play made the list for a couple reasons. One, it came from a deep bag of Coach Hayden Fry's many trick plays; and two, it was executed on the road by two freshmen against Iowa's ancient rival, which demonstrated that the future for Iowa football was bright, even if 1994 ended up as more of a down year. Moreover, the player who tossed the touchdown pass on the gadget play, Tim Dwight, went on to become one of the all-time great Iowa receivers and punt-return specialists. The exotic play gave Iowa a 42–32 lead late in the third quarter, and Iowa hung on for the 49–42 win against its border rival.

The game wasn't pretty if you were a fan of hard-nosed defensive football. But there were plenty of chills and thrills if you were a fan of big plays on offense and special teams. The numbers put up by both teams were of historic proportions. The Iowa-Minnesota series began in 1891, and

never in the history of the series had this many points been scored in one game. The previous high was 75, and as a testament to how one-sided the early matchups in this series actually were, all the points were scored by one team—Minnesota, in a 1903 blowout.

In 1994 the teams combined for 997 yards of total offense. Minnesota alone posted an amazing 562 yards of total offense and lit up the scoreboard with 42 points, but it wasn't enough. Iowa was able to offset all of Minnesota's offensive output by scoring two touchdowns on special teams to Minnesota's zero.

It didn't take long for the scoring to begin after the kickoff. Iowa was held to a punt on their first possession. Not only was Dwight an integral part of the late-game heroics on offense, but he also distinguished himself early in the game by dislodging the football from Minnesota's Rodney Heath at the goal line during a first-quarter punt from Nick Gallery. Demo Odems jumped on the loose ball in the end zone for an early 7–0 Hawkeyes lead.

Quarterback Matt Sherman secures a touchdown reception from Tim Dwight to give Iowa a 10-point lead late in the third quarter against Minnesota at the Metrodome on November 19, 1994.
Copyright: University of Iowa—CMP Photographic Service

Freshmen Matt Sherman and Tim Dwight celebrate their third-quarter touchdown against Minnesota.
Copyright: University of Iowa—CMP Photographic Service

On the ensuing Minnesota possession, running back Chris Darkins split a pair of Iowa defenders on his way to a 56-yard touchdown scamper. The game was less than three minutes old and already both teams had scored touchdowns. And the fireworks were just getting started. Not to be outdone, Iowa running back Tavian Banks raced around left end and 25 yards later he had another touchdown to put Iowa up 14–7. Minnesota added a field goal, and an eventful first quarter came to an end with the score 14–10, Iowa.

Minnesota grabbed its first lead of the game in the second quarter when quarterback Tim Schade found Chuck Rios for an eight-yard touchdown pass. However, the lead was short-lived, as Iowa answered again behind the sensational running of Sedrick Shaw who registered the next two touchdowns of the game.

Shaw's first touchdown came on a pass play from Sherman. The blitz was on, but the offensive line was able to pick it up and Sherman found Shaw in stride for a short pass near the Iowa sideline. He toed the line to stay just inbounds, then pulled a 360-degree spin move to evade a Gophers defender before making his way to the end zone for a spectacular 46-yard touchdown play. Shaw later commented that the play "was just instincts."

Iowa again drove deep into Minnesota territory on their next offensive possession. Shaw took a handoff from the 17-yard line, made a couple moves, and was gone for

another touchdown and a 28–17 Hawkeyes advantage. A 43-yard punt return by Dwight again set the Hawks up deep inside Minnesota territory just before the half ended. Although Fry and the Hawks thought they had the fifth touchdown of the half on a pass from Sherman to Anthony Dean, the officials ruled the catch out of bounds. Fry voiced his displeasure with the officials on his way to the Iowa locker room.

The scoring continued into the second half with the teams trading touchdowns during the first part of the third quarter. Then, midway through the third quarter, Minnesota added another touchdown to pull to within 35–32.

Iowa was still clinging to a 35–32 lead late into the third quarter and was on the move again, deep in Minnesota territory, when the game-changing play was called. Although he would go on to spend most

Matt Sherman and Tim Dwight

First-year players Matt Sherman and Tim Dwight would both go on to prosperous careers at Iowa, although Sherman took more than his share of criticism from fans in subsequent years—something that goes with the territory for a quarterback. The 1994 season had five different quarterbacks who saw game action, and Sherman was the fifth of the five. He entered the third-to-last game of the season in the second half and led Iowa to three scores and a 21–21 tie with Purdue. Sherman then started the last two games against Northwestern and Minnesota. The Iowa offense clicked under his direction, posting 49 points in both games. Sherman went on to be the starting quarterback for most games during the 1995, 1996, and 1997 seasons.

Dwight, an Iowa City native, was a consensus All-American return specialist. He finished seventh in the voting for the 1997 Heisman Trophy during

his senior year. That year, he led the nation with a 16.7 punt-return average and set Iowa and Big Ten records for career punt return yardage with 1,102. Dwight returned a total of five punts for touchdowns during his career, including three in 1997. He had big performances in the important games against the traditional powers, posting punt-return touchdowns against Michigan, Ohio State, and Penn State.

Dwight also contributed mightily to the offensive cause. He is the school's all-time leading receiver with 2,271 yards.

Dwight went on to a long and prosperous career in the NFL, seeing time with Atlanta, San Diego, New England, the New York Jets, and Oakland. He scored a touchdown on a kick return against the Denver Broncos in the Falcons' losing effort in Super Bowl XXXIII.

GAME DETAILS

Iowa 49 • Minnesota 42

Date: November 19, 1994

Location: HHH Metrodome, Minneapolis, Minnesota

Attendance: 43,340

Box Score:

Iowa	14	14	21	0	**49**
Minnesota	10	7	15	10	**42**

Scoring:

IA	Odems 3-yard fumble return on punt (Hurley PAT)
MN	Darkins 56-yard run (Chalberg PAT)
IA	Banks 25-yard run (Hurley PAT)
MN	Chalberg 32-yard FG
MN	Rios 8-yard pass from Schade (Chalberg PAT)
IA	Shaw 46-yard pass from Sherman (Hurley PAT)
IA	Shaw 17-yard run (Hurley PAT)
IA	Odems 34-yard pass from Sherman (Hurley PAT)
MN	Darkins 1-yard run (2-pt. conv. – Atwell, 2-yard pass from Schade)
MN	Osterman 80-yard pass from Schade (Chalberg PAT)
IA	Sherman 9-yard pass from Dwight (Hurley PAT)
IA	Porter 10-yard fumble return on kickoff (Hurley PAT)
MN	Darkins 3-yard run (Chalberg PAT)
MN	Chalberg 28-yard FG

> **I** called the play and thought, 'Here we go.' We work on it a couple days a week in practice and it usually works...Tim Dwight throws a pretty good ball and knows where to throw it. The key is selling a good fake. Everyone did their job.
>
> —MATT SHERMAN'S COMMENTS ON THE TOUCHDOWN PASS FROM TIM DWIGHT

offensive plays in his career at wide receiver, Dwight was lined up at halfback for this play. Dwight took the pitch from Sherman and did his best to sell the defense on the running play. But the defense hadn't accounted for Sherman, who snuck downfield. Suddenly, Dwight had the ball in throwing position and lofted it downfield to Sherman. The play would go down as a nine-yard touchdown pass and it put Iowa up 42–32 late in the third quarter.

Lightning ended up striking twice as the dazed Gophers gave up the ensuing kickoff on a fumble that was returned 10 yards by Bo Porter for another touchdown, extending the Iowa lead to 49–32. However, on this night, no lead was secure; the Gophers mounted a late comeback. Minnesota put up 10 points in the fourth quarter to cut the Iowa lead to 49–42 with 3:06 left.

Minnesota had the ball with time running out late in the fourth quarter. It would take a stand by a battered Iowa defense to seal the win. Iowa was able to stop Minnesota on downs deep in their own territory, sealing the game and sending Iowa into the off-season on a high note.

The heroics by freshmen Dwight, Sherman, and Banks signified good things ahead for Fry's Hawks. The 1995, 1996, and 1997 teams posted an overall record of 24–12 and reached three straight bowl games, winning two of them. The finale to the 1994 season was just a glimpse of the greatness to come from these future Iowa stars.

25 DEFENSIVE LOCKDOWN IN THE BIG HOUSE

Andre Tippett forces an incomplete Michigan pass, capping a stellar performance by the Iowa defense

To say that Michigan had Iowa's number in the 1960s and '70s would be putting it kindly. Before Hayden Fry's Hawkeyes defeated Michigan 9–7 in a defensive grudge-match en route to the Rose Bowl in 1981, Michigan had defeated the Hawkeyes nine straight times since an Iowa win in 1962 was followed by a tie in 1963. Coming into the 1981 game at Ann Arbor, Iowa had not tasted victory in the Big House since the days of Forest Evashevski.

However, these Hawkeyes—led by Coach Fry—would prove to be different. This win against longtime nemesis Michigan was the single game that let people know the Hawks were back—not only to compete for winning seasons, but also to compete for Big Ten championships. The win came down to the wire: a stellar defensive play by future Pro Football Hall of Fame player Andre Tippett clinched it on Michigan's last offensive play.

The win at Michigan, which had been sixth in the two national wire service polls, was Iowa's third of the season against a team ranked sixth in the nation. Iowa opened the year with a huge win over No. 6 Nebraska at home and followed that up with a win against sixth-ranked UCLA two weeks later. The Michigan win wasn't necessarily pretty, but Iowa wasn't in a position to be picky. The combination of a stingy Iowa defense and a freshman kicker with ice water in his veins was enough to put Iowa on top this day.

The Hawks grabbed a 3–0 lead on their first possession of the game. Iowa took over with great field position on the Michigan 38-yard line off a Michigan fumble on a punt. A 25-yard completion from Iowa quarterback Gordy Bohannon to Ivory Webb advanced the ball to the Michigan 11-yard line, but Iowa could advance no further than the 4 on a tough Michigan defense. Tom Nichol came on to connect on the first of three field goals on the day, this one a 20-yarder. Iowa built on the 3–0 lead with a 57-yard drive that led to Nichol's second field goal from 36 yards out. Iowa led 6–0 at the end of the first quarter.

Iowa linebacker Andre Tippett (99) forced an incomplete pass by Michigan with 31 seconds remaining to seal a hard-earned 9–7 victory over Michigan in Ann Arbor, Michigan, on October 17, 1981. *Copyright: University of Iowa—CMP Photographic Service*

The only scoring in the second quarter was a 17-yard touchdown toss from Michigan quarterback Steve Smith to Anthony Carter that came with 6:30 to play in the half. Michigan drove the ball 68 yards for the score, which was aided by an Iowa personal foul. Carter, a consensus All-American, was the only receiving threat for Michigan all day; he caught five passes for 91 yards, but the rest of the Wolverines as a team could muster only one pass reception. On the strength of the Carter touchdown catch, Michigan took a 7–6 lead into halftime.

Nichol would convert his third field goal in three attempts with 2:40 left in the third quarter. This field goal, from 30 yards away, was the culmination of a 67-yard drive that took five and a half minutes off the clock.

The Iowa defense, which was ranked at the top of the Big Ten during most of the season, lived up to its lofty reputation and then some against Michigan on enemy turf. The defense pretty much took over the game in the second half to preserve the win, holding Michigan's leading rusher, tailback Butch Woolfolk, under 100 yards for the first time all year. Woolfolk finished with just 56 net yards on 14 attempts.

Iowa's defense rose to the occasion three separate times to keep Michigan off the scoreboard in crucial situations. The first came on an interception by Iowa's Mel Cole off a deflected pass in the end zone midway through the third quarter. The interception halt a Michigan scoring attempt, and was the trigger for what proved to be the game-winning field goal.

Michigan's next drive following the Iowa field goal was halted on a fourth-down stop by tackle Mark Bortz on Carter early in the fourth quarter. However, the Michigan offense continued to press. Michigan was driving late in the fourth quarter toward potential game-winning points, but faced another fourth down; time was running out on the Wolverines. Tippett was

ANDRE TIPPETT

Andre Tippett and punter Reggie Roby were the first consensus All-American players under Hayden Fry at Iowa. Both earned accolades for their play during the 1981 season. Tippett was also a First Team All–Big Ten performer in both his junior and senior seasons in 1980 and 1981. Tippett still holds the Iowa record for negative yardage on tackles in a season, with 20 tackles for 153 yards lost in 1980. He played in an era where the school did not track quarterback sacks, but had they been tabulated, he undoubtedly would rank near the top of Iowa's all-time sack list.

Following his time in Iowa City, Tippett took talents to the New England Patriots after they selected him in the second round of the 1981 draft. Tippett ultimately earned All-Pro honors as a linebacker five times during his 11-year career and helped lead the Patriots to the 1986 Super Bowl versus the Chicago Bears. Tippett was elected to the Pro Football Hall of Fame in February 2008.

Iowa's quarterback on the 1981 Rose Bowl team, Gordy Bohannon, was again in the headlines some 35 years later when his son, Jason, who was a highly sought-after basketball prospect, chose to make his own way at the University of Wisconsin rather than follow the family legacy at Iowa.

GAME DETAILS

Iowa 9 • Michigan 7

Date: October 17, 1981

Location: Michigan Stadium, Ann Arbor, Michigan

Attendance: 105,951

Box Score:

Iowa	6	0	3	0	**9**	
Michigan	0	7	0	0	**7**	

Scoring:

IA   Nichol 20-yard FG

IA   Nichol 36-yard FG

MI   Carter 17-yard pass from Smith (PAT good)

IA   Nichol 30-yard FG

able to influence the Michigan pass and it fell harmlessly incomplete. There were just 31 seconds left on the clock, and Bohannon only had to kneel twice to seal the Iowa victory.

The win propelled "Hayden's Heroes" to a 5–1 record overall and sole possession of first place in the Big Ten with a 3–0 conference record. The win over Michigan, which, along with Ohio State, had dominated the Big Ten for more than a decade, surely captured the attention of the nation. Iowa would ride the momentum built by the strong start all the way to Pasadena for the Hawkeyes' first Rose Bowl appearance since the 1958 season.

The 1981 season could have been one of the all-time great seasons were it not for a letdown loss at home to Minnesota the week after the Michigan game. The Hawkeyes' hangover continued the following week at Illinois. However, Iowa then recovered with three straight victories, but the Rose Bowl berth wasn't clinched until the last hours of the Big Ten season with the win over Michigan State coupled with Ohio State's loss at Michigan.

November 1, 1958

RETURN LEAVES MICHIGAN FEELING BLUE

Willie Fleming's punt-return touchdown helps Iowa earn its first win over the Wolverines in 34 years

So, you thought Iowa's record against Michigan in the 1960s and '70s was bad? Of course it was, but unbelievably, the futility against Michigan during the late 1920s, '30s, '40s, and early '50s was even worse. From 1924 to 1957 (a period covering 14 games), Iowa did not defeat Michigan once although they did come close with ties in 1929 and 1957. Even the Big Ten–champion Rose Bowl team of 1956 could not break into the win column against the Wolverines, dropping a close 17–14 game on homecoming in Iowa City for the squad's only loss that season.

Altogether, coming into the 1958 game with Michigan, it had been 34 long years since Iowa had tasted victory against Michigan. Iowa would literally run that streak into the ground during a signature win at the Big House during their run to a second Rose Bowl in three years.

To add to the intrigue, Iowa coach Forest Evashevski, was a Michigan native. He graduated from Northwestern High School in Detroit. Evy went on to star at Michigan as a quarterback under head coach Fritz

Crisler from 1938 to 1940. During that time, he led Michigan to a record of 20–4. Crisler called Evashevski "the greatest quarterback I ever had."

Although it was Iowa's flashy passing game—led by consensus All-American quarterback Randy Duncan—that got the most publicity entering the game, it was Iowa's down-and-dirty rushing attack in the trenches that led the Hawkeyes to victory this day. The losing streak ended on the strength of an overpowering Hawkeyes rushing attack led by Iowa's "three-headed monster" halfback machine: Willie Fleming, Ray Jauch, and Bob Jeter. Iowa posted a punt return for a score and four touchdown runs, many of the spectacular variety. In the box score, they read as TDs of 72, 74, 61, 24, and three yards.

Michigan started the game strong; most of the first quarter was played on Iowa's side of the 50-yard line. However, the Iowa defense was able to keep Michigan off the scoreboard and force two punts into Iowa's end zone for touchbacks. On Michigan's third possession, the defense again forced a punt. However, Iowa would have an opportunity to return this one. Fleming fielded the 40-yard punt at Iowa's 28-yard line. He skillfully evaded multiple would-be Michigan tacklers immediately, but was nearly knocked off his feet at Iowa's 40-yard line and again 20 yards later on the Michigan 40, but again he was able to stay on his feet as a result of a well-timed pivot. At that point, Fleming found himself in the open with a clear path to the Michigan goal line. The spectacular touchdown run covered 72 yards and was the first punt return for a score since the days of Earl Smith in 1954.

Much to the chagrin of the 68,566 paying customers, most of whom were clad in maize and blue, Iowa's ground game was just getting warmed up. Two minutes later, Iowa found itself again on offense after Michigan wisely opted to angle a punt out of bounds at the Iowa 26-yard line. On Iowa's first play from scrimmage, lightning would again strike.

The first play of the drive was a handoff to Jauch. He thrust through an opening at left tackle, then cut back to his right and spotted daylight downfield. In all, Jauch cruised 74 yards for the score. He even had an escort for the last half of the run, as Don Prescott made sure no Michigan defenders would lay a hand on Jauch until the touchdown was secure. Iowa led the game 14–0 at that point.

Certainly, Iowa didn't expect Michigan to just roll over, and the Wolverines certainly didn't. The Michigan offense started to make a game of it by getting on the board just before the half on a grueling 16-play, 67-yard touchdown drive, with the score coming just 26 seconds before the

Iowa's Willie Fleming produced 240 yards on the ground at Michigan Stadium on November 1, 1958, including a memorable 72-yard punt return for a touchdown. The 37–14 win was Iowa's first at Michigan in 34 years. *Copyright: University of Iowa—CMP Photographic Service*

half ended. Michigan had to overcome two negative plays as Michigan passers were dropped behind the line of scrimmage for losses. The scoring play came on a four-yard touchdown pass from Bob Ptacek to Darrell Harper. The two-point conversion failed, and Iowa led 14–6 at halftime.

Things really started to get interesting early in the third quarter. Michigan promptly took the kickoff 74 yards on 14 plays to begin the second half. Most of the heavy lifting during the drive was done by Harper on the ground and Ptacek through the air. Michigan was able to tie the ballgame at 14–14 on a successful two-point conversion.

However, a refocused Hawkeyes team would get off the mat and issue the knockout blow. Iowa racked up three touchdowns to close the game during a glorious 16-minute stretch in the third and fourth quarters, following Michigan's tying score.

The run was set up by the defense. Michigan had possession on their own 19 and promptly lost five yards. On the next play, Hugh Drake, one of Iowa's seniors who had been to the Rose Bowl following the 1956 season, broke through the offensive line and knocked Michigan quarterback Stanton Noskin silly. The ball popped out and was recovered by Iowa's Jeff Langston. Iowa took immediate advantage of the Michigan turnover; Jeter sped around right end on the very next play to give Iowa a lead it would never relinquish.

The next several series saw both teams give the ball over to the opposition: Michigan on a pass interception and again on downs deep in Iowa territory, and Iowa on a pair of fumbles by Jauch and Jeter. It was the offensive possession for Iowa following the goal-line stand by the defense that provided the back-breaking score. Thanks to the defense, the offense took over on its own 6-yard

> There have been so many frustrations in this series for me, I just don't know what to say. This was a big one for me.
>
> —IOWA COACH FOREST EVASHEVSKI

line and drove 94 yards in eight plays, effectively putting the game away.

Duncan was able to recover from a relatively cold first half in the third and fourth quarters, as a couple of big plays in the passing game helped move the ball down to the Michigan 24. Another marvelous touchdown run by Jeter provided the scoring play, and Iowa converted a two-point conversion to make it 29–14.

Iowa capped the scoring on another long touchdown run, this one a 61-yard play by Fleming. Iowa was penalized for excessive celebration for the second straight time, but how could you blame them? Following another successful two-point conversion, the scoreboard read Iowa 37, Michigan 14.

Coach Evashevski was presented with the game ball by his players immediately after the game. A long dry spell had ended in style, and Iowa was well on their way to their second outright Big Ten title and second Rose Bowl in three years.

WILLIE FLEMING

This game was especially memorable for Willie Fleming because he was from Detroit. He was only a sophomore on the 1958 team and undersized at 5'9" and 170 pounds. But the performance he gave on the Michigan Stadium turf this day has long been remembered by Hawkeyes fans everywhere.

Unfortunately for both Fleming and the Hawkeyes, Fleming's career with Iowa ended up being brief. The 1958 season was Fleming's only season at Iowa because he encountered academic problems that prevented him from participating in future years. Evashevski thought very highly of Fleming and commented that "Willie was the best running back I had at Iowa...It's too bad he didn't finish his career at Iowa because I think he would have had all the records in his pocket if he would have. He was a great football player."

GAME DETAILS

Iowa 37 • Michigan 14

Date: November 1, 1958

Location: Michigan Stadium, Ann Arbor, Michigan

Attendance: 68,566

Box Score:

Iowa	7	7	7	16	**37**
Michigan	0	6	8	0	**14**

Scoring:

IA   Fleming 72-yard punt return (Prescott PAT)

IA   Jauch 74-yard run (Prescott PAT)

MI   Harper 4-yard pass from Ptacek
        (2-pt. attempt failed)

MI   Ptacek 1-yard run (2-pt. conv.; Myers,
        2-yard run)

IA   Jeter 3-yard run (Prescott PAT)

IA   Jeter 24-yard run (2-pt. conv.; Merz,
        2-yard pass from Nocera)

IA   Fleming 61-yard run (2-pt. conv.; Merz,
        2-yard pass from Duncan)

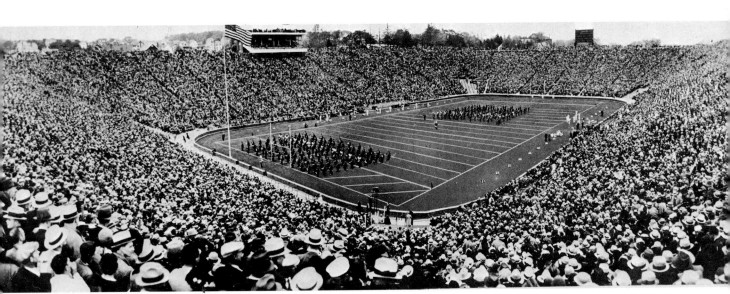

Michigan Stadium (show here in 1933) has been an especially difficult venue for the Hawkeyes, who failed to win in Ann Arbor for more than three decades starting in 1924. The 1958 upset in front of the huge pro-Wolverines crowd was a major coup for the Iowa football team. *Photo courtesy AP Images*

September 17, 1983

BOMB BREAKS NATIONAL CHAMPS

A 77-yard touchdown pass seals a wild Iowa win and hands Penn State its third straight loss

Penn State had won the 1982 National Championship but had started the 1983 season 0–2 prior to its home date against Iowa. Iowa was coming off a victory in the 1982 Peach Bowl and had started the 1983 season 1–0 after thrashing Iowa State 51–10. No disrespect to Iowa State, but the game against Penn State was expected to be a much different story. However, it ended up being much the same story for the Iowa offense led by sophomore quarterback Chuck Long. The defense would find that the Penn State offense had a few more weapons than Iowa State. However, the defense made enough big plays for Iowa to again turn Happy Valley into Happy Hawkeye Valley.

It was an offensive thrill ride from the very beginning and it was a tough day at times for both defenses. Iowa coach Hayden Fry commented after the game that "it wasn't pretty as far as our defense is concerned. They really executed against us. They picked us like chickens."

Penn State coach Joe Paterno felt similarly about his own defense: "It was the poorest tackling by a team that I've ever been associated with. In a lot of ways it was a good football game. In spots we just didn't make the plays we should make."

The offensive numbers put up in the game were mind-numbing. Iowa racked up 587 yards, which was the sixth-highest output in school history. Long set Iowa and Beaver Stadium records at the time with his 345 passing yards. The teams combined for 599 yards in the air and 1,079 total yards, which were both stadium records. Many individuals on both offenses put up impressive totals: Penn State's Doug Strang passed for 254 yards and running back D.J. Dozier logged 104 yards on the ground. Iowa's Owen Gill rushed for 131 yards and Iowa wide receiver Dave Moritz registered 119 yards receiving.

Things did not start off well for the visitors from Iowa City. Long was flagged for intentional grounding on Iowa's first offensive play, which put the Hawks in a hole at their own 4-yard line. Fry elected to use a quick kick on third down in an attempt to relieve the pressure, but the Lions took possession at Iowa's 33-yard line—and five

Iowa quarterback Chuck Long (16) enjoyed a spectacular day in leading the Hawkeyes to a 42–34 seesaw victory against Penn State at Beaver Stadium in University Park, Pennsylvania, on September 17, 1983. *Copyright: University of Iowa—CMP Photographic Service*

Ronnie Harmon celebrates a key touchdown that helped lead Iowa to a road victory at Penn State in September 1983. *Copyright: University of Iowa—CMP Photographic Service*

plays later they had a 7–0 lead on a nine-yard touchdown pass from Strang to Dean DiMidio.

However, the Hawkeyes were was unfazed and subsequently marched 80 yards for a touchdown of their own. The key play on the drive was a 40-yard completion to Moritz from a scrambling Long. Eddie Phillips plunged into the end zone from one yard out to tie the score at 7–7.

The Hawkeyes kept the momentum going on their next possession, putting together another long drive, this one for 72 yards, to make it 14–7. Now it was Penn State's turn for a long drive and they delivered, storming 89 yards in 14 plays to knot the game at 14–14.

After a controversial fumble by Long, Penn State again grabbed the lead, 21–14 at halftime. Fry was flagged for unsportsmanlike conduct while protesting the call, which set Penn State up deep in Iowa territory.

Iowa started the second half by grabbing the first of three Penn State fumbles. Long was then able to sidestep a heavy rush to sling a sidearm 26-yard touchdown pass to Phillips moments later, again tying the game at 21–21. The seesaw affair continued as the Nittany Lions stemmed Iowa's momentum with a 57-yard dash by Dozier, which set up an 18-yard scoring strike from Strang to Kevin Baugh. Now Penn State led

for the third time in the game by a touchdown, this time 28–21.

Midway through the third quarter and down by a touchdown on enemy turf, it was gut-check time for Iowa. Could they respond yet again? The answer would be a resounding yes. A Hawkeyes gang tackle forced Dozier's second fumble of the game. Paul Hufford fell on it, and the Hawks then decided to lay the game squarely on the shoulders of their young quarterback Long.

Iowa's tying score was set up by a deep pass by Long down the middle to Moritz for a 46-yard gain. Long then carried it into the end zone from five yards away. After Tom Nichol's extra point, the game saw its fourth deadlocked score of the day.

Following the well-established pattern in the game, it appeared that Penn State would answer by grabbing another lead. The Lions were on the move and had advanced to the Iowa 21-yard line before the Iowa defense dug deep and came up with another big play. Tackle George Little, a Pennsylvania native, roared into the backfield and crushed Strang, jarring the ball loose in the process. The fumble was recovered by Iowa's Mike Yacullo.

Iowa was able to take advantage of the turnover on the ensuing drive. Long hit Gill up the right sideline for a 38-yard play and Norm Granger split the Lions' defense

RONNIE HARMON

Ronnie Harmon was basically Mr. Everything during his years at Iowa from 1982 to 1985. He was one of the most versatile players in Iowa football history. He played receiver during his first two years and developed a knack for the big play, just like the one he delivered in this game against Penn State. He was converted to running back during his junior year and enjoyed tremendous production at that position as well.

Harmon is second on the list of Iowa's all-time leaders in all-purpose yards, with 4,978, just 12 yards

shy of Tim Dwight's career total. His 2,045 receiving yards and 2,271 rushing yards rank him third and seventh, respectively, in school history. Unfortunately (and unfairly), what many Iowa fans remember about Harmon is his four fumbles in his last game, the 1986 Rose Bowl against UCLA.

Harmon went on to a long NFL career, primarily with the Buffalo Bills and San Diego Chargers.

GAME DETAILS

Iowa 42 • Penn State 34

Date: September 17, 1983

Location: Beaver Stadium, University Park, Pennsylvania

Attendance: 84,628

Box Score:

Iowa	14	0	21	7	**42**
Penn St.	7	14	7	6	**34**

Scoring:

PSU	DiMidio 9-yard pass from Strang (Gancitano PAT)
IA	Phillips 1-yard run (Nichol PAT)
IA	Gill 4-yard run (Nichol PAT)
PSU	Jackson 7-yard pass from Strang (Gancitano PAT)
PSU	Strang 1-yard run (Gancitano PAT)
IA	Phillips 26-yard pass from Long (Nichol PAT)
PSU	Baugh 18-yard pass from Strang (Gancitano PAT)
IA	Long 5-yard run (Nichol PAT)
IA	Granger 23-yard run (Nichol PAT)
IA	Harmon 77-yard pass from Long (Nichol PAT)
PSU	Nichols 7-yard run (2-pt. attempt failed)

on a well-executed trap play, avoiding two defenders on his way to a 23-yard touchdown run. It was 35–28, and Iowa had a lead it would never relinquish.

The play that sealed the deal for the Hawks came midway through the fourth quarter. On the first play following a Penn State punt, Long fired deep downfield to Ronnie Harmon at the Penn State 35. With the Penn State defender in his face, Harmon leaped, grabbed the ball with one hand, and somehow managed to spin in the air and land along the sideline without losing his balance or stepping out of bounds. Once he hit the ground with the ball, the hard part was over and Harmon had a relatively easy stroll into the end zone. All told, the pass play was good for 77 yards, the longest pass completion for Iowa since 1973. The touchdown put the Hawkeyes ahead 42–28, with just about eight minutes to play in the game.

Yet there was no quit in the Penn State team. They gathered themselves and managed to engineer a nine-play drive that covered 72 yards. Skeeter Nichols scored on a seven-yard run with 5:37 to play. The two-point conversion failed and Penn State trailed 42–34. That was the last breath of life for a Penn State team that was now saddled with their third straight loss coming off their national title in 1982.

REICHARDT RETURN KEYS RECORD COMEBACK

A 99-yard kickoff-return touchdown helps the Hawks overcome a big deficit against Oregon

Oregon Ducks came calling on Iowa Stadium during the middle of the Big Ten season in 1949. It would be the first meeting between the Big Ten and Pacific Coast conference schools. Oregon had been the co-champion of the Pacific Coast Conference the season before, along with California.

The game turned out to have plenty of everything: running, passing, long kick and punt returns, and turnovers. The two schools put on an offensive clinic, although most of Iowa's points did not come until the game's last 16 minutes.

Through almost four quarters, it appeared that the Dad's Day crowd at Iowa Stadium would leave disappointed. Oregon built a 24–6 lead, and it looked bleak for the Hawkeyes. However, sparked by two long scoring plays—one that came on a punt return and the other on a kickoff return—Iowa clawed from behind to win 34–31. The comeback from an 18-point deficit remains the biggest comeback in school history.

Iowa managed to get on the scoreboard first, following a 98-yard drive for a touchdown. Most of the yards were gained by halfback Mearl Naber, but the scoring play was a 26-yard forward pass from Glenn Drahn to Don Commack. Bill Reichardt could not convert the extra point, which left Iowa with a 6–0 lead. It would be all Ducks from that point until the last play of the third quarter.

Oregon's first score came in the second quarter on a two-yard plunge by fullback Bob Sanders. The point-after attempt was good, which gave the Ducks a 7–6 lead. Oregon added a field goal to make it 10–6 at halftime.

The Ducks picked up where they left off in the third quarter. Woodley Lewis ran the ball up the middle of the Iowa defense and was met in the secondary, but could not be brought down and ended up with a 74-yard touchdown run, extending the lead to 17–6 after the successful point-after attempt.

The big plays from the Ducks continued as Oregon scored its next touchdown on a

A 99-yard kickoff return by Bill Reichardt in the fourth quarter helped turn the momentum in Iowa's favor on the way to a 34–31 come-from-behind win over Oregon at Iowa Stadium on October 29, 1949. *Copyright: University of Iowa—CMP Photographic Service*

strange play that would cover 54-yards. Johnny McKay had a big running play in hand when he fumbled. However, his teammate Lewis managed to recover the fumble 21 yards downfield and took it the last 33 yards to the goal line for the Oregon touchdown. That made the score 24–6 in favor of Oregon.

Now down 18 late in the third quarter, it was finally time for the Hawks to mount a comeback of historical proportions. Iowa forced an Oregon punt on the last play of the third quarter. Iowa co-captain Bob Longley fielded the Oregon punt on his own 6-yard line and appeared to be pinned along the east sideline with nowhere to go, but an Oregon tackler missed on a flying attempt just as Longley fielded the punt. Two other Ducks had a shot to bring Longley down as he cut to the middle of the field, but they zigged and Longley zagged back toward the sideline. From there, it was straight up the field. When it was all said and done, the touchdown play covered 94 yards. After the successful point-after attempt by Reichardt, Iowa was down 24–13 and still had plenty of hope.

The Oregon ship took on more water when the Ducks coughed up the ensuing kickoff from Reichardt, setting the Iowa offense up again at the Oregon 44. Three running plays advanced the ball to the Oregon 12, but two penalties cost the Hawks 10 yards. But Iowa was able to punch it into the end zone again on a 21-yard pass from halfback Jerry Faske to receiver Jack Dittmer, which pulled Iowa to within 24–20 after another successful point-after attempt.

Although they were seriously threatened, Oregon still had plenty of life: halfback Johnny McKay burst downfield for a 37-yard touchdown, giving Oregon a seemingly comfortable 31–20 lead midway through the fourth quarter.

BILL REICHARDT

Bill Reichardt, only a sophomore during the 1949 season, clearly made the difference in this historic comeback win for Iowa. He accounted for 16 points on two touchdowns and four point-after attempts. His spectacular 99-yard kickoff return for a touchdown in the fourth quarter was the longest at the time in the history of Iowa football. (Three players have since eclipsed the mark with a 100-yard return, including C.J. Jones in Play Number 50.)

Reichardt would use his 1949 season as a springboard for a Big Ten MVP season in 1951. That year, he rushed for a then-record 737 yards on 178 carries, caught 11 passes for 175 yards, continued to be the kick-return specialist, and converted 18 of 22 extra points. He earned the nickname of "the Bull," because he did it all.

Iowa has now had nine Big Ten MVPs, and eight have played for a winning or league-championship team. However, to underscore how dominating Reichardt's 1951 season was, the Iowa team record was just 2–5–2 in 1951.

The Iowa City native played one season with the NFL's Green Bay Packers before being drafted into the U.S. Army. Later, Reichardt returned to Iowa and maintained a high profile in the state. He was active in politics, representing Polk County (Des Moines) as a Democratic legislator from 1964 to 1970. He was also a successful and visible businessman. He served as the pitchman for his chain of men's clothing stores; many Iowans recollect his television commercials that ended with the line, "I'm Bill Reichardt and I own the store." And for sports fans, Reichardt will always be fondly remembered as the key proponent for reviving the long-dormant Iowa–Iowa State football series. Thanks to his tireless lobbying, the rivalry finally resumed in 1977.

GAME DETAILS

Iowa 34 • Oregon 31

Date: October 29, 1949

Location: Iowa Stadium, Iowa City, Iowa

Attendance: 37,976

Box Score:

Oregon	0	10	14	7	**31**
Iowa	6	0	7	21	**34**

Scoring:

IA	Commack 26-yard pass from Drahn (Reichardt PAT failed)
OR	Sanders 2-yard run (Daniels PAT)
OR	Daniels 17-yard FG
OR	Lewis 74-yard run (Daniels PAT)
OR	Lewis 33-yard fumble recovery (Daniels PAT)
IA	Longley 94-yard punt return (Reichardt PAT)
IA	Dittmer 21-yard pass from Faske (Reichardt PAT)
OR	McKay 37-yard run (Daniels PAT)
IA	Reichardt 99-yard kickoff return (Reichardt PAT)
IA	Reichardt 1-yard run (Reichardt PAT)

That "comfortable" feeling would evaporate immediately for the Ducks, as lightning again struck Iowa Stadium on the ensuing kickoff. Lewis was able to drive the kickoff deep into Iowa territory and Reichardt fielded the ball at his own 1-yard line. All 11 of the Ducks swarmed Reichardt. He started toward the sideline to escape, but quickly cut back into the middle of the field, where he somehow was able to burst through the pack of Ducks. Ninety-nine yards later, Reichardt was in the end zone.

After Reichardt made his third consecutive point-after attempt, Iowa was only down by four, 31–27. The Ducks still appeared to be rattled on their next drive, and they fumbled the ball back to Iowa quickly. The fumble by Sanders was recovered by Iowa's defensive end Bob Hoff, and the Hawkeyes were quickly back in business at the Oregon 10-yard line. Reichardt powered his way across the goal line on three plays for the go-ahead score.

After his fourth consecutive successful point-after attempt, Iowa had now come all the way back from the 18-point deficit that had been on the board just 10 minutes of game time ago. On its last 10 plays, Iowa had scored four touchdowns—a truly amazing offensive explosion. Only six minutes remained on the game clock.

As it turns out, however, the crowd was in for a fantastic finish—this game would not be secure until the final play. In the face of all this adversity, Oregon somehow managed to put together a long drive in the final six minutes. The Ducks advanced 51 yards down to the Iowa 4-yard line. One second remained on the clock.

The entire stadium was on its feet as Oregon decided to go for the win rather than attempt a potential game-tying field goal. The play call was a short pass from Jim Calderwood to Darrell Robinson. The pass skipped harmlessly over Robinson's fingertips just in front of the goal line. The historic Iowa comeback was official.

October 19, 1996

21 IOWA'S BEST OPTION: VICTORY

A 25-yard touchdown pass by a halfback helps turn Penn State's home field into Happy Hawkeye Valley

The terrible weather on a cold and rainy autumn Saturday afternoon in central Pennsylvania could do nothing to dampen the spirits of the Iowa Hawkeyes or the small contingent of Iowa fans who had made the long trip east. These Hawkeyes had just gutted their way to a come-from-behind 21–20 win over one of the most storied college football programs in the nation—and its iconic coach, the ageless Joe Paterno, whose career home record coming into the game was a dominant 151–30 that covered a span of 31 years. Penn State had been favored by 10½ points.

After the win, players and fans lingered on the field and in the stands, soaking up the atmosphere. Finally, the players headed for the warmth and comfort of the visitors' locker room at Beaver Stadium to continue the celebration there, and the unofficial Hawkeyes victory dance, the hokey-pokey, commenced. The win over No. 10 Penn State was the program's first against a team ranked in the top 10 in the national polls since 1990, when Iowa topped No. 5 Illinois

and No. 8 Michigan en route to Pasadena and the Rose Bowl.

As high as the Hawkeyes were after the game, they were equally as low after Penn State's first possession produced a 12-yard touchdown pass from quarterback Wally Richardson to running back Curtis Enis—just 2:36 into the game. However, Iowa offset that play with its own long return for a touchdown later in the first quarter. Junior bundle of energy and Iowa City native Tim Dwight returned a Penn State punt 83 yards along the Penn State sideline for the equalizing score.

Dwight also played a key role in setting up the only other Iowa score of the first half; he was on the receiving end of a Matt Sherman 65-yard bomb in the second quarter. The big play set up a five-yard touchdown run by Tavian Banks, who shouldered the rushing load for the day because tailback Sedrick Shaw was out with bruised ribs.

Penn State took a 20–14 lead into halftime, but Iowa would make the necessary

Iowa wide receiver Demo Odems caught a key pass from Rob Thein on the halfback option, setting up the touchdown that would prove the game winner as Iowa topped Penn State 21–20 at Beaver Stadium on October 19, 1996.
Copyright: University of Iowa—CMP Photographic Service

adjustments, especially on defense. The Penn State rushing attack produced a dominating 186 yards in the first half—108 of those by fullback Aaron Harris—but could muster a total of only 31 yards the entire second half. In fact, the Iowa defense held Penn State to just four first downs and a total of just 76 yards in the second half, which Penn State could not overcome.

The Iowa offense had stagnated along with the Penn State offensive unit in the wet, soggy conditions. But Iowa's offense would get the lift it needed from the defense. Iowa safety Kerry Cooks stormed through the Penn State blocking scheme on a blitz and was able to separate Penn State quarterback Wally Richardson from the ball. Iowa tackle Jared DeVries fell on the loose ball at the Nittany Lions' 33-yard line.

The Hawkeyes weren't going to let this golden opportunity slip away. The call on first-and-10 was a halfback option pass from reserve redshirt freshman Rob Thein to wideout Demo Odems. Thein took the handoff and headed off to the right, but spotted Odems open downfield at the 10. Odems had to twist in the air to catch the ball with his back to the goal line in front of the Penn State defender at the 10-yard line; he then fell backwards, landing at the 8-yard line.

Thein was put in the game specifically for this play, and it was his only play of the entire game. After the game, Coach Fry indicated that Banks could also have thrown the pass, but he felt his hands and gloves were too wet. Therefore, Thein came off the bench for the opportunity and came through with perhaps the biggest play of the game on offense.

On the very next play, Banks powered up the middle for an eight-yard touchdown run. The successful point-after attempt (an outcome not to be taken for granted in such bad weather) by Zach Bromert gave Iowa a 21–20 lead it would not relinquish. The Iowa defense clamped down the rest of the way to secure the satisfying victory.

The win, which moved Iowa to 3–0 in the Big Ten, was a staunch contrast to their last visit to Happy Valley in 1994, which ended up being a 61–21 whipping at the hands of the Nittany Lions. Two entirely different teams competed on this day, with an entirely different outcome to match.

The victory over Penn State was one of the more memorable games in the 1996 season, which was capped by a 27–0 pasting of Texas Tech in the Alamo Bowl, improving Iowa's record to 9–3 on the season.

ROB THEIN

Rob Thein was just a freshman on the 1996 team. Like Tim Dwight, he was an Iowa City native out of City High School. He was named team captain and MVP and earned elite all-state honors as a high school senior in 1994. He would go on to enjoy three additional productive seasons as a role player for the Hawkeyes at running back and fullback. During the tough 1999 year when Iowa failed to win a conference game, Thein demonstrated tremendous durability, starting all 11 games at fullback. The raw rushing numbers weren't necessarily there for Thein, but like most fullbacks,

he wasn't expected to make significant contributions by running the ball—and he helped the team in many other ways. Thein made his greatest mark as a team leader. At the conclusion of the 1999 season, he earned the Team Hustle Award and was named permanent offensive captain.

Thein would go on to throw two additional passes in his college career. Just like the first one on that rainy day in Happy Valley, the other two were also complete. Thein earned Academic All–Big Ten honors in 1997 and 1999.

GAME DETAILS

Iowa 21 • Penn State 20

Date: October 19, 1996

Location: Beaver Stadium, University Park, Pennsylvania

Attendance: 96,230

Weather: Rainy

Box Score:

Iowa	7	7	0	7	**21**
Penn St.	10	10	0	0	**20**

Scoring:

PSU	Enis 12-yard pass from Richardson (Conway PAT)
IA	Dwight 83-yard punt return (Driscoll PAT)
PSU	Conway 37-yard FG
IA	Banks 5-yard run (Bromert PAT)
PSU	Harris 49-yard run (Conway PAT)
PSU	Conway 24-yard FG
IA	Banks 8-yard run (Bromert PAT)

> This is Happy Hawkeye Valley!
>
> —IOWA COACH HAYDEN FRY, AFTER THE GAME

> We kind of had to change up there. Tavian can throw that pass too, but his gloves were soaked. I had Thein take off his gloves. It's a play we work on quite a bit. We had to pull out some of the exotics today, but we still have a few left if we need them.
>
> —COACH HAYDEN FRY

November 20, 2004

20 BADGERS BOW TO WISDOM OF SOLOMON

A 51-yard touchdown pass to Drew Tate's favorite target leads to a rout of Wisconsin to end the regular season

Iowa's 2004 regular season concluded with a home date against the Wisconsin Badgers. Iowa came into the game at 8–2 overall and 6–1 in the Big Ten, while Wisconsin was 9–1 overall and 6–1 in the Big Ten. Much more was at stake than the new Heartland Trophy, a brass bull sculpture to be awarded annually to the winner of this game. Just before kickoff, the Michigan–Ohio State game in Columbus had ended, with Ohio State—despite a subpar year by their own standards—pulling an upset win over Michigan, 37–21. The loss left Michigan with a 7–1 conference record. Therefore, the winner of the Iowa-Wisconsin game in Iowa City would claim a share of the Big Ten championship for 2004.

The Hawkeyes were able to overcome two first-quarter interceptions that set the Badgers up in Iowa territory at the beginning of their first two drives. The Iowa defense was equal to the task early. Following the first interception, Wisconsin took over at the Iowa 32-yard line. But the defense forced Wisconsin to turn the ball over on downs after gaining just two yards on four plays.

The second interception of the quarter gave Wisconsin the ball at the Iowa 35-yard line, and it was the same story from the tough defense. Wisconsin ran three plays, gained one yard, and had to settle for a long field-goal attempt that would miss. Iowa had dodged two bullets.

The offense was finally able to get on track on their third possession, when they drove 66 yards in nine plays. Iowa's primary weapon was the right arm of sophomore quarterback Drew Tate. The touchdown came on a six-yard pass as Tate rolled right and spotted Clinton Solomon near the right sideline, free inside the 5-yard line. Solomon was able to stop on a dime after making the catch, but the momentum of the Wisconsin defender carried him out of bounds. Solomon easily walked into the end zone and gave Iowa a 7–0 lead.

After the teams exchanged punts, Wisconsin took over at the Iowa 43 with 6:29 left in the half, still trailing 7–0. Stanley Booker capped the 10-play drive with a sweep to the right that resulted in a four-yard touchdown run. The extra point tied

Iowa's Clinton Solomon runs from a Wisconsin defender during a 51-yard touchdown reception in the first half on November 20, 2004, at Kinnick Stadium. Iowa's dominating 30–7 win clinched the Hawks' second Big Ten title in three years under coach Kirk Ferentz.
Copyright: University of Iowa—CMP Photographic Service

the score at 7–7 with just under two minutes to play in the half.

It appeared as though Wisconsin would take the momentum of the tying touchdown into the locker room with them at halftime. But when the Iowa offense took over at their own 40-yard line following the kickoff, they still had a minute and 43 seconds on the clock to do something about it. And do something about it they did.

A five-yard offside penalty and a short four-yard pass to Ed Hinkel brought up a third-and-one at the Wisconsin 49-yard line. Iowa was in the hurry-up offense. In a curious call on a third-and-short, Tate dropped back to pass, but faced immediate pressure and had to sidestep a defender. Keeping his eyes downfield, Tate didn't initially see anyone open and may have had a notion to run, as Iowa only needed one yard for the first down. He took one step downfield to his right as if he were going to run, then spotted Solomon deep down the middle one-on-one against the safety and decided to pass rather than run. The pass was perfect, hitting Solomon's hands midstride 40 yards downfield. Solomon waltzed into the end zone for a 51-yard touchdown and a 14–7 Iowa lead. It would be Iowa, not Wisconsin, that would take all the momentum into halftime.

The pass play was totally impromptu on the parts of Tate and Solomon. Solomon wasn't clear on which route to run. "Normally I run a crossing route with the tight end, but I honestly didn't know what route to run," Solomon said. "I saw the safety was one-on-one with me, so I figured I've got to try to beat him and get open, and I looked back and Drew and I made eye contact and he let go of the ball. Drew just put the ball out in front of me to the right, and I ran to go up and get it and made the play."

The touchdown in the two-minute offense seemed to demoralize Wisconsin, and the Badgers came out flat to start the second half. The first Wisconsin drive was a three-and-out. The Badgers' second drive of the third quarter ended on a Jovon Johnson interception. However, Iowa would give the ball right back to Wisconsin on another interception.

Wisconsin was pinned deep in their own territory. They managed one first down before another pass was picked off by Iowa's Sean Consodine and Iowa was first-and-10 inside Badgers territory. And this time, Iowa would cash in on the turnover.

Iowa marched 32 yards in six plays, again mostly thorough the air. The touchdown came on a third-and-

DREW TATE AND CLINTON SOLOMON

Drew Tate was Iowa's starting quarterback for three seasons, one of only four players ever to accomplish that feat for the Hawkeyes. During 2004, his sophomore year, Tate completed 233 passes on 375 attempts for 2,786 yards and 20 touchdowns; he also ran for two scores. Following the 2004 campaign, Tate was named First Team All–Big Ten. He would go on to register 21 wins as an Iowa starting quarterback, which puts him third on the all-time Hawkeyes list.

Tate enjoyed plenty of success during 2004, but his greatest accomplishments that year were yet to come. Iowa still had a date on New Year's Day with LSU in the Capital One Bowl, and Tate was involved in one of the most thrilling, exhilarating, unbelievable finishes in the history of college football.

Junior Clinton Solomon was Tate's go-to guy, not only in 2004, but in 2005 as well. In 2004, Solomon—who wasn't even listed on the depth chart coming out of spring practice—saw action in all 12 games and was credited with 58 catches for 905 yards and six touchdowns. He was named Second Team All–Big Ten for the 2004 campaign. Solomon's 1,864 career receiving yards (on 118 catches) is seventh on the all-time Iowa list. Tate and Solomon would hook up on another memorable touchdown connection for Iowa's first touchdown in the 2005 Capital One Bowl: a 57-yard strike early in the first quarter that got the game off with a bang, staking Iowa to an early first-quarter lead of 7–0.

GAME DETAILS

Iowa 30 • Wisconsin 7

Date: November 20, 2004

Location: Kinnick Stadium, Iowa City, Iowa

Attendance: 70,397

Weather: Cloudy

Box Score:

Wisconsin	0	7	0	0	**7**
Iowa	7	7	10	6	**30**

Scoring:

IA	Solomon 6-yard pass from Tate (Schlicher PAT)
WIS	Booker 4-yard run (Allen PAT)
IA	Solomon 51-yard pass from Tate (Schlicher PAT)
IA	S. Chandler 12-yard pass from Tate (Schlicher PAT)
IA	Schlicher 31-yard FG
IA	Schlicher 21-yard FG
IA	Schlicher 34-yard FG

goal play from the 12-yard line. Tate hit Scott Chandler over the middle at the goal line for the score, and Iowa had a 21–7 lead. The game was all but over at this point, but the Iowa defense poured it on, forcing two more fumbles later in the third and fourth quarters that would both be turned into points on Kyle Schlicher field goals.

One final field goal by Schlicher made the final score 30–7. Bedlam reigned at Kinnick Stadium, as thousands stormed the field to celebrate the victory and the Big Ten title.

The 2004 team had accomplished plenty already. The win over Wisconsin was the team's seventh straight. Who would have thought—back at the end of September, after back-to-back losses to Arizona State and Michigan left the Hawks at 2–2—that the season would end like this? Of course, this team still had one game remaining: the 2005 Capital One Bowl against the previous year's national champion, LSU. That game ended up having a fairly exciting play that actually did make this list, so stay tuned for it.

Nobody said a word about what Ohio State had done. Everybody knew, and we weren't going to let this get away. We did what we needed to do, just like we have the last few weeks. We came out and took care of our end of the deal. We stepped up and delivered.

—IOWA SENIOR FREE SAFETY SEAN CONSIDINE

September 12, 1981

HAWKEYES STIFLE HIGH-OCTANE HUSKERS

Lou King's interception in the last minute caps a magnificent defensive performance against No. 7 Nebraska

The 1981 season was Hayden Fry's third year in Iowa City. Although the Hawkeyes had shown signs of greatness in the first two years, the overall results those first two years were really nothing to write home about. The Hawks posted a 5–6 record in 1979, followed by a 4–7 mark in 1980. Perhaps the ugliest loss in the first two years of the Fry era was a 57–0 thrashing suffered at the hands of Nebraska in the second game of the 1980 season.

So, who do you think came a-calling at Kinnick Stadium to open the 1981 season? Of course, those same Nebraska Cornhuskers, with their vaunted rushing attack that ranked first nationally in 1980. Sometimes you really have to hand it to the football gods; they know just how to keep things interesting. The raw offensive numbers produced by the Nebraska rushing attack in 1980 were mind-numbing: Nebraska averaged 378 yards rushing and 506 yards of total offense per game. The 1981 edition of "Big Red" was led by future NFL star and Super Bowl champion Roger Craig and future Heisman Trophy winner Mike Rozier.

Yet, an inspired Iowa defense would allow Nebraska just 150 yards on the ground, 231 total, and only seven points on this sweltering day, to open the magical 1981 season with one of the greatest upsets in school history. Certainly most of the credit went to the Iowa defense, with Lou King making the decisive play when he intercepted the Huskers' last desperate attempt to put points on the board.

Iowa did something on their first drive that they had been unable to do in 60 minutes of football against Nebraska the year before: they put points on the board. Senior quarterback Pete Gales led Iowa down the field on a seven-play, 44-yard drive. Iowa was able to attain good field position at the Cornhuskers' 44 when King partially blocked a punt by Nebraska's Grant Campbell.

Iowa sophomore running back Eddie Phillips provided most of the offense, as he gained 34 of the yards and capped the drive with a two-yard run with 9:16 to play in the first quarter. Phillips actually got the starting nod at running back only because

Lou King's (43) interception late in the fourth quarter sealed a huge upset win over mighty Nebraska at Kinnick Stadium on September 12, 1981. *Copyright: University of Iowa—CMP Photographic Service*

first-string running back J.C. Love-Jordan was out with an ankle injury, but Phillips would finish a very strong game with 94 yards on 19 carries.

Iowa place-kicker Lon Olejniczak added the extra point and Iowa owned a 7–0 lead. Although it certainly was early, Iowa probably had Nebraska's attention because the Big Red had outscored opponents 111–6 in the first quarter last year. Iowa was able to surpass that total on one drive.

On Nebraska's next drive, a tackle by Mel Cole forced a Craig fumble, which defensive tackle Mark Bortz recovered at the Nebraska

24-yard line. However, the Hawkeyes could advance the ball no further, and Reggie Roby eventually missed a 42-yard field goal. But Nebraska certainly knew it had dodged a bullet and Iowa had definitely come to play.

This was confirmed on Iowa's next possession, when Olejniczak converted a 35-yard field goal on the first play of the second quarter to give Iowa a 10–0 lead. The field goal had been set up by a Brad Webb interception, which again gave the Iowa offense the ball in Nebraska territory, this time at the 43.

Throughout the first half, the high-powered Nebraska offense was held in check by an inspired Iowa defense. The defense worked together as a team; 10 Hawkeyes defenders registered five or more tackles on the day. In fact, the defense was so good in the first half that Nebraska only managed to penetrate Iowa territory twice in the entire 30 minutes. The shutout was kept alive when Nebraska place-kicker Kevin Seibel missed a 47-yard field goal with 1:38 remaining in the first half.

It was more of the same into the third quarter. An integral part of Iowa's success throughout the day in shutting down the Big Red offensive machine was their All-American punter, Roby. It was Roby's right leg that time after time turned field position in the favor of the Hawkeyes. He finished a hard day's work with five punts, averaging nearly 56 yards per punt.

Finally, in the fourth quarter, Nebraska was able to get on the scoreboard. On second-and-goal from the 1-yard line, Craig was ruled to have broken the plane of the goal line. The extra point following the touchdown made it Iowa 10, Nebraska 7.

The Huskers kept the pressure on Iowa for the rest of the game. Nebraska drove the ball deep into Iowa territory on three of its last four possessions following that touchdown. Iowa was able to avoid any further damage on the first of these drives, as it ended with a missed 37-yard field goal by Seibel that came with 6:30 remaining in the fourth quarter.

Later, the Huskers were able to advance the ball as far as the Iowa 34-yard line when Mark Mauer was stripped by Iowa defensive tackle Bortz. Bortz was also able to cover the fumble. Nebraska would get yet another opportunity to either tie or take the lead when Iowa running back Phil Blatcher fumbled on third down at the Iowa 41-yard line. However, Iowa was able to thwart the scoring threat at the 39-yard line on an incomplete pass, and the ball went back over to Iowa on downs. Just 1:25 remained on the clock.

LOU KING

Lou King's interception to clinch the game against Nebraska was the springboard to a record-setting season. King would go on to record a total of eight interceptions during his senior campaign in 1981, tying the school record set in 1939 by Nile Kinnick. Of course, Kinnick set the mark in just eight games, while King collected his eight picks during a 12-game season.

The disparity in games in a season is a tribute to how great Kinnick's 1939 season was. In the nearly 70 seasons since Kinnick set the Iowa standard, the record has only been tied. Note that Iowa currently plays a 12-game regular season and could earn a 13th with a bowl game, so it will be interesting to see if the record continues to withstand the test of time.

Game Details

Iowa 10 • Nebraska 7

Date: September 12, 1981

Location: Kinnick Stadium, Iowa City, Iowa

Attendance: 60,160

Weather: Sunny, 90 degrees

Box Score:

Nebraska	0	0	0	7	**7**	
Iowa	7	3	0	0	**10**	

Scoring:

IA Phillips 2-yard run (Olejniczak PAT)

IA Olejniczak 35-yard FG

NEB Craig 1-yard run (Seibel PAT)

It still wasn't over, as Nebraska still had its timeouts left. However, Iowa was unable to attain any first downs on their next possession, so on came Roby for what would end up being his final punt of the afternoon. Roby got off a beauty that went down as a 53-yard punt, pinning Nebraska deep in their own territory with just 55 seconds showing on the clock. This would be the Huskers' last gasp, as Bortz sacked Nebraska quarterback Nate Mason on first down.

Facing a deep hole now, the Nebraska quarterback attempted to force his next completion. With Iowa playing a soft zone coverage, King stepped in front of the Nebraska receiver and picked off the throw, finally sealing one of the greatest upsets in Iowa history. Gales only had to kneel down, and the game was history.

December 31, 1982

18 LONG BOMB IS JUST PEACHY

Chuck Long's strike to Dave Moritz is the first of three touchdown passes as the Hawkeyes earn their first bowl win since 1959

Winning a postseason bowl game in college football is not an easy accomplishment. Many things need to be done very well. As evidence of this fact, one could note that even a school with all the resources and all the football tradition of the Notre Dame Fighting Irish has not won a bowl game since 1994, a span of 13 years and counting. And this in an age where the Irish only need to be a .500 team to make their way to a bowl game!

It would be safe to say that Iowa had quite a bowl-game dry spell of its own between the big New Year's Day win in the 1959 Rose Bowl and the win in the 1982 Peach Bowl, which happened to be played on New Year's Eve in 1982 (how is that for symmetry?). To be fair, just getting to a bowl game was far more difficult in the 1960s and '70s, when there were only a handful of bowl games compared to today, when the holiday season is regularly filled with mediocre postseason matchups of some teams that barely finished with winning records.

Coming into the 1982 Peach Bowl, Iowa was still stinging from the sound whipping

they had suffered on New Year's Day of that same year, at the end of the 1981 season, to the Washington Huskies. That day in Pasadena, Iowa wasn't even competitive; it was all Huskies in a 28–0 shutout. As a testament to how one-sided the game really was, Iowa wasn't even able to get past Washington's 29-yard line the entire game. Thus, the Hawkeyes certainly did not lack incentive to put up a good showing in their first postseason appearance since the Rose Bowl debacle.

In spite of all this, the Peach Bowl did not start off well for Iowa, which squandered two opportunities in Tennessee territory in the first quarter. By contrast, Tennessee was able to cash in and put points on the board. The scoring play came on a perfectly executed quarterback option by Tennessee quarterback Alan Cockrell, which resulted in a six-yard touchdown run. This same option play would eventually play a vital role in another Tennessee possession deep in Iowa territory late in the fourth quarter, but the result then would be different. After the extra point, the Volunteers had the 7–0 lead and Iowa perhaps was thinking "here we go again."

Chuck Long served up three touchdown passes in the second quarter against Tennessee in the 1982 Peach Bowl at Fulton County Stadium in Atlanta, Georgia, as Iowa defeated Tennessee 28–22. *Copyright: University of Iowa— CMP Photographic Service*

Iowa's freshman phenom of a quarterback, Chuck Long, took over the game for the rest of the first half. This was all the more surprising because the Tennessee scouting report on Iowa had the Hawkeyes pegged as a run-oriented team that would pass, but only when they had to. Down 7–0 and having now gone five quarters without a score in bowl games, perhaps Fry felt like it was time to open up the playbook a bit and let Long's talents carry the day.

Well, that is exactly what happened in the second quarter. Actually, Long started red-hot right from the opening whistle, completing his first 11 passes to break his own record of nine, set earlier in the year against Northwestern. However, the touchdown passes would not come until the second quarter.

Long's first and most impressive scoring strike came on a 57-yard gem of a connection with Dave Moritz. From his left slot position, Moritz ran a deep post pattern to the middle of the field and beat the Tennessee defender by a good few steps. Long hit him perfectly in stride 40 yards downfield at the Tennessee 20-yard line, and Moritz easily jogged into the end zone for

Iowa's first score in a bowl game since the offensive explosion in the 1959 Rose Bowl.

Iowa's second score came on an 18-yard touchdown toss to Ronnie Harmon. Long was flushed from the pocket on the play; he had to roll right and release the throw on the run with two defenders bearing down on him as he spotted Harmon, who was double-covered at the back of the end zone. The ball sailed over two Tennessee defenders and into Harmon's outstretched hands just as Harmon got a foot inbounds at the back of the end zone.

Long completed the second-quarter hat trick with another touchdown toss to Harmon, this one good for an eight-yard score. On the strength of Long's right arm, Iowa led 21–7 at halftime.

Tennessee would rally in the second half. Chuck Coleman pulled Tennessee to within 21–13 on a 10-yard touchdown run early in the third quarter. However, the point-after attempt by Fuad Reveiz, who had converted on 20 straight extra points during the season, was blocked by Iowa's Nate Creer.

Following that score, Iowa responded with its only rushing touchdown of the day: a two-yard burst by Eddie Phillips that came with 8:29 to go in the third quarter. The successful point-after attempt made the score 28–13, Iowa.

Iowa coach Hayden Fry celebrates his team's victory over Tennessee in the Peach Bowl in Atlanta on New Year's Eve 1982. *Photo courtesy AP Images*

"The world's fastest football player," Willie Gault, got Tennessee on the board again before the third quarter ended. The scoring play was a 19-yard touchdown reception from Cockrell. However, Iowa was able to shut Gault down as far as the passing game was concerned; that catch was his only one of the game. (Gault also returned kickoffs and punts, but with only modest success.) The Volunteers' two-point conversion attempt failed, so the score held at 28–19.

CHUCK LONG

This is the third play in the top 50 involving Chuck Long, perhaps the greatest quarterback in Iowa history. This was Long's final game as a freshman and it really was his coming-out party, where he proved he could compete at a high level against quality Division I opponents. Long ended the game 19 for 26, for a Peach Bowl–record 304 yards and three touchdowns. Long would go on to put up huge numbers and dominate the Big Ten at times during his final three years in Iowa City.

Chuck Long is the only player known to appear in five different bowl games with one team. He got into the game for just a few plays during the 1982 Rose Bowl versus Washington, but that didn't count against his eligibility because they were his only plays of the season. Long still had four years of eligibility remaining and he put them to good use. In addition to the 1982 Peach Bowl, he lead Iowa to the 1983 Gator Bowl, the 1984 Freedom Bowl, eventually coming full circle, as he lead Iowa to another Rose Bowl during his final year in 1985.

GAME DETAILS

Iowa 28 • Tennessee 22

Date: December 31, 1982

Location: Fulton County Stadium, Atlanta, Georgia

Attendance: 50,134

Significance: Peach Bowl

> **I**t was just a super game. I have never seen a defense rise up on the goal line and sack the quarterback like that. We were very tough when we had to be.
>
> **—IOWA COACH HAYDEN FRY**

Box Score:

Iowa	0	21	7	0	**28**	
Tennessee	7	0	12	3	**22**	

Scoring:

TN	Cockrell 6-yard run (Reveiz PAT)
IA	Moritz 57-yard pass from Long (Nichol PAT)
IA	Harmon 18-yard pass from Long (Nichol PAT)
IA	Harmon 8-yard pass from Long (Nichol PAT)
TN	Coleman 10-yard run (PAT failed)
IA	Phillips 2-yard run (Nichol PAT)
TN	Gault 19-yard pass from Cockrell (pass failed)
TN	Reveiz 27-yard FG

The game would get even closer when Reveiz converted a 27-yard field goal with 10:05 left on the clock. However, from that point, the Iowa defense took over and stymied Tennessee on both of its two remaining offensive opportunities. Cockrell, who broke a Peach Bowl record with 22 completions, led Tennessee downfield to the Iowa 6-yard line, where the Volunteers faced a fourth-and-one.

Tennessee had the big horse at fullback for just this type of short yardage situation—fullback Doug Furnas had already converted three similar first downs in the second half. However, rather than the old reliable run up the middle, Tennessee perhaps got too flashy and called another quarterback option—the same play that had worked for Tennessee's first touchdown way back in the first quarter.

I think the saying goes something like: "Fool me once, shame on you; fool me twice, shame on me." Well, the Hawkeyes defense would not be fooled twice this night; Iowa's James Erb shot the gap, grabbed Cockrell by the jersey, and threw him to the ground at least one yard short of the first down.

Iowa took over with just 3:29 to play, but could not gain that precious first down that would almost have run out the clock. Reggie Roby's final punt for Iowa would be a critical one, with the game hanging in the balance. Under pressure, Roby got off an excellent 52-yard punt. Best of all, it was angled perfectly out of bounds at the Tennessee 35-yard line, denying the speedy Gault a return opportunity.

Tennessee's final gasp of a last drive never really got going, as a fumble by Cockrell on third down left the Volunteers with a fourth-and-forever (25), in which Cockrell was sacked for the final time.

The legion of 20,000 Hawkeyes faithful could finally rejoice: Iowa had won its first postseason bowl game since 1959.

November 18, 1939

17 IRONMEN SHOW METTLE AGAINST GOPHERS

Nile Kinnick's 28-yard touchdown pass leads Iowa to a come-from-behind win over Minnesota

The wins during the unforgettable 1939 season got more dramatic as the season progressed. The Hawkeyes were able to build momentum late in the season with a memorable come-from-behind win over Wisconsin on the road and a huge upset over mighty Notre Dame at home the following week. At this point, Iowa's "Ironmen" were already creating quite a buzz throughout the country. But what was perhaps the most dramatic win of the whole season came the week after the Notre Dame game in the home finale against mighty Minnesota.

Through three quarters of play, Iowa was kept off the scoreboard by a very strong Minnesota squad that had won three national titles in the 1930s. Meanwhile, the Gophers were having their way with the Iowa defense. Minnesota penetrated deep into Iowa territory twice in the first half, but had only one field goal in the second quarter to show for their efforts going into halftime.

The Minnesota offense picked up where it left off in the third quarter, but this time was able to get the ball across the Iowa goal

line on fourth-and-goal from the Iowa 6-yard line. The touchdown came on a run wide to the left; Minnesota's Sonny Franck was just able to beat the Iowa defenders to the corner of the end zone. On the strength of that score, Minnesota took a 9–0 lead as the fourth quarter began.

At that point, a never-say-die Iowa team of Ironmen were somehow able to dig deep and flip the switch. This despite seven men having to play all 60 minutes during the game, in typical "Ironman" fashion. The 60-minute club included ends Erwin Prasse and Dick Evans; tackles Mike Enich and Wally Bergstrom; one guard, Ken Pettit; the center, Bruno Andruska; and of course, their mighty leader, Nile Kinnick, who again had a hand in both Hawkeyes' touchdowns on the day and provided the one successful point-after attempt. The Hawks had to overcome the loss of one of their biggest weapons: quarterback Al Couppee was forced out of the game following a tackle on Minnesota quarterback Joe Mernik very early in the game.

Iowa's last win against their rivals from the north had occurred in 1929. Following

Kickoff at Iowa Stadium against Minnesota on November 18, 1939. Nile Kinnick led Iowa to 13 fourth-quarter points en route to a 13–9 upset of the perennial national power Gophers.
Copyright: University of Iowa—CMP Photographic Service

that narrow 9–7 win, the Hawks had dropped eight straight—and the last three games leading up to the 1939 game weren't even competitive. Until the fourth quarter, it appeared that the 1939 team would suffer the same fate as so many of its predecessors.

Finally, with a flair for the dramatic, the Hawkeyes offense made an appearance, much to the delight of the homecoming crowd (estimated at 50,000 strong). The coaching doctor, Eddie Anderson, dug deep into his playbook to spark the fourth-quarter rally. Iowa began its drive—following a

Minnesota punt that bounded into the Iowa end zone for a touchback—with 14 minutes to play in the game. The offense got rolling with two quick passes, each from Kinnick to Floyd Dean. The first toss covered 18 yards and the second 12. That brought the ball out to midfield.

On the second play on the next series of downs, Dean took the snap from center and handed off to Kinnick. Kinnick was under pressure by several Gophers linemen, but had his eye downfield where Prasse was gaining separation from the Minnesota defenders. Kinnick launched the ball downfield toward Prasse, who hauled in the pass near the 10-yard line and powered over the goal line. Suddenly, 50,000 fans came to life in unison as Prasse crossed the goal line. Kinnick's drop-kick was good. Minnesota 9, Iowa 7.

On the Gophers' next series, Enich jarred the ball loose from Minnesota's Bob Sweiger after one first down, and the Hawks again had the ball in scoring position. However, Sweiger atoned for his fumble with an interception returned out to the Minnesota 25-yard line to avert the Iowa threat. Minnesota could not sustain the drive, though, and was forced to punt after gaining one first down. Kinnick returned the Minnesota punt from Van Every to the Iowa 21-yard line, where the Iowa offense would have another opportunity to take the lead.

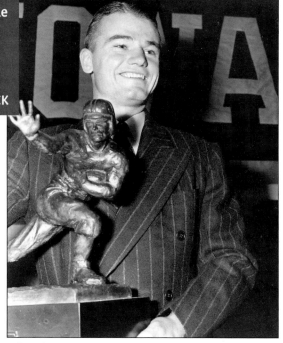

Nile Kinnick's historic 1939 season also earned him some additional hardware: the Heisman Trophy. *Photo courtesy AP Images*

NILE KINNICK: OFF THE FOOTBALL FIELD

Football certainly was important to Nile Kinnick. However, as great a football player as he was on the field, off it he proved to be an exemplary student, orator, poet, politician, patriot, and war hero. He earned honors from Phi Beta Kappa, the nation's oldest and most widely known academic honor society. Kinnick completed his undergraduate years with a 3.4 grade point average and was elected senior class president for the College of Liberal Arts, and president of the senior class presidents of the 10 colleges and schools at Iowa.

Although the NFL's Brooklyn Dodgers drafted Kinnick in 1940 and offered a big payday to play on Sundays in the NFL, he could not be persuaded to turn pro, even after meeting with the Dodgers owners—including film and figure skating star Sonja Henie, the wife of one of the owners at the time. Kinnick was set on entering law school and he was awarded the John P. Laffey law scholarship in June 1940.

Kinnick finished his first year of law school in 1941, third in a class of 103. Following completion of his first year of law school, he enlisted in the Naval Air Corps Reserve. He was called to active duty three days before the Japanese attack on Pearl Harbor.

GAME DETAILS

Iowa 13 • Minnesota 9

Date: November 18, 1939

Location: Iowa Stadium, Iowa City, Iowa

Attendance: 50,000 (est.)

Box Score:

Minnesota	0	3	6	0	**9**
Iowa	0	0	0	13	**13**

Scoring:

MN	Mernik 27-yard FG		IA	Prasse 48-yard pass from Kinnick (Kinnick PAT)
MN	Franck 1-yard run (PAT failed)		IA	Green 28-yard pass from Kinnick (PAT blocked)

> This country's okay as long as it produces Nile Kinnicks. The football part is incidental.
>
> —BILL CUNNINGHAM, OF THE *BOSTON POST*

Iowa's second play on the drive saw Kinnick and Dean hook up again on an 18-yard pass. Minnesota's Van Every then intercepted an Iowa pass, but the play was called back when a Gopher was flagged for holding Dean. The penalty moved the ball to midfield.

Runs by Iowa's Bill Green and Kinnick advanced the ball to the Minnesota 28-yard line with just 3:25 left in the game. The next play saw Green lined up far to the left of the Iowa line. As Kinnick took the snap from center, he raised his foot high in the air and lofted a high pass in Green's direction. Green was the fastest man on the Iowa team, and he easily raced past the Gopher secondary to haul in the pass in the end zone.

Although the game was far from over, eager fans rushed onto the field and hoisted Green off the ground. The officials pleaded for help to clear the field so the game could continue. Fortunately for Iowa, there was no penalty on the home team in those days for this type of display. After the field was finally cleared, Kinnick's drop-kick point-after attempt was blocked, but it didn't seem to matter too much to the rabid fans. Iowa led it 13–9, but Minnesota still had three minutes left to change that.

Minnesota's last drive began at the Iowa 26-yard line. The Gophers gained a first down on two runs, but then turned to the passing game in search of the go-ahead score. On the first play on their second series of downs, Iowa's Dean nearly intercepted, but just couldn't hold onto the pick. However, on the next play, Kinnick was able to snag and hold onto the interception that would sew up the historic win for the Hawkeyes.

Iowa closed out the two minutes remaining on the game clock on the strength of runs by…who else but Kinnick? For the second week in a row, bedlam reigned on the field at Iowa Stadium. The win was the first time Iowa could claim the Floyd of Rosedale Trophy, and it also helped propel Kinnick to the 1939 Heisman Trophy, along with almost every other major postseason award.

December 30, 1986

16 Kick Quiets Hometown Crowd

Rob Houghtlin's last-second field goal makes the difference in a dramatic Holiday Bowl win over San Diego State

Clutch place-kicker Rob Houghtlin makes the second of his three appearances in the top 50 plays here at Number 16. Houghtlin's last-second field goal under extreme pressure against Western Athletic Conference champion and hometown team San Diego State made Iowa's first trip to the Holiday Bowl in 1986 one to remember. Right up until the last-second field goal, the game itself was a classic seesaw affair that was anyone's ball game late into the fourth quarter. The game actually featured two last-minute field goals, as San Diego State had converted an apparent game-winning kick with less than a minute to play before Houghtlin's fateful kick.

Coming off an outright Big Ten championship and Rose Bowl appearance in the 1985 season, the 1986 team continued to build on its success, turning in a strong 8–3 overall regular-season record (5–3 in the Big Ten). Iowa was propelled into the Holiday Bowl as the number two bowl selection out of the Big Ten on the strength of another last-second Houghtlin kick that had allowed Iowa to beat Minnesota five weeks earlier.

The stakes would be even higher for Houghtlin and the Hawkeyes as the 1986 Holiday Bowl dragged late into the San Diego night. The Hawkeyes had become bowl veterans under coach Hayden Fry; the 1986 Holiday Bowl was Iowa's sixth straight bowl appearance. The Hawks would draw upon this wealth of experience, which allowed them to handle the spotlight brilliantly.

In spite of all the success during the 1986 campaign, there was still plenty for Iowa to be concerned about coming into the game. first and foremost, the opponent—San Diego State. The champions of the WAC were a team laden with senior leadership. The Aztecs had played all their home games on the same field in Jack Murphy Stadium. It was the second straight bowl game for Iowa on their opponent's own home field—the 1986 Rose Bowl game against UCLA was the first. San Diego State had won seven games during the year by a touchdown or less, earning them the nickname "The Cardiac Kids." One last factor for Iowa to deal with coming into the game was the fact that each

Iowa place-kicker Rob Houghtlin connects on the game-winning field goal against San Diego State in the 1986 Holiday Bowl in San Diego, California. *Copyright: University of Iowa—CMP Photographic Service*

of its 11 regular-season games had been played on artificial turf; this game would be the first on a natural grass surface. It turned out that none of this would matter, as the Hawks turned the table on San Diego State and pulled out another one at the gun. Iowa jumped on the scoreboard first on a five-yard touchdown run by Rick Bayless. The touchdown drive only covered five yards because an interception by Keaton Smiley at the San Diego State 30 was returned all the way to the 5-yard line.

San Diego State's first touchdown was also set up by the defense. A fumble by Hawkeyes quarterback Mark Vlasic put the Aztecs in business at the Iowa 8-yard line.

The touchdown came three plays later, but the point-after attempt hit the left upright, so Iowa maintained a slim 7–6 lead after one quarter.

San Diego State grabbed its first lead with 6:38 left in the half on a 44-yard touchdown pass from quarterback Todd Santos to Alfred Jackson. A successful two-point conversion put the Aztecs in the lead 14–7. Iowa answered before the half was over with a one-yard quarterback sneak by Vlasic, but Houghtlin proved he was human by missing the extra point.

The Aztecs weren't satisfied with just a one-point lead going into the half, and they subsequently ran a tight two-minute drill on the ensuing possession that culminated in a 28-yard touchdown play from Santos to freshman Monty Galbreath. An eventful first half ended with SDSU on top 21–13.

San Diego State maintained the momentum early in the second half; a tough defense sacked Vlasic twice on Iowa's opening series. The Aztecs gained good field position following an Iowa punt, and SDSU took over at the Iowa 45-yard line. Santos led San Diego State to their fourth touchdown in just nine plays, converting a fourth-and-goal at the 1-yard line to increase the Aztecs' advantage to 28–13 midway through the third quarter.

The Hawkeyes drew closer on their next possession. David Hudson jumped into the end zone with 4:58 remaining in the quarter, and a successful two-point conversion cut the lead to 28–21. However, SDSU grabbed the momentum back with a 12-play, 68-yard scoring drive, again extending the lead to 35–21.

Back and forth they went into the fourth quarter. Iowa tight end and future star Marv Cook caught the first touchdown pass of his career, a 29-yard reception from Vlasic. Following the touchdown, Iowa lined up as if to attempt the extra-point kick, but backup quarterback Chuck Hartlieb suddenly rose from his holder position and hit Mike Flagg in the back of the end zone for two points. Now Iowa trailed 35–29 with eight minutes and 39 seconds left. The Iowa defense stood firm and forced a punt on the next possession.

On the offense's next possession, Vlasic's passing led the Hawks downfield for the go-ahead touchdown, as Vlasic spread the ball among Quinn Early, Hudson, and Flagg. The touchdown came on a four-yard pass from Flagg to Vlasic. The extra point gave Iowa its first lead since early in the first quarter 36–35.

But "the Cardiac Kids" were far from finished. A 45-yard pass from Santos to Jackson, who caught the ball between two Iowa defenders at the Iowa 9-yard line, would put San Diego State in position for what appeared to be a game-winning field goal. Kevin Rahill's 21-yard kick put the Aztecs ahead again 38–36. Iowa was left with just 47 seconds on the clock.

San Diego State should have known by now that the way this game had gone, the unexpected should be expected. Iowa's Kevin Harmon promptly returned

ROB HOUGHTLIN

During his three-year career as Iowa's first-team place-kicker, Rob Houghtlin, a native of Glenview, Illinois, made last-second and last-minute field goals seem routine. Amazingly, Houghtlin made the team as a walk-on after he transferred from the University of Miami–Ohio. Houghtlin certainly had a flair for the dramatic during his tenure at Iowa. The year before this win over San Diego State, he kicked arguably the most important field goal in Iowa football history as top-ranked Iowa defeated number-2 Michigan in October 1985 (Play Number 3). Plus, in the game before the 1986 Holiday Bowl (the regular season finale at Minnesota), Houghtlin kicked yet another game-winning field goal on the last play of the game to give the Hawks a wild 30–27 victory. He converted three or more field goals in nine of the 37 games he played for Iowa.

Houghtlin's longest career field goal, a 55-yarder, came the year after this one against Iowa State. Houghtlin was Iowa's all-time leading scoring until Nate Kaeding came along in 2000–2003. Houghtlin currently ranks second on the all-time scoring list, with 290 points, behind Kaeding's 373.

GAME DETAILS

Iowa 39 • San Diego State 38

Date: December 30, 1986

Location: Jack Murphy Stadium, San Diego, California

Attendance: 59,473

Significance: Holiday Bowl

Box Score:

Iowa	7	6	8	18	**39**
San Diego St.	6	15	7	10	**38**

Scoring:

IA   Bayless 5-yard run (Houghtlin PAT)

SDSU   Hardy 6-yard pass from Santos (PAT failed)

SDSU   Jackson 44-yard pass from Santos (Hardy run)

IA   Vlasic 1-yard run (kick failed)

SDSU   Galbreath 28-yard pass from Santos (Rahill PAT)

SDSU   Gilmore 1-yard run (Rahill PAT)

IA   Hudson 1-yard run (Smith pass from Vlasic)

SDSU   Hardy 6-yard run (Rahill PAT)

IA   Cook 29-yard pass from Vlasic (Flagg pass from Vlasic)

IA   Flagg 4-yard pass from Vlasic (Houghtlin PAT)

SDSU   Rahill 21-yard FG

IA   Houghtlin 41-yard FG

the ensuing kickoff 48 yards through the middle of the Aztecs' kick-return team and up the left sideline to the Aztec 37-yard line. Two running plays advanced the ball to the 24-yard line. Iowa called timeout to stop the clock with four seconds left, and then San Diego State attempted to ice Houghtlin by using one of *their* timeouts.

As the drama built, Iowa lined up for the 41-yard field-goal attempt. The snap from center was a bit high, but Hartlieb still managed to corral the ball and get it in place for the kick. Houghtlin had to maneuver around a strong Aztecs rush as a defender dove in for the block from his left side, but the kick was away and was long enough. The ball slipped just inside the right upright as time expired.

Overcoming some anxious moments on the game's final play, Iowa had done it again on the strength of another last-second clutch kick from Houghtlin.

January 1, 2004

Russell Caps Career in Style

Senior Fred Russell's 34-yard touchdown run provides a memorable end to an Outback Bowl rout of Florida

If there is one thing that current coach Kirk Ferentz has preached over the years above all else it is that the upperclassmen, especially the seniors, need to provide leadership both on and off the field. A stellar class of seniors was able to do just that during the 2003 season, leading Iowa to back-to-back 10-win seasons and earning the Hawkeyes' first January bowl win since the 1959 Rose Bowl.

The 2003 team was brimming with senior leadership, including steady senior quarterback Nathan Chandler, dominating offensive lineman Robert Gallery, decorated place-kicker Nate Kaeding, and hard-hitting Bob Sanders on defense. However, senior running back Fred Russell was the greatest of all Iowa seniors this day; he garnered game MVP honors after rushing for 150 yards on 21 carries, including a 34-yard touchdown run to daylight late in the third quarter that would put the Hawkeyes up 34–10, demoralizing the Gators and essentially putting the game on ice.

Iowa came into the game with a chip on their shoulder and something to prove, following their dismal performance in the Orange Bowl the previous year (a one-sided loss to USC). In response to the previous year's loss, Ferentz changed the preparation plan, having the team stay in Florida for more than a week right before the game.

Whatever buttons Ferentz pushed clearly worked, as the Gators and freshman quarterback Chris Leak would take the brunt of Iowa's frustration most of the afternoon. Iowa seemed to get motivation from a perceived lack of respect on Florida's part, although the point spread coming into the game was Florida by just three and a half points. As an example of this lack of respect, coach Ron Zook referred to All-America kicker Nate Kaeding as a "reserve running back" during the week. It was a perfect formula for the Hawkeyes to put it all together against the Gators.

Russell set the tone for Iowa on the first play from scrimmage. On that play, Russell found a big hole in the Florida defense that resulted in a big 25-yard play. However, that drive stalled without any additional

Iowa running back Fred Russell (2) is sprung on a 34-yard touchdown run against Florida in the Outback Bowl in Tampa, Florida, on January 1, 2004. Russell's third-quarter score would dash the faint hopes of the Gators and seal Iowa's first win in a January bowl game since the 1959 Rose Bowl. *Copyright: University of Iowa— CMP Photographic Service*

Fred Russell is hit by Florida's Guss Scott as he crosses the goal line to put Iowa ahead 34–10 in the third quarter of the 2004 Outback Bowl. *Photo courtesy* The Cedar Rapids Gazette

first downs and Iowa was forced to punt the ball to the Gators.

On Florida's second possession, Leak and wide receiver Kelvin Knight hooked up for a long 70-yard touchdown pass to give the Gators what would turn out to be their only lead of the game.

Iowa responded on their next possession, marching 63 yards in nine plays for the tying touchdown. Chandler found fellow senior Maurice Brown wide open on a quick toss to the left for a three-yard touchdown pass, and the game was tied at 7–7. Iowa added a 47-yard field goal by Kaeding late in the first quarter to put Iowa up 10–7—pretty good for a reserve running back. It was a lead Iowa never relinquished.

Both teams' true colors started to show during the second quarter. The solid Iowa defensive unit held the high-powered Gators offense to 14 yards…in the entire quarter. Florida saw its offense go three-and-out four consecutive times during the quarter. Meanwhile, the Iowa offense continued to put points on the board. Iowa took its first possession of the second quarter and moved the ball 53 yards in nine plays. Chandler scored on a five-yard run to the left front pylon of the end zone on a play that seemed like it took about 10 minutes. He finally reached the end zone after coming all the way from the right side of the field; a late block by wide receiver Ed Hinkel at the goal line allowed Chandler to waltz into the end zone untouched. On that play, Iowa stretched the lead to 17–7, and another Kaeding field goal, of 32 yards this time, made it 20–7 at halftime.

The second half ended up being more of the same. Florida had no sooner finished its fifth consecutive three-and-out offensive possession when it got worse for the Gators. Matt Melloy charged through the right side of the Gators' punt protection and easily blocked the punt attempt inside the 10-yard line. Then he fell on the loose ball at the back of the end zone for another Iowa score, increasing the lead to 27–7.

Following the punt block for a touchdown, Florida finally converted a first down. In fact, they registered three first downs on their way to a field goal that made it 27–10 with plenty of time still remaining: 11 minutes and 19 seconds left in the third quarter. Given Florida's high-powered offense, the Gators were certainly capable of pulling off the comeback.

However, any hope that the Gator Nation had would quickly evaporate. The game-clinching drive began with a big play from Chandler to Brown, good for 41 yards to

Fred Russell

Fred Russell actually had one additional year of eligibility, if he wanted to apply for a medical hardship due to competing in only three games as a freshman in 2000. However, on the strength of his Outback Bowl performance—which was followed by an MVP showing a couple of weeks later at the Hula Bowl in Hawaii, where he ran for 101 yards and two scores—Russell believed he was ready for the next level. He finished his Hawkeyes career as the fourth all-time leading rusher in Iowa history, with 2,760 yards on 514 carries. He posted 1,000-yard seasons in both 2002 and 2003.

Russell spent time on the practice squads of the Dolphins, Bears, and Rams, and played in the NFL Europe League for Cologne. In 2007, he signed with the Saskatchewan Roughriders of the Canadian Football League.

Various other seniors on the 2003 team have gone on to more prominent NFL careers, including Sanders with the Colts, Kaeding with the Chargers, and Gallery with the Raiders.

GAME DETAILS

Iowa 37 • Florida 17

Date: January 1, 2004

Location: Raymond James Stadium, Tampa, Florida

Attendance: 65,372

Weather: Sunny, 67 degrees

Significance: Outback Bowl

Box Score:

Iowa	7	13	14	3	**37**	
Florida	7	0	3	7	**17**	

Scoring:

UF	Knight 70-yard pass from Leak (Leach PAT)
IA	Brown 3-yard pass from N. Chandler (Kaeding PAT)
IA	Kaeding 47-yard FG
IA	N. Chandler 5-yard run (Kaeding PAT)
IA	Kaeding 32-yard FG
IA	Melloy blocked punt in end zone (Kaeding PAT)
UF	Leach 48-yard FG
IA	Russell 34-yard run (Kaeding PAT)
IA	Kaeding 38-yard FG
UF	Baker 25-yard pass from Leak (Leach PAT)

the Florida 44-yard line. From there, Russell would put the Hawkeyes on his back and secure victory. The next two Russell runs produced 10 yards, moving the ball to the 34-yard line.

Russell got the ball a third consecutive time on the next play, which was designed to go off right tackle. Russell was untouched into the Florida secondary, where he cut the play back to the left side of the field and simply outran two Florida defenders. He was thrust out of bounds at the left front pylon, but not before he had gained the corner of the end zone. That 34-yard touchdown run really put a damper on the Gators' chances and the spirits of a large and partisan crowd (the Gators' campus is just a few miles from Raymond James Stadium). However, the 25,000 or so Hawkeyes fans certainly were making their presence felt at this point.

The play was a perfect exclamation point to Russell's brilliant Hawkeyes career.

From a team standpoint, the successful 2003 Hawkeyes campaign was important for many reasons. It vindicated the program for the poor bowl showing in Miami the year before; it proved that the Big Ten could go toe-to-toe with the SEC Conference; and most importantly, it demonstrated that the Iowa program under Ferentz would not be a one-year wonder—it had staying power and would be a team to reckon with for years and hopefully decades to come. On the strength of its impressive bowl win, Iowa climbed the ladder from number 13 in the polls to finish at number eight, which was the second consecutive year Iowa had finished in this spot in the national polls.

September 28, 2002

14 OVERTIME PASS LEADS TO PERFECTION

Brad Banks and C.J. Jones shine against Penn State as Iowa begins a perfect Big Ten campaign

Penn State's Beaver Stadium is the setting for the play turned in by the magical 2002 team in the first league test of the season. If the team had had its preference, the game-winning play that occurred in overtime would never have happened, because Iowa would have held a huge fourth-quarter lead and not needed overtime to win the game. However, once the extra session began, Iowa blocked out all the negative things that had occurred during the last 10 minutes of the game to refocus on the task at hand.

The result: Iowa took the first possession of the overtime for a touchdown, converting a third-and-goal from the 6-yard line on a quick pass over the middle to C.J. Jones. Then the Iowa defense stopped Penn State cold on its overtime possession. It was more interesting than it needed to be, but Iowa had another "W" at Happy Valley.

No question, the game had many twists and turns. As was the case in nearly every game during the 2002 season, Iowa got off to a lightning-fast start. Quarterback Brad Banks rolled to his right and connected with Jones on a four-yard touchdown pass in the first quarter, and Iowa had quickly taken the overflow crowd of 108,000 out of the game by grabbing the early 7–0 lead. It was the fifth consecutive week that Iowa had taken the opening kickoff and scored a touchdown.

Later in the first quarter, Iowa added a Nate Kaeding field goal from 47 yards out. Then Penn State's Larry Johnson fumbled on the next possession and Iowa took over deep in Penn State territory. Fred Russell made Penn State pay for the turnover, as he would score on a 20-yard touchdown run to increase the lead to 17–0.

A Derek Pagel interception of a Zach Mills pass over the middle set up another Hawkeyes touchdown before halftime. On third-and-nine, Banks found Ed Hinkel on a spectacular 22-yard reception. Hinkel fully extended to catch the ball and came down just inbounds for the score at the back of the end zone. The extra point was blocked, but Iowa still led 23–0.

The Nittany Lions finally scored late in the second quarter on a Mills touchdown

Iowa quarterback Brad Banks (7) tries to elude Penn State defender Michael Haynes (81) during Iowa's overtime win against the Nittany Lions on September 28, 2002. *Photo courtesy The Cedar Rapids Gazette*

pass that made it 23–7 with 1:25 left in the quarter. It appeared as though the Lions would take at least some momentum into the locker room. But Iowa took the kickoff and got in position for a long Kaeding field-goal attempt—from 55 yards out—with four seconds left on the clock. It should come as

no shock that Kaeding nailed it, clanging it off the left upright and through. It would have been good from at least 60 yards away. Kaeding ran straight into the Iowa locker room following the kick as he celebrated his 13th consecutive successful field-goal attempt, a school record.

In the second half, Penn State got on the board first with a Larry Johnson one-yard touchdown run with 10:32 left in the third quarter; it was set up by the first interception Banks had thrown all year. Yet, as had been the case with the first Penn State touchdown, Iowa quickly grabbed the momentum when Derek Pagel blocked the point-after attempt. The ball deflected to D.J. Johnson, who ran the ball the other way 99 yards for two points. Iowa increased its lead to 28–13 on the very unusual play.

Iowa then took the ensuing kickoff from Penn State and increased the lead to 35–13 on a 54-yard touchdown pass from Banks to Maurice Brown. The Hawkeyes took the big lead into the fourth quarter and were maintaining the 22-point advantage with just over seven minutes left in the fourth quarter. However, a Penn State interception off the hands of Dallas Clark and a Russell fumble at the Penn State goal line, helped open the door for a Penn State comeback.

The comeback started with a long screen pass for a touchdown to Larry Johnson that pulled Penn State to 35–20 with 7:13 left in the fourth quarter. A long touchdown pass from Mills to Tony Johnson cut into the lead again. Penn State faked the extra point and ran it in for two points, which made it just a seven-point game at 35–28 with 3:51 left in the fourth quarter.

Penn State was mounting a historic comeback, but many in the sellout crowd had already decided that they had seen enough and headed to the exits earlier in the fourth quarter. Although the departed fans would undoubtedly have liked to come back into Beaver Stadium, no reentry was allowed, so many Nittany Lions fans were left with no choice but to listen to the game in the parking lot. They missed a classic ending.

Iowa attempted to run out the clock and gained one first down, but had to punt the ball back to Penn State with 2:32 left. Zach Mills quickly led Penn State downfield on a five-play drive that covered 64 yards, connecting on a fade pattern with Bryant Johnson—the third Johnson to score on the day for Penn State—to tie the game at 35–35.

Iowa still had three timeouts and 1:20 to work with, but could not move the ball and would therefore have to settle for overtime. Yet, in the face of so many factors that would have certainly doomed an ordinary team, this Hawkeyes team on this day showed early signs as to why it would be considered nothing less than an extraordinary team. Not only was there the hostile road environment to deal with, but a similar second-half collapse two weeks before at Kinnick Stadium against Iowa State was also on the minds of everyone—the Hawks had blown a 17-point second-half lead that day.

BRAD BANKS

The quarterback of the 2002 Hawkeyes, Brad Banks, was quite a story that season. That was the only season Banks was the starting quarterback, but he made the most of his one year. He enjoyed one of the finest single seasons ever by an Iowa quarterback. He led the nation in passing efficiency with a 157.1 passer rating, and had 26 touchdown passes and only five interceptions. His stellar performance earned him a second-place finish in balloting for the Heisman Trophy. Banks won the Davey O'Brien Award as the nation's best quarterback, was named AP Player of the Year, and received the *Chicago Tribune* Silver Football as the MVP of the Big Ten in 2002. After failing to catch on in the NFL following his stellar Iowa career, Banks moved on to the Canadian Football League where the larger field was more suited to his scrambling ability from the quarterback position.

GAME DETAILS

Iowa 42 • Penn State 35

Date: September 28, 2002

Location: Beaver Stadium, University Park, Pennsylvania

Attendance: 108,000

Box Score:

Iowa	17	9	9	0	7	**42**
Penn St.	0	7	6	22	0	**35**

Scoring:

IA	Jones 4-yard pass from Banks (Kaeding PAT)
IA	Kaeding 47-yard FG
IA	Russell 20-yard run (Kaeding PAT)
IA	Hinkel 22-yard pass from Banks (PAT blocked)
PSU	B. Johnson 28-yard pass from Mills (Gould PAT)
IA	Kaeding 55-yard FG
PSU	L. Johnson 1-yard run (PAT blocked)
IA	Johnson 99-yard return of blocked PAT
IA	Brown 54-yard pass from Banks (Kaeding PAT)
PSU	L. Johnson 36-yard pass from Mills (Gould PAT)
PSU	T. Johnson 44-yard pass from Mills (2-pt. conv. – Ganter 2-yard run)
PSU	B. Johnson 8-yard pass from Mills (Gould PAT)
IA	Jones 6-yard pass from Banks (Kaeding PAT)

Iowa had the ball first in the overtime and got off to an inauspicious start, as a five-yard false-start penalty moved the ball back to the 30-yard line. But Iowa was able to march to the 6 on two completions from Banks to Brown. Russell was then stopped for no gain, and an incomplete pass to Jones left Iowa with a third-and-goal from the 6-yard line.

The Iowa offense came to the line of scrimmage showing a three-wide-receiver set, with Jones the only receiver split wide left. Jones cut across the field to his

Overtime Pass From Banks to Jones Overcomes Furious Rally

Even though Penn State had overcome a 22-point fourth quarter deficit to force overtime, the Hawks didn't lose their composure, even in the face of 108,000 Nittany Lion supporters (although many had left before the end of the game, believing the game had been decided). The winning points in the overtime session came on a 3rd-and-goal pass play. Quarterback Brad Banks (7) lined up under center, with a single-set backfield, two receivers spilt wide right, one split wide left, with a tight end also on the left side of the formation. Banks dropped back on what would be a bang-bang play. C.J. Jones (8), the only wide receiver on the left, came across the middle. The Penn State cornerback, who was running with Jones almost stride for stride early in the pattern, collided with the safety who was attempting to step up and help, springing Jones free. Banks alertly spotted the open man and fired a strike to Jones, who caught the ball at the 2-yard line and scored the touchdown that would end up being the game winner.

right against man-to-man coverage, caught the ball from Banks over the middle at the 2-yard line perfectly in stride, and waltzed into the end zone to again silence whatever remained of the crowd that had once been 108,000. The Penn State safety stepped in to try and help out his cornerback, who was in man-to-man coverage on the play, but the two actually ended up getting in each other's way as Jones caught the ball in front of both of them and quickly danced into the end zone.

Coach Ferentz admitted after the game that he had wanted to use the play earlier, but "chickened out," which he said, is why he isn't the offensive coordinator. The all-important extra point gave Iowa a 42–35 lead.

Penn State gained one first down on their possession in overtime, but the drive stalled there. Now they faced a fourth-and-four from the 5-yard line. The Lions tried to set up a screen pass to Larry Johnson—a play that had been very successful throughout the day—but Johnson was well covered and the ball fell harmlessly incomplete to the turf.

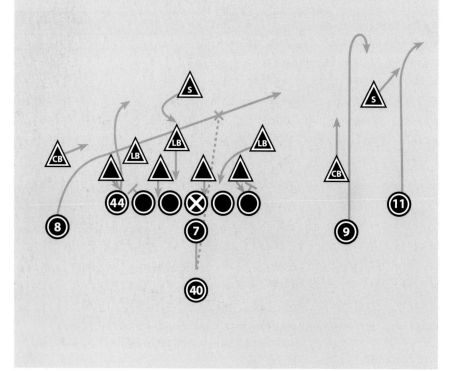

Iowa's Maurice Brown races down the sideline with a 54-yard touchdown reception. Though the score gave the Hawks a 22-point lead over Penn State, it would not hold up. The Nittany Lions roared back to tie the game and send it to overtime. *Copyright: University of Iowa—CMP Photographic Service*

January 1, 1959

13 Record Run in Pasadena

Bob Jeter's 81-yard touchdown is the centerpiece of an offensive onslaught that gives Iowa its second Rose Bowl win

A glorious 1958 season was capped with perhaps the greatest performance of the entire year in the Rose Bowl game against Pacific Coast champion California. On New Year's Day 1959, Iowa took a high-octane offense into its second Rose Bowl game in three years and dominated the Pacific Coast champions with a punishing rushing attack the likes of which the Rose Bowl had never seen before. In the single greatest running play in a day filled with great running plays for Iowa, senior Bob Jeter racked up an 81-yard touchdown run in the third quarter to put a game that was already one-sided in Iowa's favor permanently out of reach for California. The Iowa rushing attack was also ably supported by Willie Fleming.

Altogether, the offense set the following Rose Bowl records against Cal:

- Most rushing yards by a team, with 429, far surpassing the old mark of 320
- Most total yards, with 516, passing the previous mark of 491
- Most rushing yards by an individual, with 194 by Jeter, outdistancing the old standard of 151
- Longest single run, 81 yards by Jeter

The game had been billed as a showdown between two All-American quarterbacks: Iowa's Randy Duncan versus Cal's Joe Kapp. That one-on-one matchup never really materialized, as Iowa didn't need the passing game in the face of such a potent rushing attack. Duncan attempted a mere seven passes, completing five of them for 50 yards.

Duncan, on the other hand, scored Iowa's first touchdown on a two-yard run. Bob Prescott's extra point gave Iowa the early 7–0 lead. A second-quarter fumble by Kapp turned the ball over to Iowa and kept the momentum going. A 41-yard run from Jeter following the fumble moved the ball to the Cal 7-yard line. From there, Duncan would register his only touchdown pass of the game, a seven-yard toss to Jeff Langston,

Bob Jeter (11) ran wild against California in Iowa's second Rose Bowl appearance on January 1, 1959. Jeter accumulated 194 yards on just nine carries, including a Rose Bowl–record 81-yard touchdown run in the third quarter to put the game on ice for the Hawks. *Copyright: University of Iowa—CMP Photographic Service*

which made it 14–0 after another successful extra point.

Iowa was having such an easy time of it during the first half that coach Forest Evashevski inserted his second-teamers midway through the second quarter. As a testament to how one-sided the game really was, even the Iowa second team was able to punch in a touchdown; Don Horn scored on a four-yard run toward the end of the second quarter. The Iowa defense took the shutout into halftime,

Jeter's Record-Setting Rose Bowl Run

Although Iowa had the game pretty much well in hand at the time of Bob Jeter's record-setting run, leading California 26–6, the long touchdown run by Jeter late in the third quarter snuffed out any hope California might have had of a comeback. Jeter (11) took the inside handoff from quarterback Randy Duncan (25) and took the ball off right guard straight up field, breaking tackles near the line of scrimmage, before getting a key down field block from Don Norton (89) at the 25-yard line. At the California 30, Jeter cut to his left, while five California defenders who were within a few yards of him pursued him through the secondary and had a chance to tackle him just beyond the 30. However, two diving tackle attempts failed and Jeter won the foot race to the end zone relatively easily. The play was good for a Rose Bowl record 81-yard touchdown run.

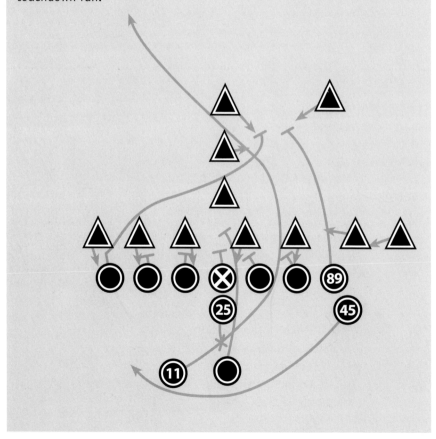

as the Hawkeyes led it 20–0 at intermission.

The Golden Bears were finally able to get on the board early in the third quarter with a touchdown against Iowa's first unit. But that would be the only score Cal was able to muster until the game's final 37 seconds.

The California score didn't faze Iowa at all; the Hawks got right back into the scoring act with a 37-yard touchdown run by Fleming, making the score 26–6. Not to be outdone, it was time for Jeter to make some Rose Bowl rushing history. With the line of scrimmage at the California 19-yard line, Jeter took the handoff and started off right guard, broke a diving attempt at a leg tackle five yards downfield, then cut sharply to his left at the Cal 30-yard line to avoid two members of the Cal secondary—and had a clear path to the goal line.

The touchdown run covered 81 yards and was the longest in Rose Bowl history. But most important, it allowed Iowa to open up a 32–6 lead and all but end the contest right then and there. Just for good measure, Fleming added his second touchdown run in the fourth quarter to give Iowa a total of six touchdowns and 38 points. The last-minute touchdown by Cal at least pushed the Golden Bears to double digits, making the final score 38–12.

Jeter finished with 194 yards on just nine carries, for an amazing

GAME DETAILS

Iowa 38 • California 12

Date: January 1, 1959

Location: Rose Bowl, Pasadena, California

Attendance: 98,297

Significance: Rose Bowl

Box Score:

Iowa	7	13	12	6	**38**
California	0	0	6	6	**12**

Scoring:

IA	Duncan 2-yard run (Prescott PAT)
IA	Langston 7-yard pass from Duncan (Prescott PAT)
IA	Horn 4-yard run (PAT failed)
CAL	Hart 1-yard run (pass failed)
IA	Fleming 37-yard run (pass failed)
IA	Jeter 81-yard run (pass failed)
IA	Fleming 7-yard run (pass failed)
CAL	Hart 17-yard pass from Kapp (run failed)

> **I** didn't have much chance to study him...every time I saw him he was running.
>
> —CALIFORNIA COACH PETE ELLIOTT, COMMENTING ON THE SPEEDY BOB JETER

average of 21.6 yards per attempt. His performance earned him game MVP honors. From a team standpoint, the Rose Bowl win and the 8–1–1 campaign was enough to earn a mythical national football title: Iowa was awarded the Grantland Rice Trophy, presented by the Football Writers Association of America to the nation's No. 1 football team. Iowa led the nation in total offense and finished No. 2 in both the AP and the UPI polls (LSU was No. 1)—the highest ranking in school history.

The win also capped a dominant three-year run by Evashevski's Hawkeyes. During the 1956, 1957, and 1958 seasons, Iowa posted a record of 24–3–2, which included two outright Big Ten titles. The team would add another Big Ten title in 1960.

EVY AND JETER

Iowa coach Forest Evashevski nearly missed the game because he was battling the flu and a 101-degree temperature just beforehand. It turned out the Hawks really didn't need too many words of encouragement from their coach. Later, when asked why Iowa won the game, Evy quipped, "I just put 13 pounds of air in the football and said 'sic 'em.'"

In the postgame celebration, jubilant Iowa fans couldn't get enough of their hero Bob Jeter, the speedy junior from Weirton, West Virginia. After the game, Jeter was stopped as he tried to get back to the locker room. He ended up being delayed 10 minutes, although he probably didn't mind too much. "Somebody got my helmet," a smiling Jeter confessed after finally getting to the Iowa locker room. "I guess I'm lucky that I kept my jersey."

November 16, 2002

12 LAYING THE GROUNDWORK FOR A TITLE

Jermelle Lewis's touchdown highlights a dominating rushing performance that delivers a perfect Big Ten season

The 2002 regular-season finale for Iowa took place on the road at Minnesota, but other than playing indoors on artificial turf instead of grass and with white jerseys instead of black, it felt like a home game to Iowa. Realizing the historical significance of this game, at least half of the record Metrodome crowd of more than 65,000 appeared to be pulling for the Hawkeyes. This was the culmination of all the hard work and dedication that had led Iowa from the abyss of a winless Big Ten season in 1999 to this: the brink of a perfect 8–0 conference season. Given how far this team had come and what was at stake, many Hawkeyes fans came to the conclusion that this game was something that simply could not be missed.

The fans' long trip north would be rewarded as Iowa unleashed a relentless rushing attack on the Gophers early and often. Iowa racked up 137 yards on 13 attempts in the first quarter alone. Fred Russell was the catalyst that led to two touchdowns on Iowa's first two possessions. Russell scored the first on a 10-yard run and set up the second with a 53-yard run on Iowa's second drive.

While Russell was out for a breather, backup Jermelle Lewis grabbed the honor of scoring the go-ahead touchdown on a six-yard run that vaulted Iowa to a 14–7 lead, which they would never relinquish.

The 11th win was a school record and closed out a perfect Big Ten season at 8–0, the team's first perfect season since Howard Jones's squad posted a 5–0 league mark in 1922. Unlike many of the prior games that had clinched Big Ten championships, Iowa's bowl destination was uncertain immediately following the game. Ohio State, with its 7–0 league record, would not conclude its season until the following week at home against Michigan. The Buckeyes could tie for the league crown with a win the following week. However, that did little to temper the joy and enthusiasm on the Iowa side following the game. The traditional accessory for a team that had just won at least a share of the Big Ten title was, of course, roses—and there were plenty of those to go around after the game.

Ironically, in the day and age of the Bowl Championship Series, neither Iowa nor Ohio State would end up at the Rose Bowl. The next week Ohio State defeated Michigan to complete an undefeated regular season and earn a trip to Tempe, Arizona, for a date with the Miami Hurricanes in the Fiesta Bowl, which was the BCS title game that year. Iowa landed in Miami for an Orange Bowl date with USC.

It was Iowa's running game that had powered the team to victory this day. Led by a veteran offensive line, Iowa gained 365 yards on the ground—including 194 by Russell, 101 from Lewis, and 39 from quarterback Brad Banks.

Because the rushing game was so strong, Banks didn't need to throw very often. But when his number was called in the passing game, he delivered flawlessly, just as he had for most of the year. Banks was nine of 17 for 100 yards and two touchdowns. He also scored on running plays of 11 and one

Iowa head coach Kirk Ferentz is carried off the field by his jubilant players after Iowa beat Minnesota 45–21, clinching a share of the 2002 Big Ten title at the Metrodome.
Photo courtesy AP Images

yards, respectively. It would be Banks's final opportunity to impress the Heisman voters.

One of the signatures of the 2002 Hawkeyes team was its fast starts, and this game played true to form. Iowa took the opening kickoff 80 yards on five plays and grabbed the early 7–0 lead on the 10-yard run by Russell. But Minnesota matched Iowa's first score on their opening possession, scoring their touchdown on an 11-yard pass from quarterback Asad Abdul-Khaliq to Antoine Burns.

But from that point, Iowa took control. A 53-yard outburst by Russell set Iowa up deep in Minnesota territory again. Russell's running mate Lewis provided the touchdown run from six yards away on an option play that came with 29 seconds remaining in the first quarter. Iowa was on its way to history with a 14–7 lead.

Turnovers played a major role in Minnesota's undoing; the Gophers gave it up a total of six times. The first came early in the second quarter on a fumble by Abdul-Khaliq that was recovered by Iowa's Howard Hodges deep in Minnesota territory at the 15-yard line. Banks quickly cashed in on the short field when he scored on an 11-yard touchdown run two plays later. Iowa extended their lead to 28–7 on a 31-yard touchdown strike from Banks to Maurice Brown, but Minnesota put together a long drive of their own right before the half to make it 28–14 at intermission.

Floyd of Rosedale

The fact that this win that clinched a perfect Big Ten season came against ancient rival Minnesota made it all the more sweet. Plus, Iowa retained the Floyd of Rosedale Trophy. Interestingly, the origin of the trophy way back in the 1930s was related to the controversial and complex topic of race relations.

Although Minnesota had dominated the series for many years, things started to look up for Iowa in 1934 when a fleet-footed halfback named Ozzie Simmons joined the team. Simmons happened to be one of the few African American players in college football in those days. During a dominating 48–12 Minnesota victory in Iowa City in 1934, many on the Iowa side thought that the Gophers unfairly roughed up Simmons. He left the game due to injury in the first half. Therefore, there was plenty of emotion on both sides leading up to the Iowa–Minnesota game in November 1935. The day before the game, Iowa governor Clyde L. Herring directed some ill-advised threats toward the Minnesota side. It was suggested that the Iowa crowd take matters into its own hands in the event that Simmons received similar rough treatment as the prior year. The Minnesota team quickly demanded that Iowa officials provide added security at the game.

Minnesota governor Floyd B. Olson tried to defuse a potentially volatile situation by offering a friendly wager on the game: a Minnesota prize hog against an Iowa prize hog. The loser had to deliver the hog to the winner in person. Governor Herring of course accepted the bet, partially to help neutralize a potentially explosive situation that he unwittingly had created. Fortunately, a clean game was played that saw Iowa nearly upset powerful Minnesota, before falling 13–6. Making good on the bet, Governor Herring ordered a prize pig from the Rosedale Farm near Fort Dodge, naming him Floyd of Rosedale in honor of the Minnesota governor. Olson donated the hog to the University of Minnesota, which commissioned a sculptor to preserve Floyd's image in a permanent statue. The resulting trophy is a bronze pig 21 inches long, 15½ inches high, weighing 94 pounds. The Floyd of Rosedale Trophy has been awarded annually to the winner of the Iowa–Minnesota football game since 1936.

GAME DETAILS

Iowa 45 • Minnesota 21

Date: November 16, 2002

Location: HHH Metrodome, Minneapolis, Minnesota

Attendance: 65,184

Box Score:

Iowa	14	14	7	10	**45**
Minnesota	7	7	7	0	**21**

Scoring:

IA	Russell 10-yard run (Kaeding PAT)
MN	Burns 11-yard pass from Abdul-Khaliq (Nystrom PAT)
IA	Lewis 6-yard run (Kaeding PAT)
IA	Banks 11-yard run (Kaeding PAT)
IA	Brown 31-yard pass from Banks (Kaeding PAT)
MN	Abdul-Khaliq 1-yard run (Nystrom PAT)
IA	Solomon 6-yard pass from Banks (Kaeding PAT)
MN	Abdul-Khaliq 1-yard run (Nystrom PAT)
IA	Kaeding 21-yard FG
IA	Banks 1-yard run (Kaeding PAT)

Minnesota was hoping to build momentum as they took the kick to open the second half, but instead found themselves in a deeper hole following another turnover. Less than one minute into the half, another Minnesota fumble, this one by Thomas Tapeh, was recovered by Derek Pagel at the Minnesota 37-yard line. Iowa converted the ensuing drive into another touchdown; Banks found wide receiver Clinton Solomon open in the end zone for a six-yard score and a 35–14 Iowa lead. It was only a matter of time before head coach Ferentz and defensive coordinator Norm Parker received the Gatorade bucket treatment.

Ferentz also got a ride on his players' shoulders, long-stemmed rose in hand. The coach commented after the game: "I was just glad they didn't drop me. It's been quite a ride."

As the clock wound down, the large contingent of Iowa fans moved the party from the stands down to the Metrodome field. Once onto the field, a crazy scene ensued. Thousands of black-and-gold–clad Iowa fans swarmed the south goal post and eventually were able to tip it over. It certainly isn't every day that legions of the visiting team's fans pull off this feat on enemy turf.

The Iowa faithful proudly paraded pieces of the posts around the Metrodome field for all to see. Eventually, fans were seen hauling pieces of the goal posts off the field and up the steps, attempting to remove them through the concourse level. Perhaps the Iowa fans were so deliriously drunk with joy (hopefully it was joy) that they forgot they had entered through *revolving doors*, which would prove difficult to get an 18-foot pole through. That didn't stop the fans from trying, but eventually the posts were left on the field.

Minnesota sent Iowa a bill for $5,000 in damages to the Metrodome goal posts. Iowa athletics director Bob Bowlsby said Iowa would accept the charge. Bowlsby added, "It's a longstanding tradition, and our fans haven't done that in a while."

October 26, 2002

11

SANDERS SPARKS ANN ARBOR ROUT

A special-teams gem in the third quarter helps Iowa hand Michigan its worst home loss in 35 years

There is no question that Iowa had a nice little season going in 2002 coming into the fifth Big Ten contest at Michigan. Iowa was taking a sparkling 4–0 conference record (7–1 overall) and a No. 13 national ranking into Michigan Stadium to face a Wolverines team that was 3–0 and 6–1 and ranked No. 8.

To really be taken seriously in this conference, everyone knows that you must beat the two traditional powers, Ohio State and Michigan. The Buckeyes and the Hawkeyes were not scheduled to meet during the 2002 regular season, so this game would be Iowa's only opportunity to shine against one of the big two.

During this game, Iowa elevated its 2002 season to a whole different stratosphere as the Hawks hung a historic 34–9 loss on the Wolverines. The bitter defeat was the worst suffered by a Michigan team since a 34–0 drubbing at the hands of in-state rival Michigan State in 1967.

As one-sided as the final score was, Michigan carried the momentum gained by a touchdown late in the first half into the

first possession of the second half, and the Wolverines converted a field goal to pull to within 10–9.

Although they were outplayed in almost every facet of the game, it appeared that Michigan was poised to vault into the lead. Following the field goal, Michigan forced an Iowa punt, so it looked as though the Wolverines would get that opportunity to grab a lead. However, things looked radically different after Bob Sanders forced a fumble as Markus Curry fielded the punt deep in his own territory. Curry attempted to return the punt just as Sanders was the lone Hawkeyes player arriving on the scene. If Curry had been able to catch the ball cleanly and get past Sanders, it would likely have been a big return for Michigan going the other way—and who knows how this game, or the 2002 season for that matter, would have ended up?

But Curry juggled the ball as he attempted to get it tucked away, and he was immediately violently spun around by Sanders and thrown to the ground. The ball flipped backward and was covered up by

Iowa safety Scott Boleyn at the Michigan 16-yard line.

Just like that, three plays later, Iowa was in the Michigan end zone on a three-yard touchdown pass from quarterback Brad Banks to C.J. Jones. It was Jones's second touchdown reception of the day and it increased Iowa's lead to 17–9.

Although it wasn't reflected in the close halftime score, Iowa thoroughly dominated the Wolverines in the first half. The Hawkeyes roared to a 10–0 first-quarter advantage on a 39-yard touchdown pass from Banks to Jones on a wide receiver screen. Jones sidestepped several tacklers before breaking into the clear and taking it to the house. The fast start immediately took a partisan crowd of 111,496 out of the game.

A 19-yard field goal by Nate Kaeding extended the lead to 10–0, and Iowa enjoyed that advantage until very late in the second quarter, when they were about to punt the ball away to Michigan deep in their

Iowa's Bob Sanders forces a fumble on a third-quarter punt that would turn the tide in Iowa's favor, leading to a big win over Michigan at the Big House on October 26, 2002. *Copyright: University of Iowa—CMP Photographic Service*

own territory with just under two minutes to play in the half. Iowa punter Scott Bradley lost concentration and dropped the ball before he could punt it away. Michigan recovered the ball on the Iowa 2-yard line, and Chris Perry scored two plays later from one yard out. Michigan's Phillip Brabbs missed the extra point, leaving the Hawks in front 10–6 at halftime.

In the Iowa State game earlier in the year and the Michigan game the year before, Iowa had become rattled following a big-impact negative play. But on this day, the players took great pride in being able to move on and

put the negative play behind them to focus on what was in front of them.

"We talked about that at the half," Ferentz said. "Last year we let that impact us in an adverse way, and today we moved on. I think that shows how we've grown as a team since then. I think we're a more mature team than we were a year ago…I told them we played a heck of a first half, there isn't any reason we can't go out there and do it again the second time around."

It turns out that was exactly what happened. The fumbled punt and immediate touchdown by Iowa early

BOB SANDERS

Bob Sanders developed quite a reputation during his days patrolling the secondary in Iowa City. What he doesn't necessarily have in physical size (he was listed at Iowa as 5'8" and 202 pounds), he more than makes up for with speed and strength. His big hits on defense were legendary. In fact, Sanders set the standard on the team for a big hit; many players and coaches would refer to a big hit on defense as a "Sanders"—kind of a nice thing to be known for, indeed.

After four stellar seasons at Iowa, Sanders took his game to the NFL, where he was drafted by the Indianapolis Colts in the second round of the 2004 NFL draft. Sanders's return from injury during the 2006 playoffs sparked the Colts' defense and

carried them all the way to a Super Bowl title against the Bears in rainy Miami. The success continued for Sanders into 2007 when he was named the AP NFL Defensive Player of the Year. In December 2007, Sanders signed a multiyear contract extension with the Colts that made him the highest paid safety in the NFL.

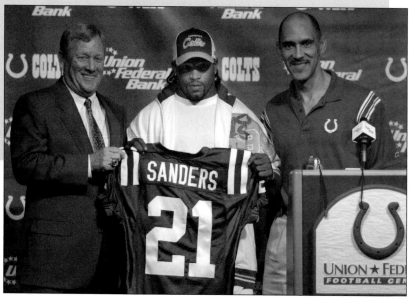

Indianapolis Colts president Bill Polian, left, and coach Tony Dungy stand with Iowa safety Bob Sanders, center, prior to a news conference in Indianapolis following the 2004 NFL draft when the Colts selected Sanders in the second round. *Photo courtesy AP Images*

GAME DETAILS

Iowa 34 • Michigan 9

Date: October 26, 2002

Location: Michigan Stadium, Ann Arbor, Michigan

Attendance: 111,496

Weather: Light rain

> Everybody did a little something today. We tried to get everybody a touch. Everybody did a little something with their turn.
>
> —IOWA QUARTERBACK BRAD BANKS

Box Score:

Iowa	10	0	14	10	**34**
Michigan	0	6	3	0	**9**

Scoring:

IA	Jones 39-yard pass from Banks (Kaeding PAT)
IA	Kaeding 19-yard FG
MI	Perry 1-yard run (PAT failed)
MI	Finley 40-yard FG
IA	Jones 3-yard pass from Banks (Kaeding PAT)
IA	Lewis 5-yard run (Kaeding PAT)
IA	Lewis 23-yard pass from Banks (Kaeding PAT)
IA	Kaeding 27-yard FG

in the third quarter pretty much took all the wind out of Michigan's sails. The Wolverines really didn't mount much of anything for the rest of the game.

After Jones's second touchdown, Jermelle Lewis ran it into the end zone off left tackle from five yards away to put Iowa ahead 24–9 with 2:58 left in the third quarter. Then, on Iowa's next possession, Lewis took a shovel pass from Banks and advanced it 23 yards, bowling over a Michigan defender at the 5-yard line on his way into the end zone.

Since the forced fumble by Sanders, Iowa had outscored the Wolverines 21–0. At this point, many in the crowd had seen enough and were ready to get out of the cold, damp autumn rain. Late in the game, the Big House turned into the Empty House. A 27-yard Kaeding field goal, his 20th straight successful one, capped the scoring with 2:49 remaining.

The team statistics on both sides of the ball supported the one-sided final score. Iowa had a 22–12 advantage in first downs, outgaining the Wolverines 399–171 and controlling the time of possession, holding the ball for over 38 minutes.

But the most impressive statistic came on the defensive side of the ball. The "no-name defense," as they were known at the time, held Michigan to a paltry 22 net yards rushing on 20 attempts. They also pressured Michigan quarterback John Navarre all afternoon and posted five quarterback sacks.

The few thousand Iowa fans who made the long trip east to Ann Arbor didn't seem to mind the empty stadium or the cold, damp weather. The Iowa players savored this victory with their fans as they left the field. With this big win over Michigan on their own turf, Iowa was now considered a legitimate contender for the Big Ten title in 2002.

10

CATCH HELPS HAWKEYES SMELL ROSES

Kenny Ploen and Jim Gibbons connect against the Buckeyes to secure Iowa's first Rose Bowl berth

They say that you never forget your first time, and this saying most definitely applies to Iowa's memorable first Rose Bowl berth, earned during the 1956 season. The Hawkeyes' first trip to the Rose Bowl was clinched on a memorable November afternoon in Iowa Stadium against legendary coach Woody Hayes and an Ohio State Buckeyes squad that boasted a 17-game conference winning streak, the longest in the history of the Big Ten. (Hayes would become known for both his winning program, but also for his violent temper. In one of the early revelations of this side of Hayes, following the game he manhandled a cameraman from a Cedar Rapids television station.) Ohio State was coming off a national championship in 1954 and seeking its unprecedented third consecutive Big Ten title, while Iowa was seeking its first since 1922.

Iowa coach Forest Evashevski challenged his team with a sign on the dressing room wall before the game: "You have 60 minutes to beat Ohio State—and a lifetime to remember it." All the pieces were in place for a truly historic Iowa victory.

The first half was nip-and-tuck and actually was evenly played. The Hawkeyes had the only realistic scoring opportunity of the half; Iowa penetrated to the Ohio State 19-yard line in the first quarter, but the ball went back over to Ohio State on downs. Both defenses had the better of the play with both sides failing to score in the first half. But the Hawkeyes would come out in the second half playing inspired football.

The only points of the entire game would come on Iowa's first possession of the third quarter. Iowa was able to advance the ball a total of 46 yards—down to the Buckeyes' 17-yard line—in eight plays. The drive was aided by a pass-interference penalty against Ohio State that gave Iowa a first down at the Buckeyes' 20.

Two plays later, on a second-and-seven play from the Ohio State 17-yard line, quarterback Kenny Ploen faked a handoff to halfback Don Dobrino, but then drifted to his left and spotted left split end Jim Gibbons streaking downfield near the left sideline. He lofted a high pass downfield toward the front part of the end zone. The

Iowa end Jim Gibbons focuses on the incoming football from quarterback Ken Ploen that would provide the winning score in the third quarter against Ohio State at Iowa Stadium on November 17, 1956. The touchdown would clinch Iowa's first-ever trip to the Rose Bowl.
Copyright: University of Iowa—CMP Photographic Service

ball floated just over the outstretched hands of the Buckeyes defender, quarterback Frank Ellwood, and fell into Gibbons's hands perfectly in stride at the goal line. Ellwood was a step behind on the play because he was apparently fooled by the well-executed fake handoff by Ploen, cheating toward the line of scrimmage to stuff the run, as Iowa had gained the majority of the yards on the drive using an overpowering running game.

Ploen and Gibbons made Ohio State pay for the costly error. In all, the scoring drive covered 63 yards in nine plays. After the game, the play was referred to by a *Cedar Rapids Gazette* writer as "a 17-yard pass to immortality."

However, Bob Prescott (whose nickname was "Automatic") missed his first kick of the season after 13 successful kicks. The snap to Ploen was just a bit high, which may have thrown off the rhythm of the kick. Iowa's lead was just a tenuous 6–0 with 10:41 left in the third quarter.

Coming into the game, no one could ever have guessed that the high-powered Ohio State offense could be kept off the scoreboard the entire game. Just one week before, the Buckeyes ran up 465 yards rushing during a 35–14 blowout of Indiana, setting another Big Ten mark. However, the Iowa defense made those six points stand up and preserved the historic win. Ohio State could muster only 47 yards rushing and six yards passing in the second half, against a most stingy Iowa defense. On the game, the Hawkeyes' defense allowed only a total of 165 yards. Ohio State advanced into Iowa territory on offense just four times during the game, and none of the four penetrated deeper than the Iowa 32-yard line. Only one Ohio State drive advanced into Iowa territory in the second half. That drive was halted on downs at the Iowa 42-yard line.

Iowa narrowly missed an opportunity to ice the game with two and a half minutes to play in the fourth quarter. The Iowa offense took over on downs at the Iowa 42-yard line. Using fullback Fred Harris as the primary weapon over the left side, Iowa had soon advanced the ball to the Ohio State 15, but then two negative plays moved the ball back to the 18. On third down, the Hawks played it conservatively and set up a potential game-clinching field goal. However, Prescott's kick came up short of the crossbar by about a foot.

Ohio State took over deep in Iowa territory for their last desperate attempt to remove the goose egg from their side of the scoreboard. The ending would have been even more dramatic for the 57,732 delirious Iowa fans were it not for an early-drive clipping penalty

KENNY PLOEN

Kenny Ploen enjoyed a historic year for Iowa in 1956, leading the team in rushing, with 86 carries for 487 yards; passing, in which he was 33 for 64 for 386 yards; and scoring, with 38 points.

During his time in Iowa City, Ploen's attributes were comparable to those of the great Nile Kinnick: both were Iowa-grown; both could throw, catch, kick, and run with the football; both played football and basketball at Iowa early in their careers; both were outstanding in the classroom (actually, Ploen came to

Iowa as a Nile Kinnick Scholar); and finally, both were involved in the military (Ploen was a cadet commander of the local R.O.T.C.).

Ploen was the MVP of both the Big Ten conference and the Rose Bowl during the 1956 season—he is still the only Hawkeyes player ever to accomplish this feat. Unlike Kinnick, Ploen went on to play professional football after graduating from Iowa in 1957. He played 11 years in Canada.

GAME DETAILS

Iowa 6 • Ohio State 0

Date: November 17, 1956

Location: Iowa Stadium, Iowa City, Iowa

Attendance: 57,732

Box Score:

Ohio St.	0	0	0	0	**0**
Iowa	0	0	6	0	**6**

Scoring:

IA   Gibbons 17-yard pass from Ploen (PAT failed)

against Ohio State that wiped out a 15-yard Ohio State gain. The penalty set the Buckeyes back to their own 25-yard line.

At this point, an Iowa defense that had been nothing short of spectacular the entire game rose up to ensure victory. An incomplete pass on first down was followed by a Frank Gilliam sack back at the 12-yard line, and another incomplete pass led to a fourth-and-forever for Ohio State with just 25 ticks remaining on the clock. This time, it was All-American Alex Karras who burst through the Ohio State line to drop Jim Roseboro at the 3-yard line.

Iowa would take over there, and pandemonium soon ensued on the field as time expired. Thirty-four years' worth of jubilation had been stored up by these fans since Iowa's last championship, during the perfect 7–0 season led by coach Howard Jones. Ploen was carried from the field by his teammates, and the goal posts at Iowa Stadium would soon be the next two victims of the Iowa Hawkeyes on this day. Harkening back to the "Ironmen" of the 1939 team, Gibbons played every down against Ohio State. He joined Harris and Dobrino in the 60-minute club this day.

That night, university provost Harvey Davis told students they could take two extra days off at Christmas. Iowa was Rose Bowl–bound!

December 29, 2001

9 KAEDING KICKS IOWA PAST TECH

Nate Kaeding's fourth field goal delivers an Alamo Bowl win over a home-state favorite

The magical 2002 Big Ten championship team didn't come completely out of nowhere. The roots of the success enjoyed by the 2002 team can actually be found in the last series of games in the 2001 season, which was capped by a thrilling last-minute win in another Alamo Bowl on the strength of a 47-yard field goal by sophomore place-kicker Nate Kaeding. Kaeding played a key role in the Iowa scoring on the day; it was his leg that had Iowa in position to win in the last minute, as he had converted three other field goals on the day to account for 13 of the 19 points Iowa scored. The game provided a glimpse of Kaeding's abilities under extreme pressure, which would lead to his gaining national recognition in 2002 as the best place-kicker in the nation.

Iowa earned an Alamo Bowl bid with a very strong finish in the Big Ten regular season, including back-to-back convincing wins at home, 59–16 over Northwestern and 42–24 over Minnesota. The big win over Minnesota brought Floyd of Rosedale home to Iowa City for the first time since

1997 and was the all-important sixth win Iowa needed to attain bowl eligibility.

The last regular-season game that year was on the road against Iowa State; the game had been delayed until late November as a result of the 9/11 terrorist attacks. The Hawkeyes dropped a narrow 17–14 decision at Jack Trice Stadium, but still were looking forward to their first bowl game under coach Kirk Ferentz, and their first overall since a 17–7 loss in the 1997 Sun Bowl to Arizona State in Hayden Fry's second-to-last year.

Their opponent in the 2001 Alamo Bowl was the same school Iowa had beaten 27–0 in their last Alamo Bowl appearance in 1996—local favorite Texas Tech. The Red Raiders featured a high-octane passing attack led by quarterback Kliff Kingsbury. A native of nearby New Braunfels, Texas, Kingsbury passed for a school-record 3,502 yards during the season and led the nation with 364 completions.

Iowa faced some adversity before the opening kickoff; their leading rusher, senior Ladell Betts (who produced a total of 1,056 rush yards in 2001), injured a hamstring

Sophomore place-kicker Nate Kaeding kicks the game-winning 47-yard field goal in the last minute to defeat Texas Tech in the Alamo Bowl in San Antonio, Texas, on December 29, 2001. It was Kaeding's fourth field goal in five attempts on the day. *Copyright: University of Iowa— CMP Photographic Service*

Those field goals are a credit to our offense. They've been great in the red zone all year. They needed me to step up, and I did all but one time.

—IOWA PLACE-KICKER
NATE KAEDING

Kaeding celebrates his game-winning 47-yard field goal against Texas Tech with 44 seconds remaining in the 2001 Alamo Bowl. *Photo courtesy AP Images*

during warm-ups and would play only sparingly. But backup Aaron Greving picked up the slack, rushing for a career-high 115 yards on 25 carries.

Iowa's offensive strategy early on favored a ball-control offense that kept the pigskin out of the hands of Kingsbury and the potent Red Raiders offense. Iowa maintained possession for nine minutes and 15 seconds after the opening kickoff, but couldn't punch it into the end zone. The Hawkeyes settled for Kaeding's first field goal of the day, a 36-yarder that gave Iowa the lead 3–0.

The Texas Tech offense was unable to get into a rhythm most of the first half. The Iowa defense kept Kingsbury off-balance by showing a variety of secondary alignments and defensive fronts.

Iowa sustained another scoring drive late in the second quarter. The drive was capped by a one-yard touchdown run by Greving with just over three minutes left in the first half, which extended the Iowa lead to 10–0. Iowa was again in position for more points just before the half ended, but Kaeding's only misfire of the day—from 31 yards out—kept the score at 10–0, but only momentarily.

When Texas Tech took over, Kingsbury connected with Nehemiah Glover deep over the middle for a 35-yard pass play that set up a 50-yard field-goal attempt just before the first half ended. Clinton Greathouse split the uprights, giving the Red Raiders some life going into the second half with a score of 10–3.

The Texas Tech offense built on the momentum with its first drive of the second half. Using a no-huddle offense and spread formations, Kingsbury drove the Red Raiders 65 yards in less than three and a half minutes and tied the game with a 20-yard touchdown pass to future NFL star Wes Welker.

However, a critical Kingsbury mistake would allow Iowa to regain the lead before the third quarter had expired. Kingsbury threw a pass right into the hands of 280-pound tackle Derrick Pickens, who returned it 11 yards to the Red Raiders' 11-yard line. The Texas Tech defense held, but Kaeding kicked a 31-yard field goal to give Iowa a 13–10 lead with 5:12 left in the period.

The Hawkeyes forced a punt on Texas Tech's next possession, and Kaeding booted a 46-yarder to make it 16–10, four seconds into the final quarter. Texas Tech managed two field goals later in the fourth quarter to draw even, the second one coming with just 2:05 to go.

The tie game would be turned over to the hands of Iowa's senior quarterback, Kyle McCann. McCann, who had had an up-and-down career over the last four years as starting quarterback, seized the moment and finished his Hawkeyes career on a high note, running a sharp

NATE KAEDING

Coralville, Iowa, native Nate Kaeding is arguably the best place-kicker Iowa has ever produced. How about this for a stat: the missed field goal near the end of the first half against Texas Tech would be his last miss until November 2002. Kaeding connected on 22 consecutive field goals during that span. The amazing streak ended on November 2, 2002, when Kaeding missed what appeared to be a chip-shot 27-yarder against Wisconsin. One other amazing statistic

to offer: Kaeding connected on five of six field-goal attempts of 50 yards or greater during his Hawkeyes career.

Kaeding's brilliant 2002 season earned the junior the Lou Groza Award as the nation's best kicker. He holds outright or shares numerous Iowa kicking and scoring records. Kaeding enjoyed another stellar season in 2003 before being drafted in the third round of the 2004 NFL draft by the San Diego Chargers.

GAME DETAILS

Iowa 19 • Texas Tech 16

Date: December 29, 2001

Location: Alamodome, San Antonio, Texas

Attendance: 65,232

Significance: Alamo Bowl

Box Score:

Iowa	3	7	3	6	**19**
Texas Tech	0	3	7	6	**16**

Scoring:

IA	Kaeding 36-yard FG
IA	Greving 1-yard run (Kaeding PAT)
TT	Greathouse 50-yard FG
TT	Welker 20-yard pass from Kingsbury (Treece PAT)
IA	Kaeding 31-yard FG
IA	Kaeding 46-yard FG
TT	Treece 23-yard FG
TT	Treece 37-yard FG
IA	Kaeding 47-yard FG

two-minute drill during a drive that covered 53 yards on eight plays to set up the winning field goal.

McCann, who completed 19 of 26 passes for 161 yards on the day, went to work, hitting Kahlil Hill for 21 yards and scrambling for 16 more to the Texas Tech 26. One play later, McCann was called for intentional grounding while trying to avoid a sack. The penalty pushed the Hawkeyes back to the 30-yard line and added more intrigue to the potential game-winning field-goal attempt to come.

Kaeding came on one play later, with 44 seconds left in the fourth quarter. Because of the penalty, the kick was a 47-yard attempt. The snap and hold were good, but Kaeding had to avoid a stiff rush that almost got to him from the right side of the Texas Tech line. In the face of the rush, Kaeding got the kick away; it had plenty of distance and slid just inside the right upright.

Similar to Iowa's last Alamo Bowl appearance in 1996, more than half of the crowd of 65,000 was clad in Texas Tech black and red. The Red Raiders faithful could do nothing at that point but sit in silence, perhaps planning their short trips home or thinking about their New Year's Eve plans. The game was sealed on an interception by sophomore Bob Sanders of a long Hail Mary pass in the end zone.

It had only been a few years since Iowa fans had seen a winning team on the field—nothing compared to the almost 20-year lull in Iowa football between the Forest Evashevski era and the Hayden Fry era. But somehow, it seemed longer. As this game would signal, the Hawkeyes were on the verge of greatness, and it was the clutch kicking of Kaeding that made the clear difference in this ball game.

October 8, 1921

Locke's Run Rocks Knute

A one-yard touchdown plunge by Gordon Locke hands Notre Dame its first loss in three years

The 1921 edition of the Hawkeyes was as star-studded a bunch as you will find on any Iowa team in school history. The leader was unquestionably Hall of Fame halfback Aubrey Devine. Devine was supported by fellow Hall of Famer fullback Gordon Locke, and blocking for them both was Hall of Fame lineman Fred "Duke" Slater. With talent like that, it's not hard to understand how Iowa posted back-to-back undefeated seasons in 1921 and 1922, under Hall of Fame coach Howard Jones.

The coming-out party for those great teams was the second game of the 1921 season against mighty Notre Dame. Notre Dame came into the game sporting a 20-game winning streak—it had not lost since dropping a 13–7 decision to Michigan State in 1918. The Irish blasted their first two opponents in 1921, Kalamazoo and DePauw, by a combined score of 113–10.

However, on a snowy day that also saw occasional hail pelt the field in an early autumn storm, Iowa was able to shock the world. Locke's one-yard touchdown plunge

in the first quarter provided the Hawkeyes' only touchdown in a 10–7 victory, perhaps the greatest game played at old Iowa Field.

This was the first-ever meeting on the football field between the two schools. Notre Dame's captain had a name that would soon become very familiar to Hawkeye supporters: All-American Eddie Anderson. Anderson would later go on to coach Iowa's legendary Ironmen in 1939.

Because Iowa's black uniforms were very similar to Notre Dame's standard navy blue uniforms, Notre Dame coach Knute Rockne decided to dress his team in green jerseys for the game. It was an unprecedented decision and history would eventually make the green uniforms famous, but not for many years, since the green jerseys did not prove advantageous in this contest.

Early in the game, the Iowa front line had the better of it against the vaunted Irish line. Devine, Locke, and Johnny Miller all contributed to the rushing attack as Iowa methodically advanced the ball to the Notre Dame 1-yard line in the first

Iowa fullback Gordon Locke provided Iowa's only touchdown in support of a 10–7 upset win over Notre Dame at Iowa Field on October 8, 1921. *Copyright: University of Iowa—CMP Photographic Service*

quarter. Although Locke was momentarily stopped at the line of scrimmage, with Slater occupying multiple men on the Notre Dame front, he powered his way across the goal line for the touchdown. Devine's drop-kick extra point made the score 7–0 against the heavily favored Irish.

Notre Dame promptly mounted a counterattack led by Chet Wynne, Dan Coughlin, and All-American Johnny Mohardt on a 50-yard drive into Iowa territory. But the Hawkeyes defense was finally able to resist the advance, and the Iowa offense took over again. Iowa drove deep into Notre Dame territory and came away with a 33-yard drop-kick field goal by Devine to increase the lead to 10–0.

Because Notre Dame found more resistance in the running game than expected, the Irish turned to an aerial assault. Mohardt attempted pass after pass and was undaunted by two Iowa interceptions at critical stages. Finally, in the second quarter, Mohardt was able to connect on a long play to Ed Kelley that ended up being a 30-yard touchdown pass. Buck Shaw was

successful on the extra point, and Notre Dame trailed just 10–7 at halftime.

As the game forged into the second half, the punishment absorbed by halfback Devine took its toll and he was forced to leave the game. Both teams had opportunities to put more points on the board in the second half, but each time the defenses rose to the occasion and made the critical play at the critical time to thwart the scoring attempt. In the third quarter, both teams traded drives that led to the opposition's 5-yard

GORDON LOCKE, AUBREY DEVINE, AND DUKE SLATER

Gordon Locke, a native of Denison, Iowa, was certainly an integral part of the undefeated 1921 team. Yet in many ways, he shared the spotlight in the Iowa backfield with fellow Hall of Fame player Aubrey Devine. After Devine graduated following the 1921 season, Locke really came into his own as a player and leader on the undefeated 1922 team. In just seven games in 1922, he scored a league-best 12 touchdowns, better than the legendary Red Grange that year. During his three-year Iowa career, which encompassed 21 games, Locke scored 32 touchdowns. Locke earned a law degree after his days with the Hawkeyes and maintained a successful practice in Washington, D.C. He was inducted into the College Football Hall of Fame in 1960.

Twenty years before Nile Kinnick's unforgettable exploits on the field, Aubrey Devine actually was Iowa's first triple-threat who could run, pass, and kick for points. His drop-kick extra point and field goal were the difference against Notre Dame.

He had one of the greatest single performances in college football history later in 1921 against rival Minnesota. Devine accounted for 465 total yards in rushing, passing, and kickoff and punt returns; scored four touchdowns; passed for two more; and

successfully converted five extra points in a 41–7 Iowa victory over the Gophers. However, Devine reportedly told former Iowa sports information director George Wine that his favorite moment came when he drop-kicked the field goal to beat powerful Notre Dame.

Devine was inducted into the National Football Foundation Hall of Fame in 1973.

Duke Slater was the third member of the Hall of Fame triumvirate that helped lead Iowa to the victory over Notre Dame in 1921. Slater did the dirty work in the trenches to clear the way for Locke and Devine. He frequently required multiple members of the opposition to block him on both sides of the line of scrimmage.

Slater, who was one of the last players not to wear a helmet, was Iowa's first African American to earn All-America honors in 1921. His skills were also good enough to earn a spot on the all-time 11-man Pop Warner team, as voted by 600 sportswriters in 1946. Slater was elected to the National Football Hall of Fame in 1951.

He was a success off the field as well, earning a law degree at Iowa in 1928. He served as a municipal court judge in Chicago after his football playing days were over.

GAME DETAILS

Iowa 10 • Notre Dame 7

Date: October 8, 1921

Location: Iowa Field, Iowa City, Iowa

Attendance: 8,000 (est.)

Weather: Snow/Hail

Box Score:

Notre Dame	0	7	0	0	**7**
Iowa	10	0	0	0	**10**

Scoring:

IA	Locke 1-yard run (Devine PAT)
IA	Devine 33-yard FG
ND	Kelley 30-yard pass from Mohardt (Shaw PAT)

> **W**e had heard so much about Devine, but the guy who hurt us the most that day was Locke.
> —NOTRE DAME COACH KNUTE ROCKNE

line, but neither could punch the ball over the goal line. Devine returned in the fourth quarter, only to be hurt again. A 40-yard field-goal attempt later in the fourth quarter by Notre Dame's Mohardt also was no good.

Notre Dame substituted Gus Desch into the game late in the fourth quarter in an attempt to spur a rally. Desch was a 1920 Olympic bronze medalist in the 400-meter hurdles, and his fresh legs spurred a final gasp by the Irish as he connected with Anderson on a play that set Notre Dame up on the Iowa 7-yard line. But once again, the Iowa defense held. The game ended with a stunning 10–7 Iowa victory.

The loss at Iowa Field to the Hawkeyes would be Notre Dame's only defeat during a span covering 40 games, from November 1918 to the last game of the 1922 season. And Notre Dame would need to wait many years for a chance to avenge the loss. Their next opportunity against Iowa would not come until 1939, against the famous Ironmen team led by Nile Kinnick.

> **I** do not believe that there is another fullback in the West or East who has carried the ball as consistently as Locke.
> —IOWA COACH HOWARD JONES

October 5, 2002

7 CLARK CATCH MAKES PURDUE BOIL

A last-minute, fourth-down touchdown pass by Brad Banks caps a dramatic comeback win

One of the most memorable plays of a memorable game in a memorable season occurred at the end of the Purdue game in 2002. The game was a wild seesaw affair that saw the visiting Boilermakers storm out to a 14–3 lead well into the second quarter before a big special-teams play got the Hawkeyes back in it. Iowa carried the momentum into the third quarter and built a 10-point lead by the fourth quarter. Then Purdue decided to "boiler up" again and scored 14 unanswered points to reclaim the lead in the fourth quarter. Just when it seemed that Iowa was out of heroics, quarterback Brad Banks quickly led the Hawkeyes downfield in the final two minutes.

Iowa had first-and-goal from the Purdue 9-yard line. But three plays later, the Hawks faced a do-or-die fourth-and-goal from the 7-yard line. The stage was set for something special.

Facing the heavy pressure of a Purdue blitz, Banks lofted a high pass to tight end Dallas Clark, who had started on the left side of the formation and cut all the way across the field toward the right end zone for his game-winning catch. A brief delay by Clark in breaking off the line of scrimmage appeared to confuse the Purdue coverage and allowed Clark to run wide open through the secondary. The Purdue blitz had left the secondary with too few defenders to cover him.

Banks was buried as he threw and didn't even get to see Clark make the catch, but no doubt he knew the outcome when the crowd came to life when Clark caught the ball. The score, with a minute and seven seconds remaining, provided what would turn out to be the decisive points.

The game was played before a sellout homecoming crowd in Iowa City. It was the second straight nailbiter to open the Big Ten year for Iowa, which was coming off a dramatic overtime victory at Penn State the week before (see Play Number 14).

Iowa grabbed a 3–0 lead on a 51-yard field goal by Nate Kaeding on its second possession. But from that point on, Purdue certainly had the better of it for most of the rest of the first half. Late in the first quarter,

Dallas Clark celebrates the go-ahead touchdown against Purdue as the Iowa bench jumps for joy in the background. *Copyright: University of Iowa—CMP Photographic Service*

Purdue quarterback Kyle Orton hooked up with John Standeford for a 61-yard touchdown strike, giving the Boilermakers a 7–3 lead. Purdue then marched 69 yards in 11 plays to extend the lead to 14–3 on its next possession. Jerod Void scored the touchdown on a one-yard run.

Plagued by a total of nine penalties for 80 yards in the first half, Iowa couldn't get anything going on offense for the rest of the half, while Purdue was able to move the ball into scoring position inside the Iowa 10 in the last two minutes of the half. Purdue was looking at a first-and-10 at the Iowa 11, knocking on the door for another touchdown—which could very well have put the game out of reach at 21–3. But the Iowa defense found a way to keep the Boilers out of the end zone, and Purdue settled for a 22-yard field-goal attempt late in the first half.

This fateful field-goal attempt would change the momentum of the game. The attempt was blocked at the line of scrimmage by Sean Considine and scooped up by Antwan Allen, who darted down the right sideline for a touchdown to wake up the big crowd and send Iowa into the locker room with the all-important momentum on their side.

Purdue took the opening kickoff of the second half, but could not gain a first down and faced a fourth-and-six at their own 16 before bringing out the punt team. The punt was blocked by the Hawkeyes, and Jermire Roberts fell on the loose ball in the end zone. The Hawkeyes' second big play on special teams (and second special-teams touchdown) put Iowa in front 17–14 with 13 minutes left in the third quarter.

Although Purdue was unable to score in the third quarter, the Boilermakers were able to win the field-position battle. Purdue had Iowa pinned inside the 5-yard line to begin its second possession of the half. Two running plays gained only two yards of breathing room, which set up a third-and-eight from Iowa's own 5-yard line and a historic play that actually made the initial draft of top 50 plays, but upon further thought, was removed in favor of the game-winning touchdown, which coincidentally would end up being produced by the same passing combination.

With their backs clearly against the proverbial wall, Banks found Clark on what appeared to be an innocent short pass in the left flat. Clark spun as he caught the pass just a few yards downfield, then turned upfield, hurdled a Purdue defender who was on the ground, and simultaneously avoided another who made a diving attempt at a tackle—all while tiptoeing the sideline, just staying inbounds. The one "move" was enough to put Clark into the secondary all by his lonesome.

DALLAS CLARK

Dallas Clark is a true Hawkeyes success story. Clark made the team as a walk-on linebacker in 2000, but was converted to tight end during the 2001 spring practice. What a move that turned out to be! In 2002, Clark enjoyed one of the greatest years of any tight end in school history. He had 43 receptions for 742 yards and four touchdowns. He was a consensus All-American and won the John Mackey Award as the nation's best tight end in 2002.

Clark left Iowa after his junior season and was drafted by the Indianapolis Colts in the first round, where he has developed into one of Peyton Manning's favorite targets. Clark won the Super Bowl with the Colts following the 2006 season and in February 2008 signed a multiyear deal with that Colts that reportedly made him the highest-paid tight end in the NFL.

GAME DETAILS

Iowa 31 • Purdue 28

Date: October 5, 2002

Location: Kinnick Stadium, Iowa City, Iowa

Attendance: 70,397

Weather: Sunny, 60 degrees

We found a way to win. Good teams find a way, even when they're not at their best, and today, with all due respect to Purdue, we weren't at our best.

—IOWA COACH KIRK FERENTZ

Box Score:

Purdue	7	7	0	14	**28**
Iowa	3	7	14	7	**31**

Scoring:

IA   Kaeding 51-yard FG

PUR   Standeford 61-yard pass from Orton (Lacevic PAT)

PUR   Void 1-yard run (Lacevic PAT)

IA   Allen 85-yard return of blocked FG (Kaeding PAT)

IA   Roberts recovered blocked punt in end zone (Kaeding PAT)

IA   Clark 95-yard pass from Banks (Kaeding PAT)

PUR   Kirsch 16-yard run (Lacevic PAT)

PUR   Goldsberry 2-yard run (Lacevic PAT)

IA   Clark 7-yard pass from Banks (Kaeding PAT)

Ninety-five yards later, Clark was in the end zone for a 24–14 Hawkeyes lead. It was his first catch of the entire game and it matched the longest touchdown pass play in school history.

During the last 15 minutes of game time, everything was going the Hawks' way and there seemed to be no way they could lose. Yet there was still over a quarter to play, and Purdue certainly had the offensive firepower to come back.

Purdue's comeback would be led by freshman backup quarterback Brandon Kirsch, who took over after Orton suffered a head injury. Kirsch was more of a run threat than Orton, and the Iowa defense had some trouble adjusting. A 16-yard touchdown run by Kirsch capped a long 13-play drive covering 89 yards,

which pulled Purdue to within 24–21 with just over 10 minutes to play in the fourth quarter.

A three-and-out by the Iowa offense gave the ball right back to Purdue. Kirsch again led the Boilers downfield for another touchdown and Purdue regained the lead it had lost earlier in the half. Purdue now led 28–24 with 5:40 remaining in the fourth quarter.

On the ensuing drive, the Iowa offense was finally able to string together multiple first downs on a drive and move the ball into Purdue territory. But the drive stalled on a sack on fourth-and-seven from the Purdue 40.

The Boilers took over in Iowa territory leading by four points, with just three minutes left in the fourth quarter. Purdue attempted to run out the clock, but

BANKS TO CLARK BAILS OUT HAWKS AGAINST PURDUE

The game was on the line as Iowa faced a fourth-and-goal from the 7-yard line in the final two minutes. The play call from offensive coordinator Ken O'Keefe was masterful. Dallas Clark (44) lined up as tight end on the left side. Quarterback Brad Banks (7) lined up under center with one running back in the backfield, two receivers split wide right, and one wide left. The slot receiver on the right went in motion to the left before the snap. Each of the wide receiver's patterns took them toward the left portion of the end zone, leaving the right side of the end zone empty. At the snap, Clark delayed a few seconds at the line of scrimmage, as if he were going to stay in to help protect the quarterback. Then, suddenly, Clark broke off the line of scrimmage and moved across the Purdue secondary to the right side of the end zone. The delay at the line of scrimmage was just enough so that the linebacker who was responsible for staying with Clark could not keep up with him as he drifted to the right portion of the end zone. There was no help because all other Purdue defenders had drifted to the opposite side of the end zone or were blitzing. The offensive line held off the Purdue blitz just long enough to allow Banks (who took the hit as he released) to loft a high, soft floater to Clark, who safely secured the ball in the end zone to provide the winning points on a memorable afternoon at Kinnick Stadium.

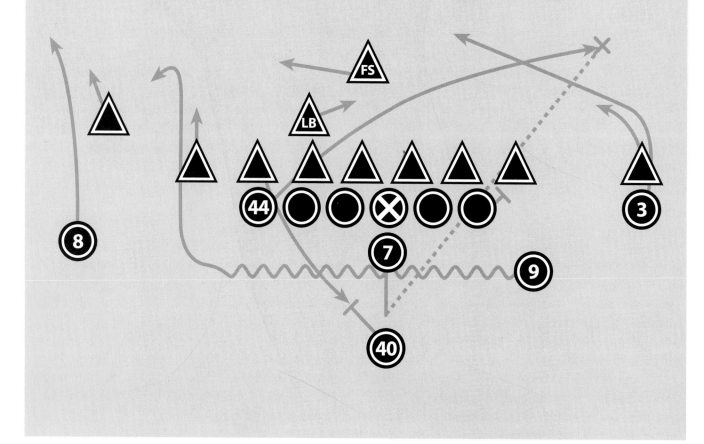

Iowa tight end Dallas Clark secures the game-winning touchdown pass late in the fourth quarter against Purdue at Kinnick Stadium on October 5, 2002. *Photo courtesy* The Cedar Rapids Gazette

three straight rushing plays could not gain a first down and the Boilers were forced to punt.

Iowa again took over with poor field position, this time at their own 13-yard line, with just 2:16 to play in the fourth quarter. With the game now on the line, the offense went to work and produced their best sustained drive of the entire afternoon. Banks scrambled for 44 yards on the first play, and the Boilers were immediately on their heels. Two pass plays to Maurice Brown and Clark, netting a total of 34 yards, put the ball on the Purdue 9 for a first-and-goal to go. But two rushing plays and an incomplete pass left Iowa with a fourth-and-goal from the 7. After calling timeout to strategize,

Banks found Clark open in the right end zone for the game-winning score.

But following the pattern that had been established all afternoon, Purdue still had 1:02 on the clock and was not finished. Kirsch had the Boilermakers driving to a potential game-tying field goal. Purdue penetrated as far as the Iowa 25-yard line, when a pass to Taylor Stubblefield deflected off his hands and into the hands of Iowa's Adolphus Shelton. The sellout homecoming crowd could finally breathe easy; the interception had put the exclamation point on one of the most dramatic Hawkeye wins in recent memory.

October 5, 1985

6 BOOTLEG IS THE RIGHT TONIC FOR SPARTANS

Chuck Long's touchdown run in the closing minute clinches a comeback win versus Michigan State

Very much like the 2002 edition of the Hawkeyes, the 1985 group was a star-studded bunch on both offense and defense. Both teams were also led by quarterbacks who would finish second in the Heisman voting: Brad Banks in 2002 and Chuck Long in 1985. Also, the similarities between the Purdue game in 2002 and the Michigan State game in 1985 are downright eerie. Both games were early-season Big Ten matchups—in fact, both were played on the same date, October 5. Both games saw multiple momentum swings and lead changes during the game and both games were won by Iowa very late in the fourth quarter on memorable plays by a Hawkeyes quarterback. Perhaps there was even more riding on the 1985 game because at the time the Hawkeyes held the No. 1 ranking in both national polls, the first time that had happened since 1960.

Iowa started quickly, jumping out to a 13–0 lead in the first half before Michigan State woke up and scored 24 unanswered points to grab the lead. Then, in the third quarter, it was Iowa's turn again; the Hawks put up 15 unanswered points to take a 28–24 lead. But Michigan State wouldn't say die. They put together a gritty 89-yard touchdown drive in the fourth quarter to grab a 31–28 lead that held until the last minute of the game.

The historic play capped a drive that began with 4:01 left in the game at the Michigan State 21-yard line. Iowa's All-American quarterback Long completed six of seven passes on the drive to get the Hawkeyes in position at the Michigan State 11-yard line. From there, running back Ronnie Harmon ran off tackle for seven yards and around the end for two more. However, on the last run, Harmon could not get out of bounds, which forced Iowa to spend its last timeout facing a third-and-one from the Michigan State 2-yard line with 31 seconds on the Kinnick Stadium clock.

The play dialed up by Coach Hayden Fry was called "fake 47 sucker pass." It called for Long to fake a handoff to the running back, then bootleg right for a run

> That might have been the greatest fake of all time in college football. I believe I could have scored on that one, and I'm really slow.
>
> —IOWA HAYDEN FRY

Iowa quarterback Chuck Long prepares to fake the handoff to Ronnie Harmon at the 2-yard line in the final minute against Michigan State at Kinnick Stadium on October 5, 1985.
Copyright: University of Iowa—CMP Photographic Service

or pass option. The fake handoff to Harmon was bought by half the people from Iowa City to East Lansing. The Spartans converged on Harmon as he dove into the center of the line, and Long had a cakewalk into the end zone around right end. The left cornerback sold out to stop the apparent run, leaving the left side of the defense completely undefended.

For dramatic effect, Long held the ball high over his head for all to see as he crossed the goal line. There were 27 seconds left on the clock, and Houghtlin's extra point extended the lead to 35–31.

If Long had not been able to score or get out of bounds on the play, Iowa would have faced a fourth down with no timeouts remaining. "I probably shouldn't say this," Fry said, "but we already called the next play. We were going to put our field-goal players on the field and fake it instead of going for the tie. Thank gosh we didn't have to. We were going for it all the way. I didn't want to tie our first game in the Big Ten."

Early on, it had appeared that the game with the Spartans would turn out just like Iowa's first three games of the season, which were lopsided Iowa wins. Long connected on a 60-yard touchdown strike to Robert Smith to give Iowa a 7–0 lead five minutes into the game. Iowa's second score came on a 17-yard pass play from Long to tight end Mike Flagg, who carried several Spartan defenders into the end zone on the play to make it 13–0.

But Michigan State stormed back on the strength of sophomore tailback Lorenzo White, who chalked up an amazing 226 yards rushing on 39 attempts, which included two touchdowns. However, White was forced out of the game with an ankle injury early in the fourth quarter; he returned for one more rush on Michigan State's last possession.

Iowa didn't fare much better slowing down his replacement. Freshman Craig Johnson racked up 89 yards on the ground on 10 carries, including a 25-yard touchdown run that put the Spartans ahead in the fourth quarter. Michigan State's passing game, led by backup Bobby McAllister, was also impressive. McAllister was 18 for 27 for 275 yards and no interceptions.

SWEET REDEMPTION

Chuck Long's touchdown at the end of this game was sweet redemption for a bitter loss to Michigan State the prior year. In those days, teams played back-to-back games at the same stadium. In the 1984 game—also at Kinnick Stadium—Iowa was denied by Michigan State on a two-point conversion try that would have secured a late victory. On the decisive play, the Spartans defense stopped backup quarterback Mark Vlasic's bootleg and Michigan State came away with the 17–16 win, costing the Hawkeyes a shot at a higher-tier bowl.

Long's swan song at Iowa was his memorable 1985 season, which was good enough for a second-place finish in the Heisman Trophy balloting. Long had 1,464 points to Bo Jackson's 1,509. It was the closest balloting in the history of the Heisman Trophy.

This game also saw a very rare punt on first down called by Hayden Fry. Iowa was pinned at their own 2-yard line at the end of the third quarter, but with a stiff wind at their back, the punt sailed 70 yards and helped to change field position around and build momentum toward an eventual Iowa win.

GAME DETAILS

Iowa 35 • Michigan State 31

Date: October 5, 1985

Location: Kinnick Stadium, Iowa City, Iowa

Attendance: 66,044

Box Score:

Michigan St.	0	10	14	7	**31**
Iowa	7	6	15	7	**35**

Scoring:

IA   Smith 60-yard pass from Long (Houghtlin PAT)

IA   Flagg 17-yard pass from Long (Houghtlin PAT Failed)

MSU   Caudell 32-yard FG

MSU   Rison 50-yard pass from McAllister (Caudell PAT)

MSU   White 23-yard run (Caudell PAT)

MSU   White 1-yard run (Caudell PAT)

IA   Smith 3-yard pass from Long (2-pt. conv. – Flagg, 2-yard pass from Long)

IA   Flagg 12-yard pass from Long (Houghtlin PAT)

MSU   C. Johnson 25-yard run (Caudell PAT)

IA   Long 2-yard run (Houghtlin PAT)

It was the Iowa offense that saved the day. Long completed 30 of 39 passes for four touchdowns and 380 yards. His 30 completions improved upon his own school record of 29, set in the Freedom Bowl against Texas in 1984.

Following Iowa's last touchdown by Long, Michigan State started the last drive at their own 38-yard line and gained 23 yards on two plays. But Iowa safety Devon Mitchell tipped McAllister's pass away from flanker Mark Ingram in the end zone, and Iowa had earned its first league win of the 1985 season and maintained its number one ranking in dramatic fashion.

> **I**t was a gutsy call by Coach Fry because I either had to get in [the end zone] or get out of bounds.
>
> —IOWA QUARTERBACK CHUCK LONG

THE GREAT SPARTAN FAKE

With their No. 1 national ranking in serious jeopardy late in the fourth quarter against a gutsy Michigan State team, Iowa faced third-and-goal from the MSU 2-yard line with 31 seconds left and no timeouts remaining. Quarterback Chuck Long (16) took the snap from under center and faked a handoff to versatile halfback Ronnie Harmon (31), but kept the ball on his hip hidden from the Michigan State defense. Harmon acted as if he had the ball while charging straight into the middle of the defense. The entire Spartans defense converged on Harmon as he dove into the line. Meanwhile, Long rolled right with the ball and had seemingly all day to stroll easily into the end zone, holding the ball high for all to see well before he crossed the goal line. The Kinnick Stadium crowd went nuts as the Hawks retained their No. 1 ranking.

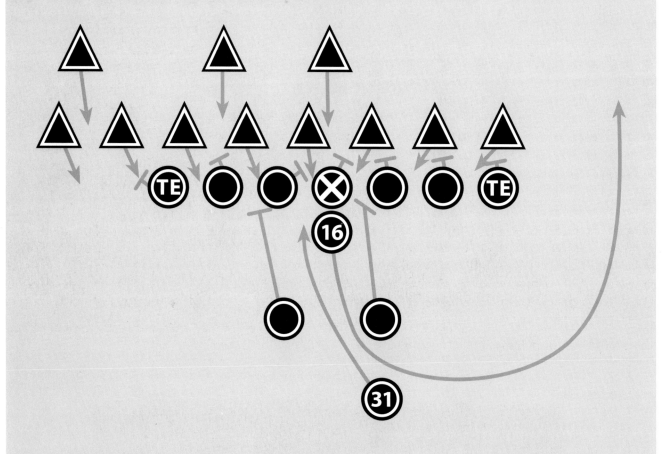

Iowa's Ronnie Harmon (31) dives into the center of the line, drawing most of the Michigan State team, while Chuck Long, left, bootlegs to his right for the winning score. *Photo courtesy* The Cedar Rapids Gazette

What a fantastic football game....Whew, I feel like I've been run over by a truck. I think the good Lord was smiling on us today.

—IOWA COACH HAYDEN FRY

January 1, 1957

 # Ploen's Rosy Touchdown Run

Kenny Ploen's 49-yard scamper leads to victory in the Hawkeyes' first trip to Pasadena

Iowa's first-ever appearance in the Rose Bowl came against Pacific Coast Conference champion Oregon State on New Year's Day 1957. It was the first Rose Bowl matchup of teams that had met in the regular season—Iowa had bested the Beavers, 14–13, in a closely contested game in Iowa City in early October.

The 1956 Hawkeyes were known more for their stingy defense than for a flashy offense coming into the game, having shut out four opponents during the regular season. However, it was the offense that would awaken in Pasadena. The Hawks were nine-point favorites, but ended up cruising to an unexpected easy win. The offense racked up five touchdowns on the way to a 35–19 triumph.

The Iowa win continued the Big Ten's dominance in the Rose Bowl (which began in 1946) against the Pacific Coast Conference. With the Hawkeyes' victory, the Big Ten had won 10 of the 11 games in the series.

Loyal Iowa fans had waited many, many years for the school's first bowl appearance,

but an estimated crowd of 15,000 Iowa fans had to wait only a few minutes for Iowa to light up the scoreboard once the game began. Many in the crowd of more than 97,000 were still settling into their seats when Oregon State coughed up the football in the game's opening moments. Iowa's Frank Gilliam was Johnny-on-the-spot, recovering the Oregon State fumble at the Iowa 40-yard line.

The Iowa offense advanced 11 yards on four plays to the Beavers' 49-yard line, setting up the play of the game. It was second-and-12 to go. From the wing-T right formation, All-American quarterback Kenny Ploen took the snap and found a hole on the right side of the Iowa line. Sprung by a block from fullback Don Dobrino, Ploen kept the ball down the right sideline. He was almost knocked off balance at the Oregon State 25, but he just managed to keep his knee from touching the turf by keeping his balance with his other hand. Regaining his balance, Ploen used blocks from teammates Dick Klein and Jim Gibbons, who took Oregon State's last hope, Tom Berry, out of the play.

Ploen then had a clear path to the end zone to complete a dazzling 49-yard touchdown run that gave Iowa early momentum.

Things would go from bad to worse for the Beavers when another fumble turned the ball back over to Iowa. The Hawkeyes promptly took the ball 66 yards in just four plays, extending the lead to 14–0 with not even half the first quarter in the books. Dobrino turned from blocker to runner and delivered the key play on the drive, a 37-yard romp down to the 9-yard line. Collins Hagler finished the drive off on a nine-yard touchdown run on the very next play.

Ploen was forced to leave the game later in the first half with a knee injury that would keep him out of the game until the second half. It was a potentially devastating blow to the Hawkeyes because Ploen led the team in rushing, passing, and scoring.

Oregon State eventually got their offense on track to score the next touchdown to pull to within 14–6. The point-after attempt by John Clarke was blocked by Iowa, and the score remained 14–6. However, Iowa was able to grab some momentum back on a five-yard touchdown run around left end to make it 21–6 at halftime. The score came on a drive led by backup quarterback Randy Duncan, demonstrating that Iowa could score without their first-string quarterback and fearless leader, Ploen.

Iowa put the game out of reach with a little razzle-dazzle on their first possession of the second half. Ploen, who had reentered the game for the start of the second half, handed off to Dobrino, who handed off to Hagler. Hagler would take the ball on a reverse 66 yards for the score. He was able

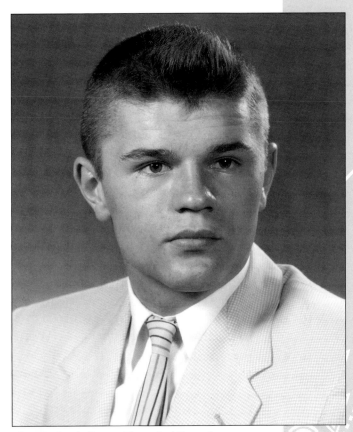

Quarterback Kenny Ploen led Iowa to a victory in its first-ever Rose Bowl appearance on January 1, 1957, against Oregon State. His spectacular 49-yard touchdown run gave Iowa an early lead it would never relinquish and helped earn him game MVP honors. *Copyright: University of Iowa—CMP Photographic Service*

to break away from the supposedly faster Beaver defensive backs near midfield and was practically untouched on his way to the end zone. It was Hagler's second touchdown of the game and after the successful point-after attempt, Iowa now led it 28–6.

Oregon State threw various new

PLOEN'S ROSY RUN

Quarterback Kenny Ploen (11) took the snap and faked a handoff to fullback Don Dobrino (20), who continued to the right side of the formation to throw a block that would help spring Ploen around right end and into the Oregon State secondary. Near the line of scrimmage, he faked a pass downfield to keep the Beavers defense honest, but continued to run, with no Oregon State defender laying a hand on him until he got 10 yards downfield. He broke a tackle at the Oregon State 40-yard line, got a block at the 33-yard line from his right end (87), almost losing his balance in the process. Barely staying on his feet, Ploen broke into the clear along the right sideline on the strength of blocks (near the 20-yard line) from teammates Jim Gibbons and Dick Klein. Ploen then cut back inside and from there had an easy stroll into the end zone to give Iowa its first-ever points in a Rose Bowl game. It was a great individual effort, but also required several downfield blocks from teammates to execute. In all, the play covered 49 yards and sent Iowa on its way to a convincing win over Oregon State in the 1957 Rose Bowl.

wrinkles at Iowa in an attempt to stay in the game. The gimmicks included having both speedy tailbacks Joe Francis and Paul Lowe in the backfield at the same time. The Beavers also used a fullback flanker and threw passes to the fullbacks for the first time. The results perhaps kept the game's final score somewhat respectable, but Iowa was never seriously threatened after taking the early 14–0 lead.

Ploen returned triumphantly in the second half to throw a perfect 16-yard touchdown pass to Gibbons on a fourth-down play in the fourth quarter, capping the Iowa scoring. Ploen would connect on nine of 10 passes on the day for 83 yards. Ploen, a native of Clinton, Iowa, earned the Most Valuable Player award in the 1957 Rose Bowl for his rushing and passing performance—this despite missing a good portion of the first half with the knee injury. Iowa's Bob Prescott was a perfect five for five on point-after attempts in the game.

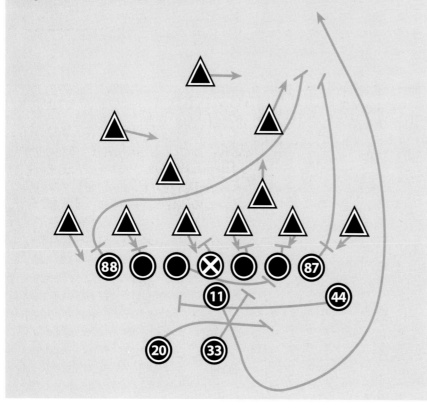

Game Details

Iowa 35 • Oregon State 19

Date: January 1, 1957

Location: Rose Bowl, Pasadena, California

Attendance: 97,126

Significance: Rose Bowl

Box Score:

Iowa	14	7	7	7	35
Oregon St.	0	6	6	7	19

Scoring:

IA	Ploen 49-yard run (Prescott PAT)
IA	Hagler 9-yard run (Prescott PAT)
OSU	Berry 3-yard run (kick failed)
IA	Happel 5-yard run (Prescott PAT)
IA	Hagler 66-yard run (Prescott PAT)
OSU	Beamer 1-yard run (kick failed)
IA	Gibbons 16-yard pass from Ploen (Prescott PAT)
OSU	Hammack 35-yard pass from Francis (Beamer run)

Game Ball Goes to Calvin Jones' Family

The team decided to send the game ball to Talithia Jones, the mother of Calvin Jones, the former Hawkeyes All-American player on the 1954 and 1955 teams who tragically was killed in a plane crash near Vancouver, British Columbia, three weeks before the Rose Bowl, on December 9, 1956. The crash took the lives of 59 passengers and a crew of three. There were no survivors, making it, at the time, the worst air accident in Canada's history.

Coach Evashevski called Jones "the greatest lineman I ever coached." Former teammate and future Iowa Coach Bob Commings commented that "Cal was the greatest football player I ever knew, and there's no two ways about it." Jones was the captain of the 1955 Iowa team, was a consensus All-America selection in both 1954 and 1955, and won the Outland Trophy as the best interior lineman in 1955. He had just finished his first season with the Winnipeg Blue Bombers of the Canadian Football League (CFL) at the time of the crash. Jones was in Vancouver to play in the CFL All Star Game. In a tragic twist of fate, he was initially scheduled to fly back to Winnipeg together with his coach, Bud Grant, on an earlier flight. Grant said that Jones reported he was unable to get ready in time and instead planned to catch a flight later that evening—the one that crashed.

November 11, 1939

4 KINNICK RUN KNOCKS OUT IRISH

The legend of the 1939 Ironmen grows as a four-yard touchdown run vaults Iowa past unbeaten and top-ranked Notre Dame

Although Nile Kinnick had enjoyed a tremendous 1939 season prior to facing Notre Dame, it was his performance against Notre Dame that really got the attention of the nation and was instrumental in his winning the Heisman Trophy. Notre Dame came in 6–0 and ranked No. 1 in the nation, having lost but once in the last 18 games. The 1939 clash between the two teams was the first since Iowa's stunning 10–7 upset of Knute Rockne's team in 1921. In fact, the Notre Dame captain of the 1921 team was right end Eddie Anderson, who in 1939 was in his first year at the helm of the Iowa program. To underscore the difference a college football coach can make, it must be noted that the 1939 Iowa team returned almost all of the same key players from a 1938 team that posted a woeful 1–6–1 overall record. Under Anderson's direction, the turnaround in 1939 led to a much improved 6–1–1 overall record. The 1939 Notre Dame team was coached by Elmer Layden, fullback on the famous "Four Horsemen" backfield at Notre Dame.

As in many of the prior games during the 1939 season, Iowa forged a 7–6 victory against all odds on the strength of Kinnick's kicking, running, and passing. Note that "kicking" was listed first on purpose; the game was a brutal, hard-nosed defensive battle on both sides that saw Iowa attempt 16 punts on the day.

Kinnick's punting performance alone was an epic contribution. On 16 punts, he amassed a total of 731 yards, for an average of almost 46 yards per punt. The 16 punts and 731 total punt yards are school records that still stand today. On the strength of Kinnick's punting, Iowa won the battle of field position time after time.

The game's most memorable play for the Hawkeyes was actually set up by a wild sequence of three total turnovers over two consecutive plays—two by Notre Dame and one by Iowa. The second of these three turnovers appeared as though it would cost Iowa yet another scoring opportunity. It was late in the first half and Notre Dame had the ball near midfield. An interception by Kinnick of a forward pass thrown by Harry

Halfback Nile Kinnick scored Iowa's only touchdown and also drop-kicked the extra point that would prove to be the margin of victory in a one-point win over unbeaten Notre Dame at Iowa Field on November 11, 1939. *Copyright: University of Iowa—CMP Photographic Service*

Stevenson gave Iowa the ball first-and-10 at the Irish 35-yard line.

To that point in the game, the Iowa running attack could only be characterized as feeble. Thinking the pass was the best option, on the very next play quarterback Al Couppee called for a long Kinnick pass. Kinnick's intended target in the end zone was fullback Bill Green. However, Notre Dame's Steve Sitko was there to make the interception. Sitko was looking for a big return, and he elected to run the ball out of the end zone. However, as he crossed his own 5-yard line, Iowa's Bruno Andruska took Sitko's legs out, forcing a fumble. Just to be absolutely sure they had it, both Buzz Dean and Dick Evans covered the loose ball

at the Notre Dame 4-yard line with only 40 seconds left in the first half.

Iowa attempted two running plays over the right side of the Iowa line for no gain. Although Iowa typically ran a no-huddle offense, they were having difficulty moving the ball on the first two plays, so Couppee called for a huddle on third down. It was one of only a handful of huddles called during the entire year.

The play that was called was a run to the left side off tackle. However, Kinnick, who normally lined up at left halfback, was lined up as the right halfback on the play. As Iowa came out of the huddle with Kinnick at right halfback, the ball was quickly snapped directly to Kinnick.

The Notre Dame defense may not have realized that Kinnick was not lined up in his usual spot. By the time the Irish knew what was happening, Iowa rookies Wally Bergstrom and Ken Pettit had opened a wide hole for Kinnick over the left side. Kinnick was met at the goal line by a Notre Dame defender, but he was able to power into the end zone, holding the ball in his left hand to protect sore ribs on his right side with his free right hand. Kinnick then drop-kicked the crucial extra point, giving the Hawkeyes a 7–0 lead.

Iowa would defend the 7–0 lead into the fourth quarter. However, Notre Dame was driving as the fourth quarter began, reaching the Iowa 10-yard line as the teams changed ends to begin the final quarter. Runs by Harry Stevenson and Milt Piepul from there would forge Notre Dame into the end zone for their only touchdown of the game.

Everyone's attention then turned to Notre Dame kicker Lou Zontini as he warmed up his kicking foot before the extra point attempt. The snap and hold were good, but the attempt sailed wide. A huge emotional release could be felt throughout the stadium as Iowa maintained the lead by the slimmest of margins.

From that point, both defenses took over, as neither team was able to get into scoring position the rest of the game. Notre Dame's fate would be sealed on Kinnick's 16th and final punt of the afternoon. With the line of scrimmage at the Iowa 34-yard line and just two minutes to play, under intense pressure with the game hanging in the balance, Kinnick boomed a punt over the head

NILE KINNICK: THE LEGEND

Secondhand information pertaining to Iowa's touchdown play suggests that Nile Kinnick wasn't the first option when the play was called in the huddle. But because Kinnick's backfield mate, Buzz Dean, had an injured shoulder, Couppee turned to Kinnick and asked if he could take it. He replied that he could but that he wanted to line up at right halfback and run left to protect injured ribs on his right side. Indeed, the famous photograph of Kinnick crossing the goal line shows him with the ball in his left hand, protecting his right side with the other.

One account of Iowa's famous touchdown suggests that Coach Eddie Anderson was screaming at Couppee as the play was called in the huddle not to give the ball to Kinnick, because everyone in the stadium knew it was going to him.

After joining the Navy, Kinnick was deployed to the *U.S.S. Lexington* in late May 1943. His life was tragically cut short in an airplane crash off the coast of Venezuela on June 2, 1943. Kinnick's plane encountered engine difficulty while on a routine training flight and he was forced to prematurely return to the carrier. However, the condition of the engine deteriorated quickly. Kinnick chose not to land on the deck of the *Lexington*, knowing that it would endanger other planes on deck. He ditched in the water and although the rescue party arrived quickly, neither the plane nor Kinnick could be found.

After years of reluctance, not wanting to have their son singled out as a hero among the many thousands of wartime casualties, the Kinnick family finally gave in and Iowa's football stadium was renamed in Kinnick's honor in 1972; it is the only stadium in the country named after a Heisman Trophy winner. Kinnick's No. 24 jersey is one of only two retired numbers at Iowa (Calvin Jones's No. 62 is the other).

Nile Kinnick is honored before each Big Ten football game to this very day. His likeness is etched onto the coin that is flipped by the officials to begin every Big Ten football game.

GAME DETAILS

Iowa 7 • Notre Dame 6

Date: November 11, 1939

Location: Iowa Stadium, Iowa City, Iowa

Attendance: 47,000 (est.)

Box Score:

Notre Dame	0	0	0	6	**6**
Iowa	0	7	0	0	**7**

Scoring:
IA   Kinnick 4-yard run (Kinnick PAT)
ND   Piepul 4-yard run (PAT failed)

of the Irish return man and out of bounds at the Notre Dame 5-yard line.

Notre Dame was able to move the ball out of the shadow of their own goal posts, but were thrown for a huge 24-yard loss in the final minute as "Iron Mike" Enich broke through the Irish line and jumped on Stevenson just before he could release his pass downfield. The last desperate attempt by Notre Dame from their own 4-yard line ended the game. Iowa had won another dramatic victory in a season full of memorable games.

In true Ironmen fashion, only 15 Hawkeyes men saw game action. There were just two substitutions in the backfield and two line replacements. The ends, tackles, center, quarterback, and—of course—Kinnick went from opening whistle to final gun against arguably the best team Iowa would face the entire season.

Nile Kinnick (left) and Erwin Prasse, offensive stars of the 1939 Iowa team, pause with the Floyd of Rosedale Trophy, awarded to the victor of the annual game between the Hawkeyes and the University of Minnesota. *Copyright: University of Iowa—CMP Photographic Services.*

October 19, 1985

NUMBER ONE OUTKICKS NUMBER TWO

Rob Houghtlin drills a 29-yard field goal as time expires and pandemonium erupts at Kinnick Stadium

Mention "The Kick" to almost any Iowa Hawkeyes football fan, and they most likely will know exactly what you are referring to. There has never been a more famous 29-yard field goal in Iowa football history.

The 1985 game against Michigan had almost everything anyone could want in a college football matchup: No. 1 versus No. 2, a tremendous coaching matchup in Iowa's Hayden Fry against Michigan's Bo Schembechler; a potent Iowa offense (the Hawkeyes led the nation in scoring) against a stingy Michigan defense that had not allowed a touchdown in the last four games; controversial officiating; multiple lead changes; and one incredibly dramatic last-second finish.

The buildup to the game had all the hype one would expect with a No. 1 versus No. 2 matchup. Unlike recent times, where the No. 1 and No. 2 ranked teams meet in the BCS championship game at the end of each bowl season, this dream matchup was more rare in 1985. And this was one of the few cases where the actual game lived up

to the pregame hype. Additional glamour was added to the game because the late-afternoon start required that portable lights be brought in for the first time ever at Kinnick Stadium.

Iowa was able to move the ball on the Wolverines' defense throughout the day, and the final offensive stats certainly showed that. Iowa ran 84 offensive plays to Michigan's 41, the Hawks outgained Michigan 422–182, and they had the advantage in time of possession: 38:05, compared to Michigan's 21:55.

But the key was that Michigan kept Iowa out of the end zone the entire game. Nevertheless, Iowa felt the officials missed a clear touchdown early in the second quarter with the game still scoreless.

Most of the damage that day was done by quarterback Chuck Long and running back Ronnie Harmon, and this drive was no different. The Hawkeyes' drive reached the Michigan 18, where they faced a third down. Long scrambled away from the rush and quickly tossed the ball deep into the end zone where Scott Helverson leaped high in

I knew it was good from the beginning, like a golfer who knows he hits a good drive. After I watched the ball go through, I turned around to signal good and all I remember is people jumping up and down.

—ROB HOUGHTLIN

Rob Houghtlin connects on the game-winning kick against Michigan in October 1985.
Copyright: University of Iowa—CMP Photographic Service

the air to grab the ball over the Michigan defenders. Although television replays indicated that Helverson got the required one foot inbounds upon landing, the officials ruled after some delay that Helverson had landed out of bounds.

There were staunch protests from Iowa, but the play stood. Unlike today, there was no way to correct the call back then by using instant replay. Iowa was forced to accept the call and continue the fight. The Hawkeyes settled for a 35-yard field goal by Houghtlin to give Iowa the first points of the game.

Unfortunately for Iowa, the momentum of getting the game's first points was quickly overshadowed on the ensuing kickoff, as Michigan's Tom Wilcher took the kickoff back 60 yards to set the Michigan offense up in Iowa territory. Michigan cashed in on the good

Rob Houghtlin reflects on his impending last second field-goal attempt that, if good, would give No. 1 Iowa a 12–10 victory over No. 2 Michigan at Kinnick Stadium on October 19, 1985. *Photo courtesy* The Cedar Rapids Gazette

GAME DETAILS

Iowa 12 • Michigan 10

Date: October 19, 1985

Location: Kinnick Stadium, Iowa City, Iowa

Attendance: 66,350

Weather: 60 degrees, overcast

Box Score:

Michigan	0	7	0	3	**10**
Iowa	0	6	0	6	**12**

Scoring:

IA	Houghtlin 35-yard FG
MI	White 5-yard pass from Harbaugh (Gillette PAT)
IA	Houghtlin 27-yard FG
IA	Houghtlin 36-yard FG
MI	Gillette 40-yard FG
IA	Houghtlin 29-yard FG

field position with the game's only touchdown, but more controversy aimed at the officials erupted from the Iowa side during the drive.

Several times, Michigan quarterback Jim Harbaugh asked for and was granted permission to walk away from the line and halt the 25-second clock because of "excessive crowd noise." The rule was a terrible one because it relied completely on the referee's judgment as to what was considered "excessive."

Aided by these calls by the referee, on third-and-goal from the Iowa 5-yard line, Harbaugh scrambled away from the Iowa pursuit and shoveled a pass to fullback Gerald White for a touchdown. The successful point-after attempt gave Michigan the lead 7–3. Iowa drew to within a single point at halftime on another short field goal by Houghtlin, this one a 27-yarder.

Both defenses exerted themselves in the third quarter, and neither team put up any points. But an Iowa drive that began late in the third quarter ended with 14:20 to play in the fourth quarter on Houghtlin's third field goal of the day—this one from 36 yards out. Iowa had its first lead since the second quarter at 9–7.

But again Michigan took advantage of good field position following the kickoff to answer the Iowa score. On a drive that began at their own 37, Michigan advanced into Iowa territory but was thwarted at the 23. They had to settle for a 40-yard field goal to reclaim the lead 10–9 with 10:55 to play.

Michigan was looking to put the game away with six minutes left to play. Facing a third-and-two at their own 35, Iowa All-American Larry Station broke through the Michigan line to drop tailback Jamie Morris for a

A Historic Celebration

One of the prices paid for the victory was some collateral damage sustained during the wild postgame celebration. Seven players were hurt in the postgame pileup following the winning kick. The most seriously injured was the holder, backup quarterback Mark Vlasic, who missed the next two games. Fortunately for Vlasic, he would go on to post a nice career of his own after Chuck Long graduated following the 1985 season. Vlasic was promoted to starting quarterback for the 1986 season and was named one of five team captains that year. He helped lead Iowa to a 9–3 season, including the dramatic Holiday Bowl win over San Diego State. Vlasic was also an academic All-Big Ten selection in 1986. Following his time in Iowa City, he spent time in the NFL with the San Diego Chargers and Kansas City Chiefs in the late 1980s and early 1990s.

Rob Houghtlin celebrates with teammates and fans following his field goal on the last play of the game that gave No. 1 Iowa the win over No. 2 Michigan in October 1985. *Photo courtesy* The Cedar Rapids Gazette

two-yard loss. Iowa regained possession following a 45-yard Michigan punt on their own 22-yard line with 5:27 remaining in the fourth quarter.

Once again led by the heroics of Long and Harmon, Iowa methodically drove downfield against the decorated Michigan defense. Long converted two third downs on the drive with passes to tight end Mike Flagg. Iowa again faced another third down from the Michigan 22, but a six-yard run by David Hudson kept the drive alive as darkness fell and the lights began to take full effect.

Iowa reached the Michigan 12-yard line, but was out of time. Hayden Fry called for timeout with two seconds showing on the clock, and it was now Houghtlin's turn to make Hawkeyes history.

The game was in the hands of a sophomore walk-on kicker with a sore leg that hadn't allowed him to practice in the weeks leading up to the game. Houghtlin quickly jogged onto the field to set up his tee, but Fry called him back over to the sideline to calm his nerves and try to keep him loose.

Then Iowa lined up for the kick—and Michigan called timeout to ice the kicker. According to Fry, Houghtlin confidently commented after the timeout that the Michigan strategy of icing him wasn't going to work. Iowa lined up again for the field goal, but Schembechler *again* called timeout. This time, Houghtlin came back over to the Iowa sideline and commented to Coach Fry that he would make this kick for his grandfather, who had died not long ago.

Again, the two teams prepared to line up for the game's final play. Houghtlin was hunched over his kicking tee in an apparent moment of prayer and reflection before kicking. He then hit the ball straight through the uprights and into the annals of Hawkeyes history.

As complete darkness fell on Kinnick Stadium that evening, the scoreboard blazed the final score for all to see: Iowa 12, Michigan 10. Security estimated that 30,000 people made their way to the field to celebrate the victory, in one of the wildest scenes ever inside the historic stadium.

In the huddle before Rob's kick, we were telling each other to block like crazy because Michigan would be coming 100 miles an hour. There must have been a pileup four feet high. I looked up as the ball was going through the uprights and my knees felt weak.

—IOWA TACKLE MIKE HAIGHT

November 14, 1987

Cook's Catch Tops OSU

Marv Cook's last-second touchdown converts an improbable fourth-and-23 and gives Iowa a thrilling win in Columbus

Perhaps numerous college teams have plays in their history affectionately referred to in generic terms like "The Kick" or "The Catch." Iowa is somewhat fortunate in that there have been two game-ending plays that could be referred to as "The Catch." One of them is yet to come in the countdown and the other checks in here at Number 2.

The Catch occurred in a stadium that had been (and continues to be) a house of horrors for Iowa: Ohio Stadium in Columbus, Ohio. Coming into the 1987 clash with the Buckeyes at the Big Horseshoe, Iowa had won just once in Columbus in the last 20 tries. The last win there had been way back in 1959 under coach Forest Evashevski.

Iowa had fallen behind by a 14–3 score midway through the second quarter on two touchdown receptions from quarterback Tom Tupa to flanker Everett Ross; the second play was good for 60 yards. But a nifty 50-yard touchdown run by Kevin Harmon got Iowa back in it. Rob Houghtlin kicked three field goals in the first half, with the third

coming from 22 yards out as the half expired to give Iowa 15–14 halftime lead.

The teams traded touchdowns in the third quarter. Late in the fourth quarter, it looked for all the world that the streak of futility in Columbus would continue for the Hawkeyes when the Buckeyes grabbed a 27–22 lead on a 14-yard touchdown run by freshman tailback Carlos Snow. The score came with just two minutes and 45 seconds to play.

Iowa's Harmon gave the Hawkeyes some hope with a 35-yard kickoff return, giving Iowa good field position. From that point, Iowa's junior quarterback, Chuck Hartlieb, went to work. Hartlieb connected on short passes to Rick Bayless and Mike Flagg. On the 14-yard pass play to Flagg, Ohio State drew a flag for having 12 men on the field, which tacked on a 15-yard penalty, moving the ball down to the Buckeyes' 30-yard line.

Things really started to get crazy from that point. First, there was a holding penalty against Iowa, then Ohio State tackle Ray Holliman nailed Hartlieb, forcing a fumble

Iowa tight end Marv Cook snags a pass from Chuck Hartlieb in the game's final seconds to cap a dramatic come-from-behind victory over Ohio State at Ohio Stadium in Columbus, Ohio, on November 14, 1987. *Copyright: University of Iowa—CMP Photographic Service*

that was recovered by fullback David Hudson way back at the Iowa 49-yard line. There sure aren't a ton of plays in the playbook to convert the second-and-31 that faced the Hawks. However, a 27-yard strike from Hartlieb to Marv Cook brought up a manageable third-and-four from the Buckeyes' 24-yard line. But, Kevin Harmon was stopped short on the third-down play, bringing up a critical fourth-and three play, with the game hanging in the balance. Another connection between Hartlieb and Cook kept the drive alive, and Iowa earned another set of downs from the Ohio State 15.

A relentless Ohio State defense kept coming. On the next play, Hartlieb was blindsided by defensive end Eric Kumerow for an eight-yard sack. Coach Fry was forced to use Iowa's final timeout to stop the clock with 47 seconds remaining.

Hartlieb would later admit that the punishment he received from Ohio State on the game's final drive had left him feeling a bit "woozy," which made the stunning turn of events at the end of the Iowa drive all the more incredible. The Hawkeyes were put in an even deeper

hole following a five-yard loss on a sweep. An incomplete pass on third down brought up a fourth-and-23 from the Ohio State 28-yard line with precious few ticks left (16 seconds, to be exact).

Hartlieb dropped back to pass and looked deep downfield to his left as long as he could to draw attention away from Cook, who was running a pattern down the right sideline in man-to-man coverage with the Ohio State strong safety. Although they had been successful on the blitz earlier in the drive, Ohio State chose to drop back into coverage rather than blitz. This allowed Hartlieb the time he needed for the patterns to develop—and to release the ball untouched.

Hartlieb threw the ball at Cook's back; Cook made a slight adjustment while the ball was in the air to turn inside toward the ball and come slightly back to meet it, as the strong safety's momentum took him downfield and away from Cook. Cook hauled the ball in at the 9-yard line, but he still had multiple Buckeyes defenders between him and the goal line.

Two Buckeyes converged on Cook as he approached

ON FURTHER REVIEW:

One of the Ohio State defenders that day in November 1987 was free safety Bo Pellini. Pellini would later serve as a graduate assistant at Iowa before working his way to the Nebraska head coaching position in 2008 after winning a national championship as LSU defensive coordinator during the 2007 season. Pellini firmly believed for years that Marv Cook had been brought down just short of the end zone. Replays confirmed a close play, but the officials who had the best view of all ruled it a touchdown.

Ironically, it was reported that coach Hayden Fry nearly substituted Mike Flagg for Cook before the

fateful final play, but ultimately changed his mind and opted for the smaller, faster Cook.

The bitter last-second defeat would prove to be the downfall of Ohio State coach Earle Bruce. The loss dropped the Buckeyes to an overall record of 5–4–1, 3–4 in the Big Ten. Bruce was fired two days after the game, though he did coach Ohio State to a season-ending victory over traditional rival Michigan the following week.

GAME DETAILS

Iowa 29 • Ohio State 27

Date: November 14, 1987

Location: Ohio Stadium, Columbus, Ohio

Attendance: 90,000

Weather: Sunny

Box Score:

Iowa	3	12	0	14	**29**
Ohio St.	7	7	7	6	**27**

Scoring:

OSU	Ross 24-yard pass from Tupa (Frantz PAT)
IA	Houghtlin 39-yard FG
OSU	Ross 60-yard pass from Tupa (Frantz PAT)
IA	Harmon 50-yard run (Hartlieb pass failed)
IA	Houghtlin 41-yard FG
IA	Houghtlin 22-yard FG
OSU	Ellis 20-yard pass from Tupa (Frantz PAT)
IA	Hudson 1-yard run (Houghtlin PAT)
OSU	Snow 14-yard run (Koch run failed)
IA	Cook 28-yard pass from Hartlieb (Houghtlin PAT)

> **I** didn't know for sure he was in. I was running downfield trying to get another play off.
>
> —IOWA QUARTERBACK CHUCK HARTLIEB

the end zone. They all collided together near the end zone, but Cook was just able to power across the plane of the goal line for the score as he fell to the ground. Had he not gotten into the end zone, it is doubtful that Iowa would have had time for another play—the score came with just six seconds left on the clock, and Iowa was out of timeouts. Houghtlin added the extra point to make the final score Iowa 29, Ohio State 27. The game-winning touchdown was the ninth time in the game that roommates Hartlieb and Cook had connected. The nine plays were good for 159 passing yards. Overall, Hartlieb finished the day with 20 of 37 for 333 yards. The stellar passing performance set a school record with his fourth 300-yard passing game of the 1987 season (in fact, Hartlieb would make it a total of five the next week against Minnesota).

> **I**'ve broadcast hundreds of football games in over 50 years, most of them Iowa games, and that tops my list of all-time great plays. The fact that it happened at Ohio State makes it all the more incredible.
>
> —VETERAN IOWA FOOTBALL BROADCASTER JIM ZABEL, OF WHO IN DES MOINES

COOK'S CLUTCH CATCH

It was fourth-and-forever from the Ohio State 28-yard line with just 16 seconds left on the clock and Iowa needed a touchdown or the game would end with yet another Hawkeye loss at the Big Horseshoe. Quarterback Chuck Hartlieb (8) took the snap from under center and dropped back to pass, looking initially to his left before turning to find tight end Marv Cook (84) down the right side. He had plenty of time to survey the field and follow through on a good throw to Cook, who caught the ball at the 9-yard line while shielding the defender from the ball with his body. The Ohio State defender fell down trying to defend the pass and Cook then turned inside, while two Ohio State defenders converged on him at the 2-yard line. But both defenders decided to tackle the big tight end high rather than cut him down low. He managed to drag the would-be tacklers across the goal line with him, just getting the ball across the plane as he fell to the ground.

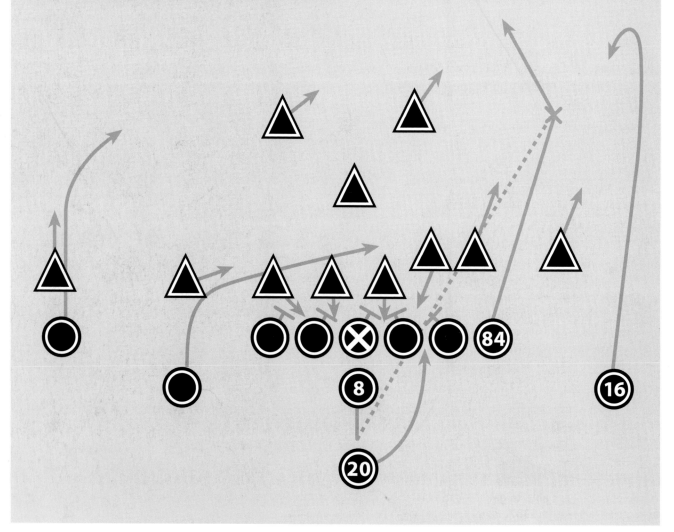

Marv Cook was just able to get the ball across the goal line in the final seconds to provide the winning points against Ohio State in 1987. *Photo courtesy* The Cedar Rapids Gazette

January 1, 2005

1 HOLLOWAY'S HAUL STUNS LSU

Drew Tate finds an unlikely touchdown target and Iowa steals the Capital One Bowl from the defending national champs

It couldn't have been a more perfect setting for the greatest play in the history of Iowa Hawkeyes football. It occurred on the most important day of the entire calendar year as far as college football fans are concerned—the pinnacle, the ultimate college football day: New Year's Day. Just for dramatic effect, the Hawkeyes waited until several other New Year's Day games occurring earlier in the day had been completed. At 3:36 PM Iowa City time, when Drew Tate took the final snap of the game and dropped back to pass, the Capital One Bowl game between Iowa and LSU was the only college football game in progress. Millions across the country were tuning in to ABC to view the game; perhaps some were also tuning in to catch the pregame show for a historic nontraditional Rose Bowl battle between traditional powers Michigan and Texas, the game scheduled to follow the Capital One Bowl.

Even before the final play, the game might have been considered a classic comeback…on LSU's part. Although the offenses struggled to move the ball at times, both teams executed various big plays when they needed them.

The big plays started early. Just as everyone was settling into their seats, Tate hooked up with Clinton Solomon for a 57-yard touchdown connection, staking Iowa to an early first-quarter lead just over two minutes into the game. LSU then registered two field goals to make it 7–6.

Iowa's special teams were very strong all day. Their second blocked punt of the day—by Miguel Merrick, with just over a minute to play in the second quarter—was scooped up by Sean Considine inside the LSU 10. He ran it into the end zone for a touchdown to make it 14–6.

Unfortunately for the Hawkeyes, LSU got a long 74-yard touchdown run by Alley Broussard on their first play from scrimmage on the ensuing drive. The point-after attempt failed, and Iowa would take a 14–12 lead into halftime.

Iowa built a 24–12 lead early in the fourth quarter following a four-yard touchdown run by Marques Simmons, capping a 10-play, 72-yard drive. Then LSU sent redshirt

This is like a dream. It's my first touchdown—ever—and we win the game against LSU in a bowl. You can't write a better script than that.

—IOWA WIDE RECEIVER WARREN HOLLOWAY

Iowa's Warren Holloway crosses the goal line on the last play of the game as incredulous LSU fans react in the background. The 56-yard completion from Drew Tate gave Iowa an improbable 30–25 victory over LSU in the Capital One Bowl in Orlando, Florida, on January 1, 2005. *Copyright: University of Iowa—CMP Photographic Service*

freshman quarterback—and future number one overall draft pick—JaMarcus Russell on as quarterback in place of Marcus Randall, who had been injured earlier in the game. Russell was LSU's third quarterback of the game, and he led the Tigers on back-to-back touchdown drives, with both scores coming on touchdown passes to Skyler Green. The

second touchdown capped a grueling 12-play drive that covered 69 yards. The two-point conversion attempt failed, but LSU still had a 25–24 lead with just 46 seconds left in the fourth quarter

It appeared as though a strong Iowa effort would all be for naught—until Tate, Holloway, and company proved yet again that the game of football is a 60-minute contest. It certainly didn't look good for the Hawkeyes as they began the last drive with 39 seconds remaining in the fourth quarter. Iowa's final drive began on their own 29-yard line. Two quick passes from Tate to Ed Hinkel and Warren Holloway gained 20 yards to the Iowa 49. However, the pass to Holloway was over the middle and did not gain a first down, so the clock was running. Although Iowa still had two timeouts remaining, inexplicably, they chose to spike it rather than calling timeout. That proved to be a costly decision because the offense wasn't set and was subsequently called for a five-yard false-start penalty, pushing the ball back to the Iowa 44-yard line.

The previous spike play never happened, so once the ball was reset after the penalty, the officials wound the clock. It moved to under 10 seconds before Iowa could get the snap off. Whether Tate was aware of it or not, this would be the final play of the game. The winning pass play was far from a low-probability "Hail Mary" pass. There were four receivers split wide in the formation: Hinkel, Holloway, and Scott Chandler were split wide right and Clinton Solomon was the lone receiver split wide left. The play was called "All Up."

The LSU defense rushed a total of six men, including a blitzing defensive back from the right side of the defense, but unlike much of the game up to that point, could not get near Tate as he surveyed the field for several

IN THE AFTERMATH

The dramatic touchdown catch by Warren Holloway was his first-ever as a collegian. The fifth-year senior from Homewood, Illinois, finished the game with four catches for 72 yards. Once they realized that Holloway had made the grab, the Iowa radio booth referred to him as "the forgotten man" because of the emergence of other options like Clinton Solomon, Ed Hinkel, and Scott Chandler as Tate's favorite targets during the year. Clearly, Holloway had shed that term forever.

Tate finished the game connecting on 20 of 32 passes for 287 yards, two interceptions, and two touchdowns. Tate was named the game's MVP, and he was just a sophomore on the 2005 Capital One Bowl championship team. Tate led Iowa to a 10–2 record in 2004, and certainly big things were expected of Tate and the Hawkeyes during his junior and senior years.

Unfortunately, the team could not duplicate the overall success of the 2004 campaign or the magic of the Capital One Bowl finish in subsequent bowl games. The Hawkeyes posted a 7–5 record in 2005 (including a close loss to Florida in the Outback Bowl) and a 6–7

record the following year in 2006 (which included another close loss to defending national champion Texas in the Alamo Bowl).

Although the team accomplishments in Tate's last two years were disappointing given the high bar set during the 2004 season, he should be remembered more for his part in the improbable miracle touchdown to beat LSU than his disappointing junior and senior seasons.

The LSU loss was Nick Saban's last as LSU head coach. He had accepted the head coaching position with the NFL's Miami Dolphins the week before, but agreed to stay on at LSU to coach the bowl game. Saban has since returned to the college coaching ranks; he was hired as Alabama head coach in 2007 after an unsuccessful attempt at turning around the fortunes of the Dolphins.

Iowa's dramatic win over LSU was enough to move the Hawkeyes up to the No. 8 slot in the year-end wire service polls, the third consecutive year Iowa finished No. 8 in the polls.

GAME DETAILS

Iowa 30 • LSU 25

Date: January 1, 2005

Location: Florida Citrus Bowl, Orlando, Florida

Attendance: 70,229

Weather: 75 degrees, mostly sunny

Significance: Capital One Bowl

Box Score:

LSU	0	12	0	13	**25**
Iowa	7	7	3	13	**30**

Scoring:

IA	Solomon 57-yard pass from Tate (Schlicher PAT)	LSU	Broussard 74-yard run (PAT failed)
LSU	Jackson 29-yard FG	IA	Schlicher 19-yard FG
LSU	Jackson 47-yard FG	IA	Simmons 4-yard run (Schlicher PAT)
IA	Considine 7-yard blocked punt return (Schlicher PAT)	LSU	Green 22-yard pass from Russell (Jackson PAT)
		LSU	Green 3-yard pass from Russell (Russell pass failed)
		IA	Holloway 56-yard pass from Tate

> **I** don't know if you could write a better script. Nobody would believe you if you did.
>
> —IOWA COACH KIRK FERENTZ

> **W**e just called four verticals and Solomon was supposed to run a skinny post. They had a safety on him. I was going back to Chandler, but the safety playing that side of the field jumped on him. And then, Warren's guy ran over to the flat. I just threw it up to Warren, and I think once Warren caught it, he wasn't going down. I was scared I overthrew him, but he did an unbelievable job not going down.
>
> —IOWA QUARTERBACK DREW TATE'S DESCRIPTION OF THE GAME-WINNING PLAY

seconds. The primary target on the play was Solomon, who was running a skinny post down the left side. However, he was unable to shake the LSU cornerback and one of the safeties was also there downfield to help out. Tate next looked to Chandler, basically running straight up the field from his right split end position,

but he too was closely covered by the safety on the other side of the field.

Not calling the timeout actually worked to Iowa's advantage because LSU wasn't able to clearly set their defensive scheme, and the secondary appeared to be confused on the coverage. The LSU defensive back

ALL UP

The situation facing the Iowa offense was about as desperate as it gets. Down by one with less than 10 seconds to play and more than 50 yards away from the end zone, the officials had wound the clock after the ball was set following a false-start penalty on Iowa. As Drew Tate (5) took the snap out of the shotgun and dropped back to survey the field, only 8 seconds remained. This likely was going to be Iowa's last shot. Iowa had three receivers lined up trips right, with Warren Holloway (86) between Ed Hinkel (11) and Scott Chandler (87). Holloway essentially ran straight up the field, past the LSU defensive back who perhaps expected safety help behind him. But, the safety help never came on Holloway, as both safeties were already occupying Chandler and Clinton Solomon (88), who had also run deep pass patterns. Although it appeared that Tate may have overthrown his target, Holloway was able to make an adjustment while the ball was in the air, running under the ball to haul it in at the 15. He maintained his balance as the cornerback running down the field with Hinkle, also running the deep route, laid a hand on his back and attempted to make a tackle, to no avail. Holloway waltzed into the end zone as time expired and bedlam reigned at the Citrus Bowl.

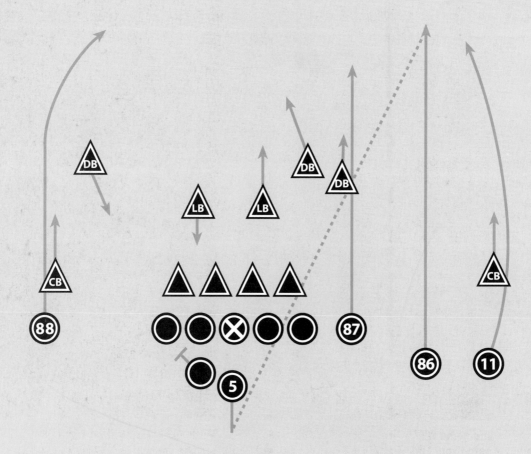

responsible for covering Holloway let him go, apparently thinking they were in a zone coverage and he had safety help behind him. In reality, the safeties had already occupied Solomon and Chandler, leaving no one left to take Holloway.

Tate heaved the ball deep downfield. Some in the press box—and the quarterback himself—initially thought he had overthrown Holloway. But Holloway was able to run under it perfectly in stride at the 15-yard line between Chandler and Hinkel. He kept his

We just went to the Land of Oz.
—IOWA RADIO PLAY-BY-PLAY MAN GARY DOLPHIN

balance and shed the arm tackle of LSU's Travis Daniels, who was closely covering Hinkel all the way down the field. From there, he waltzed into the end zone for the winning points just as the Citrus Bowl clock turned to 0:00. The Iowa sideline, an estimated 30,000 Iowa fans in the stands, the Iowa radio booth, and thousands of Iowa fans watching live on television went absolutely berserk.

Drew saw it the whole time. He saw the defense wasn't ready. He saw a gap in the coverage. And he took advantage.
—WARREN HOLLOWAY

Iowa quarterback—and game MVP—Drew Tate (5) celebrates with wide receiver Warren Halloway (86) after Holloway caught the game-winning touchdown as time expired against LSU during the Capital One Bowl on January 1, 2005 in Orlando. *Photo courtesy Getty Images*